Why M.Destiny doesn't work
pp 147-8

UNITED STATES
DIPLOMATIC HISTORY
VOLUME 1

UNITED STATES
DIPLOMATIC HISTORY
VOLUME 1

READINGS FOR THE
EIGHTEENTH AND
NINETEENTH CENTURIES

EDITED BY
GERARD HOWARD CLARFIELD
DEPARTMENT OF HISTORY
UNIVERSITY OF MISSOURI

HOUGHTON MIFFLIN • **BOSTON**
ATLANTA • DALLAS • GENEVA, ILL. • HOPEWELL, N.J. • PALO ALTO

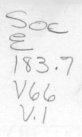

Cover photograph by Donald Dietz.

Furniture courtesy of William A. Turtle and Company,
Cambridge, Massachusetts.

FOR JOSEPH AND SHIRLEY

Preface

The history of American foreign relations during the period 1775–1900 chronicles a nation's rise from colonial status to sovereignty, stability, and eventually genuine power. Beginning as a set of vaguely united seaboard colonies, America expanded both territorially and economically until, at the dawn of the twentieth century, she dominated the Western Hemisphere and was fully the equal of any of the great states of Europe and Asia. On many occasions during this period America resorted to war. Moreover, crises that threatened to erupt into conflict were frequent and often prolonged.

This book focuses on six of the most critical moments in the history of pre–twentieth century American foreign policy. It is not intended to replace a general text but is designed to supplement, to widen, and to deepen the reader's understanding of some of the most serious problems that confronted America's early diplomats.

Other than this emphasis on moments of diplomatic crisis, there has been no attempt to create any artificial structure or pattern in the readings. The part introductions are broadly interpretive, designed to provide a framework of understanding for the individual readings. The readings themselves have been chosen from a wide variety of primary and secondary materials, in good part with an eye toward stimulating the reader's interest. Beyond this they fall into two categories. Some are simply descriptive, easy to understand, and informative. Others are more interpretive, subject to discussion and controversy.

As for the major divisions, each explores at least one, but frequently more than one, dimension of an issue. The part on the diplomacy of the American Revolution reveals the role of foreign policy in securing

American independence and the very generous concessions won at Paris in 1783. It also, however, provides examples of the Machiavellian flavor of diplomatic practice in the late eighteenth century. The unit dealing with the crisis over neutrality in the 1790's exposes the outlines of early American policy, the commitment to economic expansion and political nonentanglement, and the difficulties created by such mutually contradictory policies. It also raises the persistent question of the relationship between foreign and domestic policies. The third section, which deals primarily with the events leading to the War of 1812, focuses on the question of causation but investigates as well an issue which persists throughout American history: the utility of economic sanctions as a substitute for military force in achieving foreign policy goals.

An exception to this general approach occurs in the fourth part which deals with America's expansion into the Pacific in the 1840's. The single, critical question here is causation. Beginning with the theory that American foreign policy during the period was determined by a popular and romantic passion for expansion, the section suggests alternate economic and political views as well.

The last two sections, dealing with the diplomacy of the American Civil War and post-war expansionism, return to the earlier pattern. One part focuses on the critical question of the Civil War: Would the great European powers, particularly England and France, intervene on the side of the South? But several other issues also appear. First, there is the question of American attitudes toward the rights of neutrals during a time when the United States was a major belligerent and England was at peace. Second, there is the recurring question of the value of economic sanctions as a means of accomplishing foreign policy ends. The Southern embargo on cotton provides the vehicle for discussion.

The final segment of the book focuses on the history of post-war expansionism and considers the impact of industrialization on foreign policy. The quest for foreign markets did, in all likelihood, encourage America's outward thrust. But was it the major consideration in America's decision to go to war against Spain in 1898? How much did other political and emotional factors count? Perhaps an even more important question concerns the degree to which the search for markets influenced the decision to assume the responsibilities of empire at the war's end.

This book has been deliberately designed to be brief and to fit the needs of students and teachers using other reading materials as well. None of the problems discussed is treated exhaustively. Each section, however, should provide a useful and interesting beginning for further investigation.

Gerard H. Clarfield

CONTENTS

PART 1   AMERICA'S REVOLUTIONARY DIPLOMACY

INTRODUCTION   2
1. AUTOBIOGRAPHY/JOHN ADAMS   7
2. BENJAMIN FRANKLIN/CARL VAN DOREN   9
3. MILFORD SHELBURNE PLAYS THE HOST/
   RICHARD B. MORRIS   18

PART 2   NEUTRALITY IN JEOPARDY

INTRODUCTION   43
1. TRUCE WITH BRITAIN/ARTHUR BURR
   DARLING   48
2. THE DAMNATION OF MR. JAY/FRANK
   MONAGHAN   64
3. THE FRENCH MISSION OF 1799–1800: CON-
   CLUDING CHAPTER IN THE STATECRAFT OF
   JOHN ADAMS/STEPHEN G. KURTZ   69

PART 3   WAR AND PEACE WITH ENGLAND

INTRODUCTION   82
1. MARITIME ISSUES AND THE WAR OF 1812/
   A. L. BURT   90

2. THE EMBARGO ACT: DECEMBER 22, 1807   105
3. AGRARIAN DISCONTENT IN THE MISSISSIPPI VALLEY/GEORGE ROGERS TAYLOR   107
4. THE REPUBLIC IN PERIL/ROGER H. BROWN   124
5. THE MONROE DOCTRINE: DECEMBER 2, 1823   142

PART 4   **THE AGE OF MANIFEST DESTINY**

INTRODUCTION   146
1. PUBLIC DINNER TO COMMODORE STOCKTON/ *NILES NATIONAL REGISTER*   149
2. HARD WAR AVERTED—EASY WAR GAINED/ CHARLES G. SELLERS   156
3. EMPIRE ON THE PACIFIC/NORMAN A. GRAEBNER   167

PART 5   **THE AMERICAN CIVIL WAR AND BRITISH NEUTRALITY**

INTRODUCTION   179
1. THE CONFEDERATE STRUGGLE AND RECOGNITION/*LONDON QUARTERLY REVIEW*   185
2. SQUALL ACROSS THE ATLANTIC: THE *PETERHOFF* EPISODE/STUART L. BERNATH   201
3. NORTHERN DIPLOMACY AND EUROPEAN NEUTRALITY/NORMAN A. GRAEBNER   214

PART 6   **POST–CIVIL WAR EXPANSIONISM**

INTRODUCTION   226
1. YEARS OF PREPARATION/WALTER LAFEBER   230
2. THE UNITED STATES LOOKING OUTWARD/ ALFRED THAYER MAHAN   236
3. HYSTERIA/ERNEST R. MAY   247
4. INSULAR IMPERIALISM AND THE OPEN DOOR: THE CHINA MARKET AND THE SPANISH-AMERICAN WAR/THOMAS McCORMICK   261

UNITED STATES
DIPLOMATIC HISTORY
VOLUME 1

PART 1
AMERICA'S
REVOLUTIONARY
DIPLOMACY

INTRODUCTION

By the time the thirteen colonies became independent in 1776, Americans had already developed some firm convictions about the role they wished to play in world affairs. The American experience as a member of a vast international trading community, as a colony and political satellite of Great Britain, and as a place where a new and, it was thought, just and virtuous society was being carved from nature provided the foundations for an ambitious and distinctive foreign policy. That policy was designed to serve three purposes: to fulfill the needs of a practical commercial people, to provide the political flexibility necessary for avoiding involvement in European political affairs, to reflect America's view of herself as unique, an example of political and social morality to a world dominated by corrupt despotisms.

One of the most distinctive elements in early American foreign policy was the commitment to nonentanglement in the political affairs of Europe. Of course, tradition, experience, and the three thousand miles of ocean that separated America from Europe seemed to dictate the wisdom and practicability of such a policy. However, ideology too played a role. As republicans Americans believed they had no reason to become involved in the dynastic squabbles that perpetually troubled the monarchies of Europe. Moreover, despite the economic connection between America and Europe, many were convinced that the republic, by acting with care and circumspection, actually might be able to remain unentangled. Thomas Paine, reflecting broadly held opinion in his pamphlet *Common Sense*, made just this point. He recalled that during the late seventeenth and eighteenth centuries America had been involved needlessly in a series of wars, the result of her connection with Great Britain. Independence, he believed, would allow Americans to live in peace and prosperity, divorced from the wars of Europe, in which they had no interest. Neither Spain nor France, England's two major antagonists, could be considered America's enemies. On the contrary, once separated from England, Paine was convinced, America might not only remain at peace with those two governments but could easily cultivate a profitable trade with them as well. In part Paine pinned his hopes for noninvolvement on the ocean barrier. He believed too, however, that ideological differences separated America from the great nations of Europe and that these would prove immensely significant in helping to keep America at peace. War, he suggested, was in no nation's real interest. It was rather the sport of a few princes who indulged in it solely to augment their personal power. Thus Europe's monarchs, unconcerned with the general welfare of their people, followed policies designed to suit only their own pride, passions, or prejudices and kept Europe in a continuing state of confusion. As a republic, America might avoid all this. The policies of a free government would represent the best interests of its inhabitants. True republican foreign policy was peace-loving, concerned only with encouraging moral and economic progress.

The winning of independence from the world's most formidable power, an awesome task, would test Americans' commitment to the policy of nonentanglement and the ideological assumption that monarchism was the root cause of war. It was clear from the beginning of the war for independence that America had certain foreign policy advantages. France, smarting from defeat at the hands of England in the Seven Years' War, was anxious for revenge and interested in supporting the rebels. America's success would at a stroke strip England of the diadem of the British Empire and restore France to the premier position among the states of Europe. Though this was evident to many American leaders, most were reluctant to seek any kind of formal alliance. French troops, though on American soil for the purpose of driving the English out, would be a danger to American liberty. An alliance with France would mean plunging into the tangled thicket of European politics, the very thing American policy makers hoped to avoid. Thus although they sought to tap France as a source of war materiel and financial support, they accepted the early advice of John Adams (selection 1) and resisted the impulse to seek an alliance.

A string of military defeats and the inability of the Continental Congress to obtain supplies for Washington's pathetically small army forced a reconsideration of early views of an alliance. The French, however, were not easily convinced to fight. Weakened by a century of conflict with England and beset by serious financial difficulties, they were in no mood blithely to enter another war against England with their only ally the foundering United States. Benjamin Franklin, the best known of the American representatives in Paris, received sympathy from the French people and even from France's Foreign Minister, the Comte de Vergennes, but was unable to maneuver the French government into committing itself to the American cause. Ultimately, the victory of General Horatio Gates and his army of New Englanders over General John Burgoyne and the surrender of Burgoyne's army at Saratoga in upstate New York, provided the able Franklin (selection 2) with the leverage he needed to force a treaty from France.

The alliance was little more than a marriage of convenience. The government of Louis XVI had little sympathy for America's republican experiment, and Americans were suspicious of their new Catholic ally. Although Vergennes actively supported the principle of American independence, he was not eager to see the development of a truly powerful United States. He sought instead a weak and threatened satellite for France. Further weakening the ties that linked the United States and France was the fact that Vergennes had to consider the desires of France's other ally, Spain, whose interests were also at variance with those of the United States. Authorities in Madrid blanched at the thought of a successful revolution in the Western Hemisphere, for revolutionary contagion might easily spread to their empire in that part of the world. Yet, in order to entice Spain into participating in the war, Vergennes had to defer to her interests because he desperately needed Spanish support if he was to challenge Britain for control of the seas. Thus, although he was committed to winning American independence, he lent his support to Spain's efforts to cripple the American republic by hemming her in behind the Appalachian Mountains and denying her the right to use the North Atlantic fisheries, vital to New England's commercial interests.

After six years of indecisive conflict in America and division at home, London decided to begin serious negotiations leading to a peace settlement. Talks began late in 1781 in Paris, where three American negotiators—John Jay, Benjamin Franklin, and John Adams—sat down with Britain's representative, Richard Oswald. Vergennes hoped to control these talks, and as they began he had a reasonably good chance of succeeding. In the period before serious discussions began he had worked with great success through his envoy in Philadelphia, the Chevalier de la Luzerne, to influence the drafting of the American negotiators' instructions. Congress' instructions to the envoys effectively tied their hands, requiring them to consult with Vergennes and be guided by his advice throughout the negotiations. Yet despite the fact that he seemed in a position to dictate even the pace of the talks, the French Foreign Minister did not ultimately have his way. This was due in large measure to the efforts of one of the Americans in Paris, John Jay.

Before coming to France, Jay had spent two frustrating years in Spain attempting to wring recognition and aid from Spain's chief minister, the unwilling Floridablanca. It was an experience that enhanced his innate suspicion of European diplomatists. Of great moment to Jay, and the issue over which he quickly came to doubt the sincerity of Vergennes, was the question of American recognition. Oswald, the British negotiator, was not empowered to treat with the representatives of a sovereign power. His commission authorized him to talk with representatives of the American colonies. Jay, fearing that the talks might be used by the British as a delaying tactic and that recognition might be withheld, insisted that Oswald's commission be amended to empower him to deal with representatives of an independent power. In effect he wanted recognition as a precondition to negotiation. Vergennes, when consulted, thought the matter of little consequence and urged Jay and his colleagues to proceed with the talks notwithstanding Oswald's unsatisfactory commission.

Of itself Vergennes's casual unconcern might not have aroused Jay's suspicions. But when the New Yorker learned, almost simultaneously, of the secret mission to London of Joseph-Matthias de Rayneval, Vergennes's undersecretary, he suspected duplicity. While the American delegation futilely conducted discussions with Oswald, Vergennes might well be in direct communication with Britain's Prime Minister, the Earl of Shelburne, arranging a separate peace settlement at America's expense. These doubts led Jay to set aside his instructions and open a private channel of communication to London (selection 3). This crucial decision laid the groundwork for what amounted to a separate peace between Britain and the United States, which, though it violated the spirit if not the letter of the alliance with France, nevertheless was arranged on terms very favorable to the American republic.

The visits of Rayneval and then of Jay's representative, Benjamin Vaughan, placed Shelburne in an enviable diplomatic position. All the cards were open to him, and his alternatives were clear. The French and Spanish were urging him to cooperate with them in limiting the future growth of the United States. Certainly here was an appeal to passion difficult to ignore. Many in England would have liked nothing better than to see America founder as an independent nation. Why Shelburne did not take this tack is not easy to explain. It is likely, however, that he believed Britain's national interest better served by a generous and openhanded position toward the Americans. A peace settlement such as Vergennes suggested had serious political drawbacks for Britain, for it would perpetuate Anglo-American hostility and cement the alliance between France and the United States. The Americans would be left with no alternative but to cling to France for protection against England. Shelburne may well have hoped to divide the allies and influence the political balance in Britain's favor. The simplest way to accomplish this was by adopting a friendly and generous attitude toward the United States. Then too, Shelburne, who was deeply impressed by the laissez-faire philosophy of the Scottish economist Adam Smith, must have believed that it was of great importance to England to restore her vanished trade with America. How could this be accomplished if Britain was narrow, resentful, and inflexible at the conference table? Shelburne, probably influenced primarily by these calculations, astounded many, not the least of whom was the Comte de Vergennes, by his generosity in arranging a settlement with the Americans. His first move was to satisfy Jay about the form of Oswald's commission. He then agreed to a preliminary treaty with the United States that granted formal recognition, sweeping boundaries, and access to the North Atlantic fisheries.

The treaty was an astonishing success for American diplomacy, made possible by the shrewd insights of Shelburne and the able manner in which Jay and his colleagues manipulated European rivalries in the service of America's national interest. Yet, although America emerged successful in her first brush with eighteenth-century power politics, the experience served only to confirm earlier views of the duplicity of European statecraft. It made more pressing America's already established desire to remain aloof. It demonstrated too, however, that noninvolvement was going to prove more difficult than had earlier been imagined.

AUTOBIOGRAPHY
JOHN ADAMS

Some Gentlemen doubted of the Sentiments of France, thought She would frown upon Us as Rebells and be afraid to countenance the Example. I replied to these Gentlemen, that I apprehended they had not attended to the relative Situation of France and England. That it was the unquestionable Interest of France that the British continental Colonies should be independent. That Britain by the Conquest of Canada and their naval Tryumphs during the last War, and by her vast Possessions in America and the East Indies, was exalted to a height of Power and Preeminence that France must envy and could not endure. But there was much more than pride and Jealousy in the Case. Her Rank, her Consideration in Europe, and even her Safety and Independence was at stake. The Navy of Great Britain was now Mistress of the Seas all over the Globe. The Navy of France almost annihilated. Its Inferiority was so great and obvious, that all the Dominions of France in the West Indies and in the East Indies lay at the Mercy of Great Britain, and must remain so as long as North America belonged to Great Britain, and afforded them so many harbours abounding with Naval Stores and Resources of all kinds and so many Men and Seamen ready to assist them and Man their Ships. That Interest could not lie, that the Interest of France was so obvious, and her Motives so cogent, that nothing but a judicial Infatuation of her Councils could restrain her from embracing Us. That our Negotiations with France ought how-

From L. H. Butterfield, ed., *The Adams Papers, Diary and Autobiography of John Adams*, vol. 3, (Cambridge, Mass.: The Belknap Press of Harvard University Press, 1961), pp. 328–329. Used by permission of Harvard University Press.

ever, to be conducted with great caution and with all the foresight We could possibly obtain. That We ought not to enter into any Alliance with her, which should entangle Us in any future Wars in Europe, that We ought to lay it down as a first principle and a Maxim never to be forgotten, to maintain an entire Neutrality in all future European Wars. That it never could be our Interest to unite with France, in the destruction of England, or in any measures to break her Spirit or reduce her to a situation in which she could not support her Independence. On the other hand it could never be our Duty to unite with Britain in too great a humiliation of France. That our real if not our nominal Independence would consist in our Neutrality. If We united with either Nation, in any future War, We must become too subordinate and dependent on that nation, and should be involved in all European Wars as We had been hitherto. That foreign Powers would find means to corrupt our People to influence our Councils, and in fine We should be little better than Puppetts danced on the Wires of the Cabinetts of Europe. We should be the Sport of European Intrigues and Politicks. That therefore in preparing Treaties to be proposed to foreign Powers and in the Instructions to be given to our Ministers, We ought to confine ourselves strictly to a Treaty of Commerce. That such a Treaty would be an ample Compensation to France, for all the Aid We should want from her. The Opening of American Trade, to her would be a vast resource for her Commerce and Naval Power, and a great Assistance to her in protecting her East and West India Possessions as well as her Fisheries: but that the bare dismemberment of the British Empire, would be to her an incalculable Security and Benefit, worth more than all the Exertions We should require of her even if it should draw her into another Eight or ten Years War.—When I first made these Observations in Congress I never saw a greater Impression made upon that Assembly or any other. Attention and Approbation was marked on every Countenance. Several Gentlemen came to me afterwards to thank me for that Speech, particularly Mr. Caesar Rodney of Delaware and Mr. Duane of New York. I remember those two Gentlemen in particular because both of them said, that I had considered the Subject of foreign Connections more maturely than any Man they had ever heard in America, that I had perfectly digested the Subject, and had removed, Mr. Rodney said all, and Mr. Duane said, the greatest part of his objections to foreign Negotiations. Even Mr. Dickinson said to Gentlemen out of Doors, that I had thrown great light on the subject.

BENJAMIN FRANKLIN
CARL VAN DOREN

In July Vergennes told the king that secret assistance was no longer enough to keep up the war in America and that France must either withdraw altogether or else do more—that is, declare war on England. What was needed was an offensive and defensive alliance with the United States and Spain, each of them agreeing not to make peace without the consent of the others. The king was willing only if Spain would join them. But Spain held back, having made a truce with Portugal and being still opposed to independence for any American colonies. The news from America did not encourage France to go on alone. Burgoyne easily took Ticonderoga in July. Howe, though dilatory, promised to capture Philadelphia. If Philadelphia as well as New York were to be in the hands of the British, and New England isolated by Burgoyne, the rebellion must fail, Vergennes assumed. He continued his waiting for some hopeful occasion to strike.

To the French Franklin still showed the calm, smiling face which reassured and charmed them. Even when bad news came and Gérard (or someone) said: "Well, Doctor, Howe has taken Philadelphia," Franklin replied: "I beg your pardon, Sir, Philadelphia has taken Howe." Pleased with Franklin's spirit in public, Paris thought his wit better than it was. Privately he knew that American affairs were in the worst way. Letters from Congress said they did not see how they could continue without alliances and loans. Few letters arrived. British men-of-war had almost cut off the service of communications, and a

From *Benjamin Franklin* by Carl Van Doren, pp. 584–593. Copyright 1938 by Carl Van Doren, copyright © renewed 1966 by Barbara Van Doren Klaw. All rights reserved. Reprinted by permission of The Viking Press, Inc.

squadron outside the mouth of the Loire effectually shut up American vessels in the port of Nantes: privateers eager to invade the Channel, cargo ships with munitions for the United States. While the British army threatened to divide New England from the other colonies, the British navy threatened to divide Washington, heading the Revolution at home, from Franklin, heading it abroad. Both of them suffered from lack of supplies and money. Both of them had to endure quarrels and cabals among their associates. Both of them had fallen back on the last deep resources of their minds and wills.

Late in September the commissioners presented a memorial to Vergennes, pressing him to recognize the independence of their country and to grant a loan—they mentioned fourteen million livres—which would bring real relief. Through the sly Bancroft and the protesting Stormont the ministers heard about the memorial before it reached them. Vergennes, in a temporizing answer, told the envoys they did their work unguardedly. It must not leak out. They argued among themselves over the ministerial reproof. Lee thought they laid their affairs "open to all the world"; Deane that the accusation was untrue; Franklin that Vergennes had only found a pretext for refusing help. The month went on with no decisive answer.

On 25 October Lee had a long talk with Franklin at Passy and that day wrote out at unusual length in his journal what Franklin had said about the American beginnings of the Revolution which Lee, in England, had not seen. "He seemed to agree with me in thinking that France and Spain mistook their interest and opportunity in not making an alliance with us now, when they might make better terms than they could expect hereafter. That it was well for us they left us to work out our own salvation; which the efforts we had hitherto made, and the resources we had opened, gave us the fairest reason to hope we should be able to do.

"He told me the manner in which the whole of this business had been conducted was such a miracle in human affairs that, if he had not been in the midst of it and seen all the movements, he could not have comprehended how it was effected. To comprehend it we must view a whole people for some months without any laws or government at all. In this state their civil governments were to be formed, an army and navy were to be provided for those who had neither a ship of war, a company of soldiers, nor magazines, arms, artillery, or ammunition. Alliances were to be formed, for they had none. All this was to be done, not at leisure nor in a time of tranquillity and communication with other nations, but in the face of a most formidable invasion, by the most powerful nation, fully provided with armies, fleets, and all the instruments of destruction, powerfully allied and aided, the commerce with other nations in a great measure stopped up. . . .

"Nor was this all; they had internal opposition to encounter which alone would seem sufficient to have frustrated all their efforts. The Scotch, who in many places were numerous, were secret or open foes as opportunity offered. The Quakers, a powerful body in Pennsylvania, gave every opposition their art, abilities, and influence could suggest. To these were added all those whom contrariety of opinion, Tory principles, personal animosities, fear of so dreadful and dubious an undertaking, joined with the artful promises and threats of the enemy, rendered open or concealed opposers, or timid neutrals, or lukewarm friends to the proposed revolution." But Franklin was convinced that the Revolution was supported by a genuine majority. "Consequently the feebleness, irresolution, and inaction which generally, nay, almost invariably attends and frustrates hasty popular proceedings, did not influence this. . . . Those who acted in council bestowed their whole thoughts upon the public; those who took to the field did with what weapons, ammunition, and accommodations they could procure. . . . Dr. Franklin assured me that upon an average he gave twelve hours in the twenty-four to public business." Multitudes of men, "not of inferior abilities," had worked as hard.

"The consequence was that in a few months the governments were established; codes of law were formed which, for wisdom and justice, are the admiration of all the wise and thinking men in Europe. Ships of war were built, a multitude of cruisers were fitted out, which have done more injury to the British commerce than it ever suffered before. Armies of offence and defence were formed, and kept the field through all the rigours of winter in the most rigorous climate. Repeated losses, inevitable in a defensive war, as it soon became, served only to renew exertions that quickly repaired them. The enemy was everywhere resisted, repulsed, or besieged. On the ocean, in the Channel, in their very ports, their ships were taken and their commerce obstructed. The greatest revolution the world ever saw is likely to be effected in a few years; and the power that has for centuries made all Europe tremble, assisted by twenty thousand German mercenaries and favoured by the universal concurrence of Europe to prohibit the sale of warlike stores, the sale of prizes, or the admission of the armed vessels of America, will be effectually humbled by those whom she insulted and injured, because she conceived they had neither spirit nor power to resist or revenge it."

The voice of Franklin sounds through the words of Arthur Lee. In the light of all that is now known about those first years, Franklin's version of the Revolutionary beginnings seems at many points romantic. But versions like his were a part of the Revolution itself. Here was the grand style by which the humorous philosopher lived, in the midst of his realistic cares and plans. That grand style in the Revolutionary leaders was a force which the cynical British ministry could not learn to take into account.

In November news came by way of England that Philadelphia had fallen to Howe. Franklin, all of whose property was in the town, with his daughter and her younger children so far as he knew, was the firmest of the commissioners when they met on the 27th to make up their next dispatches to Congress. "He was clearly of opinion," according to Arthur Lee's journal, "that we could maintain the contest, and successfully too, without any European assistance; he was satisfied, as he had said formerly, that the less commerce or dependence we had upon Europe the better, for that we should do better without any connexion with it." Nor would he consent to warn the French ministry that without a French alliance the envoys must make terms with England: "the effect of a such a declaration upon them was uncertain; it might be taken as a menace, it might make them abandon us in despair or in anger." Better wait till the news was better, and they could make better terms. Just before noon on 4 December Jonathan Loring Austin arrived from Boston with the news that Burgoyne's entire army had surrendered at Saratoga.

Beaumarchais, who was there or came soon after Austin, rushed off to Paris, presumably to speculate on the report, and drove so recklessly that his carriage was overturned and his arm injured. Bancroft left for London, certainly in part to look after his own speculations. (He had already written a London friend that Burgoyne was in danger and that stocks were likely to fall.) The envoys at once drew up a dispatch for Vergennes. Lee wrote to the Spanish ambassador. Two days later Conrad-Alexandre Gérard of the foreign office called at Passy, bringing Vergennes's congratulations and inviting the Americans to renew their proposal for an alliance. Franklin drafted the proposal on the 7th, and on the 8th Temple delivered it. Sir George Grand, dining with Franklin that day, told him that a note just come from Vergennes referred to the envoys as "our friends," not "your friends" as formerly. On the 12th the envoys went by stealth—for fear of possible spies—to a place some distance from Versailles and sent word to Gérard. A coach called for them and took them to a house half a mile out of town, where Gérard and Vergennes were waiting. Nothing could be done of course, Vergennes said, without Spain, but he complimented and encouraged them. His courier could travel to and from Madrid in three weeks. In only five days Gérard came to Passy to say that the king's council had decided upon the alliance, though they would, as a mark of respect to Spain, not technically conclude it till the courier returned. Vergennes's haste was due largely to the presence in Paris of Paul Wentworth, chief of the British spies.

Wentworth now distrusted Bancroft because Bancroft had withheld from him the private information about the danger Burgoyne was in. A speculator in stocks himself, Wentworth resented being left out of what might be a lucrative secret. At least Bancroft had meant to leave him out, even though Wentworth had got hold of the message to Bancroft's partner. George III, who hated speculation, disliked both Bancroft and Wentworth for their financial activities. And he disliked them, too, for the information they had furnished about the prospect of a French alliance, which he obstinately refused to believe in. But after the news of Saratoga the king could no longer oppose North's plans for a prompt though belated move toward conciliation. Wentworth was sent to Paris, without authority to offer terms but with instructions to learn how Franklin and Deane stood, and to watch developments. Arthur Lee's spy-secretary had reported Lee to be so set on absolute independence that there could be no point in dealing with him. Wentworth left London on 6 December, and was in Paris by the time the American commissioners had their clandestine meeting with Vergennes.

Within a few days Wentworth had had two conferences with Deane. The spy said the British ministry had been forced into the war with America against their will, and now wanted to undo that mistake. They were ready to return to the imperial status before 1763 and repeal the obnoxious acts passed since then. Wentworth suggested a general armistice by land and sea, the British troops to be withdrawn everywhere except from the New York islands. Long Island might remain temporarily British as a kind of barrier fortress, and the smaller islands neutralized. This was to last while a commission went from England to readjust American affairs on the "grand basis of the Navigation Acts." The British would still have their colonial monopoly over the Americans, who would still be colonists. Deane said that America must be independent. Wentworth promised that any Americans who helped to bring about an understanding might expect everything from the Crown in the way of reward: titles of honour, wealth, high administrative posts.

Franklin, who knew that Deane was seeing Wentworth, refused himself to see him. Nobody knew better than Franklin how much the best policy honesty was. He turned over to Vergennes a letter to Bancroft from an unidentified correspondent in London asking whether the Americans would accept something "a little short of independence." This was on the 17th, the very day Gérard came to Passy to say that the French had decided, but must formally wait for Spain. The presence of British emissaries in Paris gave rise to the rumour that, if France did not recognize American independence, the Americans might be reunited with England and join in the conquest of the French and Spanish islands in the West Indies. Vergennes, without crediting it, used the rumour to influence the king. A reunion between Great Britain and the colonies, Vergennes knew, would put a French war on England out of the question. And Vergennes could not be sure—any more than Franklin was—what Wentworth's errand amounted to. Had he been sent to coax the envoys out of a French alliance, or only to cause the French to distrust them? Might he not—even—have been craftily brought over by Franklin for the purpose of troubling and hurrying up the French? Was he, as Wentworth pretended, merely an agreeable cosmopolitan speculator, or was he a British spy? Vergennes's own spies watched Wentworth so closely that he burned his papers, and his friends avoided him. He was worried over being thought a spy. Stormont, to give Wentworth a character, presented him to Louis XVI. Vergennes, to have a closer look at him, asked him to dinner.

Franklin waited. So long as Bancroft was in London it was hard for Wentworth to find out much about the commissioners. After Bancroft's return Wentworth learned that letters had come to Franklin from the British opposition. On 25 December Wentworth wrote to Eden that it would be wise to promise the envoys anything, no matter whether the promises were to be kept or not. The alliance must be prevented. In spite of Wentworth's efforts, made through Bancroft, Franklin still refused an interview. By the 31st Vergennes had his answer from Spain, which was against signing the treaty. France must act alone. Franklin gave Vergennes a few days more, and then consented to talk with Wentworth on 6 January, stipulating that Wentworth must not say a word about personal rewards to the commissioners. The master spy came to Passy.

"I called on Franklin yesterday," Wentworth reported to Eden (using numbers for names: 72 for Franklin), "and found him very busy with his nephew [grandson], who was directed to leave the room, and we remained together two hours. . . . Franklin received me very kindly. I introduced the conversation by some compliments, to which he is very open. . . . I concluded with wishing to be honoured with his opinion of the temper of the Congress, the terms and the means he would suggest to induce reconciliation. Hinted that his opinion, in my opinion, would be that of the Congress." Wentworth reminded Franklin that he had formerly favoured an imperial union rather than American independence. "He said that any of the different opinions he had given would have done at the time they were given, because they were, as they necessarily must be, formed from the circumstances of the epocha; that Mr. Barclay and Dr. Fothergill had one set in writing which only subjected him to abuse. Another set was obtained by Lord Hyde and Lord Howe, and again by Lord Howe in America." As to the present, propositions in writing were impossible, and Franklin had learned to be cautious about verbal ones, which were "liable to be not sufficiently or over-explained." After recalling many details of the Barclay-Fothergill negotiations, Franklin, according to Wentworth, "worked himself up into passion and resentment. I told him . . . that his resentments should be lost in the cause of his country; that this was too great to mix private quarrels with. . . . He replied that his warmth did not proceed from a feeling of personal injuries, but that, they going all along with the barbarities inflicted on his country, the remembrance of these roused in an old man, constitutionally phlegmatic, the resentments of high-mettled youth; and it should serve to convince me of the resentments of those on the spot, seeing the regular system of devastation and cruelty which every general had pursued. Here he lost breath in relating the burning of towns, the neglect or illtreatment of prisoners." They spoke of Major Thornton, Lee's secretary, who had gone to London with a letter to North about American prisoners held by the British.

How large, Wentworth went on, Franklin's satisfaction must be "if he could turn the torrent of vigour and resolution of an opulent and courageous people into affection, union, and prosperity. Britain and America could be the greatest empire on earth. He answered he believed he might do a great deal, but that the spirit of America was so high nothing but independence would be at all listened to." Other nations were willing to make "candid and fair" terms with the United States. "Nay, the savages of America would soon be more so than the savages of G[reat] Britain. Here he apostrophized again, and talked of Englishmen to be barbarous!" Wentworth tried to moderate him by changing the subject, and read—on a pledge of secrecy—a letter from Eden, who was not named. Franklin thought it a sensible letter, as far as it went. "He said he was glad to find honour and zeal so near the throne." A row of dashes in the letter probably hinted to Eden of things which Franklin said about George III but which Wentworth did not care to write. By this time Wentworth had given up reporting Franklin's talk so fully as at first. "I never knew him so eccentric"— that is, so out of centre with royal and ministerial opinion. "Nobody says less, generally, and keeps a point more closely in view, but he was diffuse and unmethodical today." Wentworth offered to try to get safe conduct for Franklin to go to London. Franklin said he might deal with a commission properly authorized. As it was, he had no powers himself and could merely hold polite conversation. Any discussions between representatives of England and America would have to be "on the broad bottom of reciprocal advantages." Before anything had been settled Deane came in, and he and Franklin dined with Wentworth and Bancroft, the two spies. "The conversation at dinner was offering bets that 7 [America] would be 107 [independent]; that Vandalia was to be the paradise on earth"; and that Chaumont with his whole family would emigrate.

Wentworth, who noted and reported a letter lying on Franklin's table and all the bits of news he picked up at dinner, seems not to have perceived that Franklin was playing with him, talking against time at canny length. The spy returned to London with no real answer, and perhaps without the uncomfortable knowledge that Franklin had seen him for the effect the meeting would have on Vergennes. The next day after the interview, when Wentworth thought it not worth while to call again as he had intended, the king's council voted in favour of a treaty and an alliance.

On the 8th Gérard came to Deane's lodgings in Paris to meet the commissioners. Having put three questions, he withdrew for an hour so they might discuss them. "Dr. Franklin began to write," Lee's journal says, "and the other two talk." Franklin wrote out two questions with their answers. The commissioners had not yet agreed on the second, when Gérard returned. Gérard thought the first question and answer sufficient for the time being. "*Question*. What is necessary to be done to give such satisfaction to the American commissioners as to engage them not to listen to any proposition from England for a new connexion with that country? *Answer*. The commisioners have long since proposed a treaty of amity and commerce which is not yet concluded. The immediate conclusion of that treaty will remove the uncertainty they are under with regard to it, and give them such a reliance on the friendship of France as to reject firmly all propositions made to them of peace from England which have not for their basis the entire freedom and independence of America, both in matters of government and commerce." The king, Gérard now said he was at liberty to tell them, had given his word that the treaty would be concluded. After a year's delay, Gérard did not say, the French desired the alliance as much as the Americans did, and were offering it, asking only the pledge that America would not make peace with England. Franklin had won a diplomatic campaign equal in results to Saratoga.

3
MILORD SHELBURNE PLAYS THE HOST
RICHARD B. MORRIS

Rayneval had more pressing business on his hands than the settlement of the Spanish-American dispute. On September 7th he left for
England incognito. Three days later as "Monsieur Castel" he took up
lodgings in London. Addressing a letter to Shelburne that very day,
he asked permission to call upon him promptly at his country home in
Wiltshire in order to give him a letter from Vergennes. Significantly,
he signed the note as "Secretary of the Council of State of His Most
Christian Majesty."[1] Bowood Park provided the setting for the discussions which began on September 13th and continued for almost a
week.[2]

Like so many other well-guarded secrets Rayneval's absence was
noted almost at once in Paris and caused a buzz of speculation. Vergennes had shared the secret with Aranda, and even provided the
Conde with a copy of his instructions to Rayneval.[3] To cover himself
Vergennes also informed the ambassadors of the comediating countries of the mission, but he made a point of not telling his American
allies. Word spread quickly, however. By the ninth, two days after
Rayneval had set forth on his trip, Jay had learned of it from Matthew
Ridley, who got around in the best circles of Paris, as well as from

[1] See V to R, Sept. 6, 1782. CP A 538: 117–118; to S, Sept. 6, 1782. LP 71; S to G,
Sept. 13, 1782. CG, VI, 123–125. See key to footnotes, p. 39.
[2] CP A 538, passim.
[3] A to F, Sept. 8, 1782. AHN, E, 4215, apt. 2, no. 2294, p. 32.

From pp. 323–329 ("Rayneval had . . . in close harmony") in *The Peacemakers* by
Richard B. Morris. Copyright © 1965 by Richard B. Morris. Reprinted by permission of Harper & Row, Publishers.

other sources.[4] Jay's suspicions had already been aroused on learning that on the morning of Rayneval's departure the Conde de Aranda had, "contrary to his usual practice, gone with *post horses* to Versailles," and was two hours in conference with Vergennes and his undersecretary. It seemed only obvious to put two and two together. Assuredly the Spanish ambassador had not taken post horses to turn over to Rayneval a new recipe for *gazpacho*. Jay rushed to Passy. He and Franklin agreed to take no public notice of the journey, but the doctor, unable to contain his curiosity, dashed off a note to Lafayette to find out the purpose of Rayneval's trip.[5]

To Jay the gossip about Rayneval's secret mission sounded an alarm bell in the night. From his own knowledge he had every reason to fear that a quick deal was in the offing between the other belligerents at the expense of the United States. Distorted accounts of Rayneval's visit which leaked out to the British press seemed to support such an interpretation.[6] Apart from rumor, Jay's suspicions seemed confirmed both by the Rayneval memorandum on the West and by a copy of an intercepted cipher dispatch from Barbé-Marbois to Vergennes, which a member of the British mission thoughtfully placed in Jay's hands. The communication, certainly no more indiscreet than countless others from the pens of the Secretary of Legation or the Chevalier de La Luzerne himself, was dated March 13, 1782. Therein Barbé-Marbois referred to the instructions of Congress to the peace commissioners as leaving "the King master of the terms of the treaty of peace, or truce, excepting independence and treaties of alliance." His letter shed further light on the growing breach between the French and Americans over the fisheries. Barbé-Marbois denounced the New England faction in general and Sam Adams in particular for stirring up trouble by insisting on sharing in the fisheries off the Grand Bank. He warned that England might even be tempted to make such a concession just to stir up jealousy between America and France. Such embarrassment might have been avoided had France been so prudent as "to have de-

[4] Matthew Ridley to JJ, n.d. [Sept. 13, 1782]. Mass. Hist. Soc.; Ridley, Diary, Sept. 13, 1782; [Edward Bancroft] to O, Sept. 9, relayed to S in dispatch of Sept. 11, 1782. LPB; JJ to RRL, Nov. 17, 1782. *RDC*, VI, 29.

[5] Ridley, Diary, Sept. 21, 1782.

[6] Thurne forwarded to Baudouin a clipping from a London paper, September 17, 1782, asserting that France's purpose in sending R was "to treat for a separate peace, and to totally renounce their connections with America." CP A 538: 200–201.

clared at an early period to the Americans that their pretension is not founded and that his Majesty does not mean to support it." The King, Barbé-Marbois advised now, should express "his surprise that the Newfoundland fisheries have been included in the additional instructions" of Congress and that the United States should have set forth such pretensions "without paying heed to the King's rights." Such a declaration, he urged, should be made before peace came, and, if at all possible, while the redcoats still held New York, Charleston, and Penobscot.[7]

Almost from the moment this interception was placed in John Jay's hands doubts were cast on the letter's authenticity. Vergennes was later to insist that, even if authentic and correctly deciphered, the translation was forced, that Marbois' opinion was "not necessarily that of the King," and, finally, that "the views indicated in the dispatch" had not been followed.[8] Franklin, closely reflecting Vergennes' views, felt that the channel of communication to Jay made the letter suspect, that it could well have been doctored, and that in any event the "forward, mistaken zeal of a secretary of legation should not be imputed to the King."[9] True, doctored and forged interceptions were by no means uncommon in these war years, but Barbé-Marbois' letter does not fall into that category. Its authenticity is today beyond question. Despite the denial of an eminent French diplomatic scholar that no copy of this dispatch was found in the French diplomatic archives, one of the quintuplicate copies did reach France from Philadelphia some time during the summer of '82 and may still be read in the *Correspondance politique, États-Unis* series, at the Quai d'Orsay.[10] The red-faced secretary of legation categorically denied having written the letter,[11] but after the storm abated was reputed on at least two occasions to have admitted authorship.[12]

[7] The decoding and translation with minor variations appear in RDC, V, 238–241, and Jay, *Life*, I, 490–494.

[8] V to L, Sept. 7, 1783. D, V, 296–297.

[9] BF to Samuel Cooper, Dec. 26, 1782. CP EU 22: 588–589; BFS, VIII, 649.

[10] CP EU 20: 407–417. There is a copy in CO 5/40. The copy that JJ forwarded to RRL with his letter of Sept. 18, 1782, is in PCC 110: 2. See also AP, IV, 358. Cf. RDC, V, 241n., 242n.

[11] Madison, *Writings* (Hunt, ed.), I, 463–464n.

[12] Boston *Patriot*, Aug. 24, 1811. In a conversation with William Beach Laurence, editor of Wheaton's *International Law*, mentioned by Jay, "The Peace Negotiations of 1782–83," in Justin Winsor, ed., *Narrative and Critical History of America* (Boston, 1888), VII, 120.

Massive evidence in the diplomatic archives reveals that the views expressed by Barbé-Marbois on the fisheries and Rayneval on the boundaries were not purely personal to the authors but expressed the deep-seated convictions of their court on both issues. One of the books that John Adams studied abroad with unusual absorption was a French tract published with government approval in 1780, entitled *Observations sur le Traité de la Paix Conclu à Paris*. The author urged that the forthcoming treaty secure for France the unlimited freedom of fishing in North America and advocated the establishment of strongholds in the Gulf of St. Lawrence and Newfoundland for the defense of French fishing ships otherwise exposed to harassment from the British while the New Englanders were finding means of appropriating all the riches of the sea.[13] Repeatedly had Vergennes found it necessary to caution Congress through his envoys at Philadelphia on pressing their claims to the fisheries. From the moment the colonies issued their Declaration of Independence, Vergennes contended, they ceased to share the fisheries. Insisting that France's guarantee bore only on independence, Vergennes wrote La Luzerne as recently as August 12th, "We will not sacrifice our own fisheries and we will not prolong the calamities of war to force England to sacrifice hers."[14]

By early September, when the Marbois dispatch was placed in Jay's hands, the French were deep in discussions with Fitzherbert over the fisheries. They were currently proposing revisions of the Newfoundland fisheries arrangements without any reference whatsoever to the United States, including a demand for a cession giving France *exclusive* possession of that section of Newfoundland where French fishermen were still privileged to dry their fish.[15] Fitzherbert, in a conference with Vergennes and Rayneval toward the end of August, took occasion to remind the Frenchmen that the Americans were likely to advance a claim to participate in the fisheries. "Nothing could be farther from the wishes of this Court," Rayneval replied, "than that such a claim should be admitted." He added gratuitously, "You, too, in your

[13] Zoltan Haraszti, "More Books from the Adams Library," *Boston Public Library Quarterly*, III, no. 2 (April, 1951), 109–126; Boston *Patriot*, Aug. 21, 1811.
[14] V to L, Sept. 1779; Oct. 7, 1781; June 28, Aug. 12, 1782. Jay, *Peace Neg.*, pp. 149–152; CP EU 19: 41–46; incomplete in *D*, IV, 679n.; CP EU 21: 336–345; incomplete in *D*, V, 92; CP EU 22: 52–57; L to V, Jan. 1, 9, 11, 18, 25, 28, 1782. CP EU 20: 3–20, 43 *et seq.*, 74, 106–110, 152–163, 208–213.
[15] See Memoirs on Newfoundland Fisheries, Aug. 15, 20, 1782. CP A 538: 36–49, 59; AF to TG, Aug. 17, 1782. FO 27/3.

hearts, are not only bound in interest to reject it, but you might do so consistent with the strictest principles of justice on the ground of your being the sole and undoubted proprietor of the Island of Newfoundland, and consequently of the fishery upon its coasts. . . . Of course, I only speak for myself," Rayneval added with his customary caution. Fitzherbert took the disclaimer with a grain of salt. It was "natural to suppose," he reported to Grantham, "that his ideas and language upon this and other political subjects must be nearly the same with those of his principle."[16] This underhand gesture against an ally was one that an adversary was not likely to forget. Retrospectively Fitzherbert commented, "M. de Vergennes never failed to insist on the expediency of a concert of measures between France and England for the purpose of excluding the American states from these fisheries, lest they should become a nursery for seamen."[17]

On the matter of boundaries Vergennes seemed as restrictive as had Rayneval. First of all, he was concerned that the Americans should not acquire Canada. "You know our system with regard to Canada," he wrote La Luzerne. "It is unchanging. Whatever will halt the conquest of this country accords with our views. But you will agree, Monsieur, that this way of thinking ought to be an impenetrable secret from the Americans. It would be a crime that they would never pardon. It is convenient, then, to make an outward show to convince them that we share their views, but to checkmate any steps that would put them into effect in case we are required to cooperate." His interpretation of Canada was so broad as to exclude the Americans from the Great Lakes, which he considered "a part of Canada." As regards the claims to the West put forward by Jay, claims resting on the sea-to-sea provisions of the old charters, Vergennes dismissed them as "foolishness not meriting serious refutation." These ideas are for your ears alone, La Luzerne was again cautioned. Do not reveal this information "because for the present we do not wish to intervene in the discussion between Aranda and Jay."[18]

Without being privy to this correspondence John Jay was convinced that Rayneval's memoir on the boundaries voiced the official French

[16] AF to TG, Aug. 29, 1782. FO 27/3. For S's reaction to the Barbé-Marbois interception, see S to TG [Aug. 26, 1782], GP L 30/14.

[17] Quoted by John McVickar, in the *New York Review* (Oct., 1841); Jay, *Peace Neg.*, p. 206.

[18] V to L, Oct. 14, 1782. CP EU 22: 368–373. This portion of the letter was omitted from D.

position. At the proper time, he felt, France was prepared to assume the role of arbiter between Spain and America, to contest America's extension to the Mississippi as well as her claim to the free navigation of that river, and most "certainly" to support Britain's claims north of the Ohio. In the event that America would not agree to a division of the West with Spain along Rayneval's lines, then Jay feared that France would favor splitting the territory lying north of the 31st parallel and below the Ohio between Spain and Britain.[19]

With the evidence before him, both direct and circumstantial, Jay now acted swiftly. On September 9th he learned of Rayneval's secret trip. The next day he was handed the intercepted Barbé-Marbois dispatch. Wasting not a moment, he immediately broke off his discussions with Aranda. Like a woman scorned, the Conde fell into a fury. He accused Jay of bad faith and lacking talent for diplomacy, and put the blame for the breakdown on the New Yorker's exalted opinion of his own public character. On one of those rare occasions when the Conde and Spain's first minister saw eye to eye, Floridablanca sent back a consoling note, ridiculing Jay, his pretensions, and his unending cries for recognition and money. In turn, Jay attributed the impasse to Spain's shortsightedness. "There is a tide in human affairs," he wrote the French chargé at Madrid, "which waits for nobody, and political mariners ought to watch it and avail themselves of its advantages."[20]

While the Jay-Aranda negotiations were broken off in Paris, the Rayneval-Shelburne talks were proceeding smoothly. Rayneval's visit was prompted, not by the American issue, despite the apprehensions of the French court about America's pretensions, but by the conviction on Vergennes' part that the Allies should now get out of the war if decent terms were offered them. For a certainty the French Minister was as much concerned about Spain's inflexible position on Gibraltar as he was about prolonging the war to satisfy America's demands. The day Rayneval left for England Vergennes wrote Montmorin at Madrid: "Let us not lose the occasion if it presents itself to end a war honorably, a war promoted less by ambition than to reestablish ourselves in that position of equality becoming to great powers."[21] This

[19] R to James Monroe, Nov. 14, 1795. William C. Rives, *History of the Life and Times of James Madison* (Boston, 1873), I, 655–660.
[20] F to A, Sept. 2, 1782; A to F, Sept. 1, 8, 15, 1782. AHN, E, 3885, exp. 1; JJ to Bourgoing, Sept. 26, 1782 (extract), Bancroft-America, IV, 171, NYPL.
[21] V to M, Sept. 7, 1782. CP E 608: 315–318.

Vergennes—Spain   Rayneval—France
Jay—US   Shelburne—Eng.

was a thinly veiled warning to Spain not to hold out for unreasonable terms.

Rayneval was instructed to ask Shelburne point-blank whether the notions about peace he had discussed with Admiral de Grasse conformed to his present intentions. Should Shelburne disavow them, then Rayneval was to demand his passport and leave England. In other words, he was to feel out Shelburne rather than enter into negotiations, and he was to remind the Earl that it was the King of France's intention of treating only in conjunction with his allies. For that assignment a stay of eight or ten days would suffice, Vergennes figured. The Comte gave Rayneval a personal letter assuring Shelburne that the bearer possessed his "full confidence."[22]

Although Rayneval quickly discovered that Shelburne had no intention of making the generous concessions that de Grasse had attributed to him, and even insisted that he had been misquoted by the Admiral,[23] he did not break off his talks and ask for his passport as instructed. The Frenchman was fascinated by his clever host and seemed captive to the conciliatory mood he sought to arouse. Rayneval's stay at Bowood and a subsequent visit some months later converted him into an ardent admirer of Shelburne. He found the Earl "a minister of noble views" and "winning manners," neither "an intriguer" nor an "equivocator," "whatever persons say who imagine that they know him, but imagine wrongly."[24]

Certain later critics have belabored Jay for his assumption that Rayneval went to England to arrange a deal about the West and the fisheries. In refutation these critics have pointed to Rayneval's formal instructions by which he was told to pursue the conversations begun by de Grasse. These written instructions contained nothing about America's claims, and only passing references to America are found in the contemporary account Rayneval has left us of his conversations with Shelburne. These talks dealt largely with Franco-Spanish grievances, with the West and East Indies, the Newfoundland fisheries, the

[22] See "Ouvertures de M. le Comte de Grasse et propositions de L'Espagne alors remises à M. le Comte de Vergennes," Sept. 4, 1782 (in A's hand), AHN, E, 4203, apt. 1, p. 35; V to R, S, and TG, all dated Sept. 6, 1782. CP A 538: 117–118, 121–124; LP 71; *D*, V, 105.

[23] S to G, Sept. 13; G to S, Sept. 14, 1782. *CG*, VI, 123–125; R to V, Sept. 15, 1782. CP A 538: 193–194.

[24] R to V, Sept. 13, Dec. 25, 1782. CP A 538: 146–162; 539: 314–317; R to S, Sept. 28; S to V, Sept. 21, 1782. LP 71.

slave trade, Dunkirk, Gibraltar, and freedom of commerce. Indeed, Jay's detractors have contended that America did not even come up in the conversations.[25]

Jay's sons and grandsons took up the cudgels in his behalf, and were seconded by the articulate progeny of John Adams. With proper allowance for the filiopietistic impulses of Jay's champions, it is now perfectly clear that Jay's critics were unwilling to draw reasonable inferences from the circumstantial evidence at hand and were careless in their reading of Rayneval's own account of his trip. On September 8th Aranda made the significant observation to Floridablanca that regardless of Jay's obduracy the English would be consulted about America's territorial claims and that nothing further could be done with the Americans until Rayneval's return.[26] It was probably no coincidence that a copy of Rayneval's historical memoir found its way into the *Angleterre* section of the *Correspondance politique*, wherein the paper relating to Rayneval's mission are filed. It seems a reasonable inference that the undersecretary took this document with him when he went to see Shelburne.

Rayneval's own report of his conversations belies the assertions that he did not advert to America. The subject of America came up almost at once. Shelburne conceded that he had "always been opposed to independence, that it was the hardest pill to digest, but that he recognized the necessity of swallowing it, and that this object would be decided unconditionally." Later on in the talks independence was again referred to, but taken for granted by both parties.

After luncheon on the first day of their talks the two diplomats took a stroll through the Earl's wooded park, which gently sloped downward to the man-made lake in which Shelburne took special pride. The talks now turned on the fisheries. Without a doubt the Americans would put in some claims here, Shelburne remarked, but he hoped the King would not yield anything to them. Rayneval replied that, while he did not know the views of Congress on the fisheries, he could take it on himself to say that "the King would never support an unjust demand." Thus, while Shelburne was privately repudiating the decision taken by his own Cabinet to concede to the Americans a share

[25] Sparks, III, 208–212; *North American Rev.*, LXVI (Jan., 1830), 15; James Brown Scott, "Historical Introduction," in *The American Secretaries of State and Their Diplomacy* (New York, 1927), I, 73, 74.

[26] A to F, Sept. 8, 1782. AHN, E, 3885, exp. 1.

in the fisheries, a decision taken hardly more than a week earlier, Rayneval, emboldened by the Earl's apparent accord on this point, declared, *"We do not want the Americans to share in the fisheries."*

After dinner the issue of the mediators came up. Shelburne, in Rayneval's account, "exhibited great coldness for the Court of Vienna," and the two parties readily agreed that peace could be achieved without mediation. "Only three persons should make the peace," Shelburne insisted. By three he included himself, along with Vergennes, and Rayneval as the channel of communication between the two ministers. However flattering Shelburne's posture may have seemed to Rayneval, it was a characteristic sample of Shelburne's penchant for backstage operations, of his readiness to by-pass Alleyne Fitzherbert and Lord Grantham in the Anglo-French negotiations just as he had been prepared to by-pass Thomas Grenville and even the loyal Oswald.[27]

Shelburne continually dangled before the French the prospect that after the peace an Anglo-French *entente* or even a political amalgam of the two might "act as arbiter of the public peace." We could then take a firm stand toward Russia and Prussia, the Earl pointed out, and prevent the kind of partition that had been taking place in Poland. The idea of an *entente* was again reverted to by Shelburne in his closing talk with Rayneval on September 18th. "Let us cease fighting each other," he urged, "and we will lay down the law to the rest of Europe." He reminded Rayneval of the "time when no one dared shoot off a cannon in Europe without the consent of England and France. . . . If we are in accord we can once again assume our former place and we will stop all the revolutions in Europe." Rayneval found the idea of an *entente* a congenial one.

On the second day of their conferences Shelburne and Rayneval agreed that secrecy was necessary to establish the preliminaries of peace. Rayneval pointed out that there were ways of putting the Americans and the Dutch off the track by keeping them in ignorance of the negotiations between England, France, and Spain. The idea seemed to please Shelburne.[28]

At the closing conference on September 18th the talks again reverted to the Americans, whose pretensions were remarked upon during the course of the opening day's talks. Shelburne confided to

[27] Conferences between R and S, Sept. 13, 16, 18, 1782. CP A 538: 146–162, 172–192, 197–198.
[28] Conference between R and S, Sept. 14, 1782. *Ibid.*, pp. 163–170.

Rayneval how much trouble the Americans were stirring up over the boundaries and the fisheries, and expressed the hope that the King of France would not support them. Rayneval answered that he had no doubt of the King's intention to do what could be done to "contain the Americans within the bounds of justice and reason."

"What do you think of their pretensions?" Shelburne asked his guest.

"I do not know what they are relative to the fisheries," Rayneval answered, "but whatever they might be, it appears to me that there is a sound principle to uphold in this matter: Recognize that the fisheries in the high seas are *res nullius,* while the fisheries on the coast belong by right to the proprietor of the coast, except where modified by agreement."

Having blasted America's claims to shore rights for drying fish as well as to fishing within coastal waters, Rayneval turned to the boundaries. To sound out Shelburne he expressed his own belief that the Americans would stand on the provisions of their ancient charters. "That would be silly," Shelburne remarked. Rayneval reported that he did not pursue this line of discussion "because I did not wish either to sustain the American pretension or to deny it." He did not switch the subject, however, before pointing out that the British government might find that the negotiations of 1754 relative to the Ohio offered a measuring stick to settle what should be allotted the United States. As Rayneval interpreted it, the rule would have quashed America's claims to the lands lying north of the Ohio. It is scarcely a coincidence that this same emphasis on the 1754 negotiations appears in the memoir Rayneval had put in Jay's hands before departing for England.

Emboldened by the support of the French court implied in Rayneval's remarks as well as by the heartening news to come from Gibraltar, Shelburne was to renege the Cabinet offer of August 30th, and to put up one more desperate stand along the Ohio. Counting on French support in withholding the "back lands" from America, Shelburne instructed Oswald at a later date to learn through Fitzherbert just how Rayneval and his court stood as regards America's territorial claims. According to Shelburne's own account, Rayneval gave him to understand that, once independence was granted, the French "were disposed to assist us as to the Boundaryes."[29] Indeed, the anti-American overtones of Rayneval's remarks did not pass unnoticed by Shel-

[29] S to TT, *c.* Oct. 28, 1782 (incorrectly dated *c.* Sept. 15, 1782). FO 95/511.

burne. "He appears rather jealous than partial to America upon other points, as well as that of the Fishery," he reported to George III after his very first conference with the Frenchman.[30] Subsequent talks gave Shelburne no cause to modify his observation. So much, then, for the charge that Jay's superheated imagination magnified an innocuous mission into an anti-American plot.

While Rayneval's conversations with Shelburne provided further confirmation for the British of the widening rift between France and America over terms of peace, they also exposed to view the tightrope on which Shelburne himself was teetering. Regardless of his own convictions about the need for American independence, Shelburne had to pursue a political course demanding acrobatic agility of a high order. He had to deal daily with a King unaccustomed to hearing unpalatable truths and to prepare to face some months off a Parliament and a public still ill-prepared to accept terms of submission. Some of these problems Shelburne mentioned to Rayneval in his closing talk. It was terribly difficult to talk to the King, he told the Frenchman. His ministers had never spoken to him save to refer to his grandeur and his power. They had always elevated him above the greatest monarchs, told him that he commanded infinite resources whereas France was exhausted and without credit. He was informed that by continuing the war he would inevitably smash the French Navy. All these ideas, Shelburne explained, had been drummed into the head of George III in the past. To counteract them was indeed a "delicate and difficult" undertaking, but, he reassured his listener, he had the courage to attempt it and up to a point he flattered himself that he had succeeded. With French assistance, he now hoped he could bring about the King's complete conversion.[31]

The letters passing between Lord Shelburne and George III during these fateful weeks disclose how the former constantly sugar-coated the pill and pursued a zigzag course to overcome the King's suspicions. Thus Shelburne found Rayneval "a well-instructed, inoffensive man of business," who stressed Vergennes' eagerness to "expedite everything which can contribute to an instant and final conclusion" of hostilities. When the conferences started, he told the King, he had been "as clearly of opinion against a peace as I ever was against American independence, till in fact the resolutions of the House of Commons

[30] S to G, Sept. 13, 1782. CG, VI, 125.
[31] Conference between S and R, Sept. 18, 1782. CP A 538: 172–192.

decided the point." Now he reminded the monarch of the state of the army and navy, of the troubles in Ireland, and the temper of the Commons. All these factors pointed to the necessity of a quick peace with France.[32]

Let us not be "too eager to advance the negotiation," the King cautioned his First Lord of the Treasury, and do not be "deceived by the appearance of Monsr. de Rayneval. I owne the art of Monsr. de Vergennes is so well known that I cannot think he would send him if he was an inoffensive man of business; but that he has chosen him from having that appearance whilst well-armed with cunning, which will be the more dangerous if under so specious a garb." Do not rush affairs at the sacrifice of our national interests, he warned a few days later. As for himself, George III could do nothing but pray to heaven for guidance "that posterity may not lay the downfall of this once respectable Empire at my door; and that if ruin should attend the measures that may be adopted, I may not long survive."[33] His deep-dyed suspicions of the French notwithstanding, George III had been cleverly maneuvered into a state of resignation about yielding Gibraltar provided there was equivalent compensation and even to seeing the advantage of pressing the French negotiations to strengthen the hand of the British with the Americans.

John Jay had been quick to perceive the peril to American interests at the peacemaking should France and England arrive at a secret understanding. To divine the nature of the Rayneval-Shelburne conversations was beyond the Americans, who lacked the same kind of intelligence service from inside of Bowood Park that Dr. Edward Bancroft had so obligingly provided the British for years from within Franklin's Passy household.[34] Yet the New Yorker was convinced by a perusal of the Rayneval memoir that France was prepared to frustrate America's major aspirations, aside from independence, and his views were shared by Benjamin Vaughan.[35] Jay conjectured, as he later wrote Secretary Livingston, that Rayneval was sent to England:

> 1st, To let Lord Shelburne know that the demands of America to be treated as independent previous to a treaty were not approved or coun-

[32] S to G, Sept. 13, 1782. *CG*, VI, 125.

[33] G to S, Sept. 14, 16, 23, 27, 1782. *CG*, VI, 125, 129, 135, 137.

[34] S was promptly posted on the status of the V-JJ controversy, and told by an insider that America would take it amiss should Britain cede the back country to Spain. [Edward Bancroft] to S, Sept. 9, 1782. LPB.

[35] BV to James Monroe, Sept. 18, 1795. Monroe Papers, VIII, 964. LC.

tenanced by this Court, and that the offer of Britain to make that acknowledgment in an article of the proposed treaty was in the Court's opinion sufficient.

2dly, To sound Lord Shelburne on the subject of the fishery, and to discover whether Britain would agree to divide it with France to the exclusion of all others.

3dly, To impress Lord Shelburne with the determination of Spain to possess the exclusive navigation of the Gulf of Mexico, and of their desire to keep us from the Mississippi; and also to hint the propriety of such a line as on the one hand would satisfy Spain and on the other leave to Britain all the country north of the Ohio.

4thly, To make such other verbal overtures to Lord Shelburne as it might not be advisable to reduce to writing, and to judge, from the general tenor of his lordship's answers and conversations whether it was probable that a general peace, on terms agreeable to France, could be effected in order that, if that was not the case, an immediate stop might be put to the negotiation.[36]

Convinced that Vergennes would rather "postpone the acknowledgment of our independence by Britain to the conclusion of a general peace than aid us in procuring it at present," Jay took the most audacious step of his career. He dispatched Benjamin Vaughan to England on a mission so secret that neither Vergennes nor Franklin was apprised of it. Vaughan was sent to counteract Rayneval. He was instructed to tell Shelburne that "the manner as well as the matter of the proposed treaty" was important, and that without unconditional acknowledgment of independence "neither confidence nor peace could reasonably be expected." Such acknowledgment Jay labeled "the touchstone of British sincerity." Vaughan was to point out to Shelburne how vain it was to count on France's acting as a moderating influence, for America "never would treat on any but an equal footing," and he was to show how it was in France's interest to postpone such acknowledgment to the very conclusion of the treaty, thereby obliging the Americans, both by the terms of their treaty with France as well as for their own safety, to continue in the war to the end. These considerations, Jay made clear, underscored the "obvious interest of Britain immediately to cut the cords which tied us to France, for that, though we were determined faithfully to fulfill our treaty and engage-

---

[36] JJ to RRL, Nov. 17, 1782. JP; *RDC*, VI, 29.

ments with this court, *yet it was a different thing to be guided by their or our construction of it.*"

Adverting to the terms he anticipated Rayneval would be taking up with Shelburne, Jay instructed Vaughan on the fisheries. "We could not make peace," the agent was told, at the expense of England's dividing the fisheries with France and excluding America. He also gave Vaughan instructions on the boundaries and the navigation of the Mississippi. To contest the American claims to either would be "impolitic," he was told. Shelburne was to be enticed into making these concessions by holding out to him "the profits of an extensive and lucrative commerce." Not "the possession of vast tracts of wilderness," but commerce was the true objective of "a commercial European nation," Jay shrewdly reminded Shelburne, the free trader. Dangling the prospects of an immense amount of trade into the interior of the country, Jay now intimated, and without authority either from Congress or his colleagues on the peace commission, that America was prepared to share that interior trade with England, including the free navigation of the Mississippi. England should abandon any idea of retaining any part of the back country or of insisting on extending the bounds of Canada "so as to comprehend the lands in question." Nothing could prevent the Americans from gradually taking possession of the area, Jay prophesied, and to hold on to it would be to sow the seeds of future war. By implication Jay now waived all claims to ancient Canada itself. In short, Vaughan was instructed to impress Shelburne "with the necessity and policy of taking a decided and manly part respecting America."[37]

That Jay should have picked for so delicate a mission a man who was the unavowed agent of the British First Minister may seem astonishing at this day when there is much less tolerance of divided loyalties than in Jay's time. Yet the New Yorker had complete reliance on Benjamin Vaughan's basic friendliness to the American cause, and his trust was not misplaced. Vaughan immediately dashed off a few lines to Shelburne. "In the utmost haste," he informed the Earl that "an affair has occurred which gives much alarm here. M. de Rayneval, Count de Vergennes' principal secretary, will probably soon be with your lordship, as we suspect on deep business. . . . Will your lordship,"

[37] For a sharp criticism of JJ's offer to share the navigation of the Mississippi with the British, see George Bancroft, *History of the United States of America* (New York, 1897), V, 568.

he asked, "be kind enough to take no sort of measure till one of us comes over, or a courier arrives?"[38]

Jay talked over Vaughan's prospective visit with Richard Oswald, but hid it from Franklin. "It would have relieved me from much anxiety and uneasiness," he confessed to Secretary Livingston, "to have concerted all these steps with Dr. Franklin, but on conversing with him about M. Rayneval's journey, he did not concur with me in sentiment respecting the objects of it." To invite Franklin's opinion on the necessity of the trip would have been to court a possible veto. To have confided in him would have jeopardized the secrecy of the project.[39] Needless to say, Jay did not apprise Vergennes of his plans nor Lafayette. The latter was used by the Comte to pump Jay about the Rayneval mission. On the twenty-first Lafayette remarked casually to Jay that a courier had just come over from England and he wondered what the dispatches were about. "The best way to find out would be to write Mr. de Rayneval in England," Jay replied dryly.

"Why do you believe he is there?" Lafayette asked.

"It's on everybody's lips, and I can't help but suppose it to be true."

"Well, then, why do you think he has gone over?" Lafayette prodded.

"I don't know."

"Well, guess."

"I'd rather not."

Vergennes proved almost as uncommunicative to the Marquis about the Rayneval mission as had Jay. "What did Shelburne say about America?" Lafayette reported that he asked the Comte.

"*Assez convenable,*" was the cryptic reply.[40]

A week before Jay had decided to send Vaughan over to see Shelburne he had finally hit on a satisfactory formula to end the impasse over independence. On September 2nd he informed Oswald that, if Franklin would consent, he was prepared to accept "a constructive denomination of character to be introduced in the preamble of the treaty" which would merely describe their constituents as "the Thirteen United States of America." While Oswald readily agreed, Jay reminded him that he had no authority to treat with the Americans "under that denomination." Jay now narrowed his insistence down to "an explicit authority" to be stated in Oswald's commission.

[38] BV to S, Sept. 9, 1782. BV Papers, Amer. Philos. Soc.
[39] JJ to RRL, Nov. 11, 1782. JP; *RDC*, VI, 32.
[40] Ridley, Diary, Sept. 21, 1782.

"How about using the term 'provinces' instead of 'states,' or the expression 'states or provinces'?" Oswald suggested.

"No, neither will answer," Jay replied.

"Then let me have in writing a draft of the alteration you propose."

Jay did so at once, and Oswald forwarded the draft of the new commission to the Home Office. Jay's alteration would have empowered the Scot "to treat of Peace or Truce with the Commissioners and Persons vested with equal powers by and on the part of the Thirteen United States of America."[41] Obligingly, Jay also offered to turn over to Oswald a draft of a letter he might send back "to satisfy His Majesty's Ministers of the propriety of their conduct." The draft again stressed America's insistence on being treated on the basis of equality and restated Jay's objections to having such acknowledgment deferred until the first article of a treaty. To do so would mean, Jay pointed out, "that we are not to be considered in that light until after the conclusion of the treaty, and our acquiescing would be to admit the propriety of our being considered in another light during that interval." Jay presumed that the British court would not wish to press a measure which could not "be reconciled with the received ideas of national honor." Hence he gave his assurances that, had Oswald been commissioned "in the usual manner," the negotiations would have gone forward. The removal of this obstacle, Jay concluded, was a trivial matter to Great Britain, "but so essential and insuperable with respect to us."[42]

Jay showed the draft letter to Franklin, and the pair thrashed the matter out on the evening of the ninth and again the following morning. The doctor, still incapacitated from his severe attack, persuaded Jay not to turn it over to Oswald. The letter was "too positive, and therefore rather imprudent," Franklin argued. Suppose we have to back down? After so peremptory a rejection we would do so with ill grace, he pointed out. Behind his objections, Franklin confessed, lay a deep uneasiness about whether such a move might be considered a violation of the commissioners' instructions which fettered them to the French court. Jay quickly dismissed both objections. He could conceive of no situation, he rejoined, where it would be proper, "and therefore possible," for America "to treat in any other character than

---

[41] Proposed alteration by JJ, dated by O, Sept. 10, 1782. FP, XII, 341–342; LP 70; FO 95/511. See also BF to O, Sept. 8, 1782, with O's comment. FO 97/157.

[42] Draft by JJ (undated) turned over to O on Sept. 10th and forwarded by him to S the next day. LP 71; Jay, *Life*, II, 466, 467.

that of an independent nation." He reminded the doctor, once again, that as regards the instructions, he "could not believe that Congress intended we should follow any advice which might be repugnant to their dignity and interest."

Leaving Passy without Franklin's signature to the draft letter, Jay returned to Paris, dropping in at Oswald's at noontime. "I can't let you have the letter. You had best phrase it in your own way," Jay informed the British commissioner, who could not conceal his disappointment. Oswald tried now to pin the commissioners down to a definite commitment.

"In your conference with the Doctor this morning," he asked Jay, "did you and he agree that upon my receiving from his Majesty a new commission under the Great Seal such as the last, with an alteration only of my being empowered to treat with you as Commissioners of the Thirteen United States of America, naming the states by their several provincial distinction, did you both agree in that case to go on with the treaty, and without any other declaration of independence than as standing as an article in that Treaty?"

"Yes," Jay reassured Oswald. "With this we will be satisfied. Immediately upon such commission coming over, we would proceed with the Treaty, and should not be long about it. I might add that perhaps we should not be so hard upon you in the conditions we exact."

Then Oswald turned back to Jay's draft letter. He insisted that he needed it to convince his government of the good faith of the American commissioners. Jay was at length persuaded to turn over to him an unsigned copy of the draft. "With some difficulty I got [it] out of his hands after it had been settled with his Friend that it was not proper to go before any public Board." In transmitting to the Home Secretary Jay's proposed alteration of the commission along with his draft letter, Oswald warned his government that if they rejected Jay's compromise formula "there will be an end to all further confidence and communication with the Americans."[43] "With great difficulty," Oswald wrote Shelburne, "they have yielded to this mode of compromise. . . . I hope His Majesty will grant it. If it is refused, Mr. Fitzherbert as well as me, may go home, and in my opinion it will not be an

[43] Endorsement on draft forwarded by O to S, Sept. 11, 1782. LP 71: 15. JJ to RRL, Nov. 17, 1782. *RDC*, VI, 18–21. O to TT, Sept. 10, 1782. FO 95/511; 97/157; 27/2. "Sketch of an alteration proposed by Mr. Jay to be made in His Majesty's Commission," Sept. 10, 1782. FO 95/511; LP 70; FO 97/157.

easy matter for any other to take up the same clue for extracting the Nation out of its difficulties which I think is within our reach." In that same letter Oswald pointed out that the Spaniards apparently wanted a cession from England before the American treaty was ironed out, and that this was the apparent motive behind Rayneval's visit. "If that gentleman goes over," he added, "there can be no difficulty in amusing him."[44]

While these negotiations were going on Vergennes was using Lafayette as an intermediary with the American commissioners to make clear that, although he had no objection to making independence a preliminary, he wanted to be sure that all the preliminaries were signed simultaneously. The Comte still felt that the issue that Jay had raised could be settled if only Oswald would write a letter agreeing to treat with the American commissioners "in their capacity as plenipotentiaries of the United States," with the understanding that George III's renunciation of the territory of the United States would be contained in the first article of the treaty. Jay was not content with such "expedients,"[45] nor with the ambivalent role of Lafayette. Under the character of an American and as aid to Franklin by Congressional designation,[46] the Marquis claimed an insider's role in the British-American negotiations, while as a loyal Frenchman he was constantly leaking confidential information to Vergennes. "This mongrel character of French Patriot and American Patriot," as John Adams uncharitably put it, made Lafayette increasingly suspect in American circles in Paris. "As we have a competent number of commissioners," Jay tactfully advised Secretary Livingston, "it ought not to be necessary to trouble the Marquis." Adams put it with his customary bluntness. "There ought to be no Go-between," he declared.[47] What made the situation especially delicate was Jay's conviction that Franklin was passing on to Lafayette a full account of all the moves the New Yorker made, so far as they were known to him. Accordingly, Jay said

[44] O to S, Sept. 11, 1782. LP 71. TT referred O's "two large packets" dealing with the change in form of the commission to G, and indicated to S the likelihood that G would want a Cabinet opinion. TT to S, Sept. 14, 1782. LPB.

[45] JJ to RRL, Sept. 18, Nov. 17, 1782. *JPJ*, II, 348, 385–386. Lafayette to BF (*ante* Sept. 18, 1782), FP, no. 2594. LC.

[46] *JCC*, XXI, 1134–1136.

[47] JJ to RRL, Oct. 13, 1782; *JPJ*, II, 349; JA to Warren, April 16, 1783, *Warren-Adams Letters*, II, 214, 215.

nothing to his aged colleague about handing over the unsigned draft to Oswald.[48]

Jay's altered proposal gave an urgency to Vaughan's trip. On September 11th Vaughan wrote Shelburne to inform him of his intention of following "a few hours after the present courier," and apprising him of the rumor that Rayneval's journey had for its object an "underhand bargain" between England and Spain. "This is a crisis of the first consequence," Vaughan declared. He urged Shelburne to hold up his negotiations with the Frenchman, but advised him that he should act with "instantaneous despatch" in dealing with the American commissioners and in modifying the form of Oswald's commission to suit Jay's demands. " 'America must have a character,' to use the words of Mr. Adams," Vaughan remarked. Finally, he cautioned Shelburne in language close to that of Oswald's, "If this moment is rudely managed, or slightly passed over, I conceive peace in *consequence* takes its flight." In short, in this crisis the alternatives were "good sense" or "ruin."[49]

That night Vaughan left for London.[50] His arrival in England obliged Shelburne to suspend his zigzag course. A decision to issue a new commission in the form Jay had proposed was not one to be made casually by England's First Minister. Shelburne had, first of all, to consider the King's feelings. Next he had to pay heed to public opinion. During September he continued to receive anonymous letters warning him that "America must be preserved to England," and even threatening him with assassination should he concede independence.[51] So intimate a follower of Shelburne's as Thomas Orde cautioned his chief about the alarm prevailing both in the city and over the countryside as a result of rumors of "the extent of the concessions made by this country." People might digest independence as the price of peace, Orde pointed out, but would with difficulty be reconciled to an unconditional grant so damaging to "our national pride should no concessions be gained thereby." At least there should be an implied agreement on all the issues under discussion *before* the "irretrievable surrender of sovereignty," he pleaded.[52] Another intimate, Lord Ash-

---

[48] Ridley, Diary, Sept. 14, 21, 1782. Ridley was in error in asserting that JJ did not let O know that BF opposed sending on the draft letter. *Ibid.*, Sept. 26, 1782.
[49] BV to S, Sept. 11, 1782. Amer. Philos. Soc.
[50] Ridley, Diary, Sept. 11, 1782.
[51] See anonymous letters to S of Sept. 5, 23, 1782. LPB.
[52] T. Orde to S, Sept. 26, 1782. LPB.

burton, warned Shelburne that to issue the commission in the form Jay proposed and Vaughan was now urging in person would put "the Executive Government" in a dubious light should peace not be attained, but he did reluctantly agree that the alteration came within the terms of the Enabling Act.[53] Fortuitously for the cause of peace, the Lord Chancellor, who, as might be anticipated, showed no enthusiasm for the new form, was out of town when the Cabinet took action, as was the unpredictable Duke of Richmond. Thurlow, still suspicious of the American commissioners, considered Jay's demands for preliminary independence to be "frivolous," and felt that the British would henceforth be negotiating from weakness, especially in view of their failure to secure advance commitments on the Tories and the debts.[54]

Vaughan's personal appeal, Oswald's threats, and Jay's sober arguments all added up to compelling reasons for complying with the New Yorker's wishes, and overriding the grumblers within the Ministry. A special meeting of "a considerable number" of the Cabinet who happened to be in town was called for the night of September 18th, less than a week after Vaughan's arrival in England, and on the day of Rayneval's final conference with Shelburne. The Cabinet voted to change the commission and to empower Oswald "to treat, consult, and conclude with any Commissioner or person vested with equal power by and on the part of the Thirteen United States of America," named in geographical order from north to south. Significantly, the Cabinet did not consider the new phraseology to amount to "a final acknowledgment of independence," but merely as providing the American commissioners during the negotiations with "the title they wished to assume." This may have been technically correct, and Shelburne was later to insist on this point in defense of his course before Parliament. Neither Townshend nor Shelburne admitted any such thing to Oswald, however, when on the following day a new commission was sent over to Paris embodying the change that Jay had desired.[55]

How decisive a factor was the Vaughan mission in persuading Shel-

---

[53] TT to TG, Sept. 15, 1782. GP L 30/14; Ashburton to S, Sept. 16, 18, 1782. Add. Sydney Papers, 3: 11. CL; LPB.

[54] Thurlow to TT, Sept. 18, 22, 1782. TT Papers, Huntington Lib.

[55] Minutes of Cabinet Meeting, Sept. 19, 1782, in TT's hand forwarded by S to G. *CG*, VI, 131. TT to Thurlow, Sept. 20, 1782 (draft); to Richmond, Sept. 23, 1782; Add. Sydney Papers, 3: 13, 14; Thurlow to S, *c.* Sept. 23, 1782. LPB; TT to O, Sept. 19; to S, Sept. 24, 1782. LP 70; LPB; FO 27/2; 95/511; 97/157; PCC 106; CP EU 22: 248–252 (in French and English); Hartley Papers, III, CL.

burne to back down on the issue of independence? The motivations of a figure as inscrutable as Shelburne cannot be pinned down with certitude. The papers of Shelburne and Townshend disclose that it was the "private letters from Paris," presumably brought by Vaughan, which impelled Shelburne to take the forward step. Vaughan himself had no doubts whatsoever about it. Writing many, many years later, he recounted that Shelburne only asked him, "Is the new Commission necessary? and when I answered 'Yes,' it was instantly granted."[56] Shelburne may well have been on the verge, but Vaughan's presence seems to have precipitated the decision to jump. "Mr. Vaughan greatly merits our acknowledgments," Jay reported home.[57]

His business with Shelburne completed, Vaughan returned to Paris on September 27th with word that there was "every disposition in Lord Shelburne for peace." As solid evidence he could point to the new commission for Oswald which the courier had brought and the copy for Mr. Jay. Even Franklin, who had been grumbling about "standing out for the previous acknowledgment of Independency" and been overheard remarking that it was "a pity to keep three or four millions of people in war for the sake of form," was content with the new commission,[58] for which he could scarcely claim credit.[59] Franklin's implied criticism of Jay for stalling the negotiations on a technicality was hardly fair, for, as we now know, it was Townshend who kept Oswald from disclosing his full hand, and it was Jay who speedily devised a compromise formula to end the impasse. Despite some reservations on the part of the doctor about legal quibbling, Jay's solo performance did not lessen Franklin's admiration for him one whit, and the pair henceforth worked together in close harmony.

---

[56] Hale, *Franklin in France*, II, 146, 147.

[57] JJ to RRL, Sept. 28, 1782. JJ Letterbook, JP; PCC 110: 2. The commission, dated Sept. 21, reached Paris on the same day as BV, Sept. 27. *RDC*, V, 779; *JPJ*, II, 348; Sparks, VIII, 128.

[58] BF to RRL, Sept. 26, 1782. *BFS*, VIII, 602; BV to S, Oct. 3, 1782, Amer. Philos. Soc. James Parton, *Life of Franklin* (New York, 1864), II, ch. XV, speaks of the doctor "during the month wasted upon *this nonsense*."

[59] Ridley, Diary, Sept. 21, 1782.

KEY TO FOOTNOTES

NAMES

A	Conde de Aranda
AF	Alleyne Fitzherbert (Baron St. Helens)
BF	Benjamin Franklin
BV	Benjamin Vaughan
CG	Conrad Alexandre Gérard
DH	David Hartley
F	Conde de Floridablanca
G	George III
H	Earl of Hillsborough
HL	Henry Laurens
JA	John Adams
JH	Sir James Harris (1st Earl of Malmesbury)
JJ	John Jay
K	Prince Wenzel Anton Kaunitz-Rietberg
L	Chevalier Anne César de La Luzerne
LV	Duc de La Vauguyon
M	Comte de Montmorin
MA	Marie Antoinette
MDA	Comte Mercy d'Argenteau
MT	Maria Theresa
O	Richard Oswald
R	Joseph Matthias Gérard de Rayneval
RRL	Robert R. Livingston
S	William Petty, 2nd Earl of Shelburne (1st Marquess of Lansdowne)
ST	David Murray, Lord Stormont
TG	Thomas Robinson (2nd Baron Grantham)
TT	Thomas Townshend (Baron Sydney)
V	Charles Gravier, Comte de Vergennes
W	Thomas Thynne (3rd Viscount Weymouth)

SOURCES

Adm.	Admiralty Papers (Public Record Office, London)
A.G.	Archives du Ministère de la Guerre (Château de Vincennes)
AGI	Archivo General de Indias (Seville)
AHN, E	Archivo Histórico Nacional, Estado series (Madrid)
A.M.	Archives de la Marine (Archives Nationales, Paris)
AMON	*Archives ou Correspondance Inédite de la Maison d'Orange-Nassau*, 5th ser., ed. by F. J. L. Kramer (Leyden, 1915)
AN	Archives Nationales (Paris)
AP	Adams Family Papers (Massachusetts Historical Society)
ARH	Algemeen Rijksarchief, The Hague
BFAW	*Benjamin Franklin's Autobiographical Writings*, ed. by Carl Van Doren (New York, 1945)
BFB	John Bigelow, ed., *The Complete Works of Benjamin Franklin* (10 vols., New York, 1887–88)
BFS	Albert H. Smyth, ed., *The Writings of Benjamin Franklin* (10 vols., New York, 1905–07)
BM	British Museum
BN	Bibliothèque Nationale
CG	*Correspondence of King George the Third (1760–1783)*, ed. by Sir John Fortescue (6 vols., London, 1928)
CL	William L. Clements Library, University of Michigan
CO	Colonial Office Papers (Public Record Office, London)
CP	Correspondance politique, Ministère des Affaires Étrangères (Paris)
	CP A Correspondance politique, Angleterre
	CP Aut Correspondance politique, Autriche
	CP E Correspondance politique, Espagne
	CP EU Correspondance politique, États-Unis
	CP H Correspondance politique, Hollande
	CP R Correspondance politique, Russie
D	Henri Doniol, *Histoire de la Participation de la France à l'établissement des États-Unis d'Amérique* (5 vols., Paris, 1886–92)
DC	Manuel Danvila y Collado, *Reinado de Carlos III* (5 vols., Madrid, 1893–94)
Diary	*Diary and Autobiography of John Adams*, ed. by L. H. Butterfield (4 vols., Cambridge, Mass., 1961)
FC	*Memorials and Correspondence of Charles James Fox*, ed. by Lord John Russell (3 vols., London, 1853)
FO	Foreign Office Papers (Public Record Office, London)
FP	Papers of Benjamin Franklin (Yale University Library)
FS	Lord Edmond Fitzmaurice, *Life of William, Earl of Shelburne* (3 vols., London, 1876)

GP   Grantham Papers (Bedfordshire Rolls Office)
HLP   Henry Laurens Papers (South Carolina Historical Society)
HMC, R Royal Commission on Historical Manuscripts, *Reports* (London, 1874
        ——)
HP   Sir Lewis Namier and John Brooke, *The History of Parliament: The
        House of Commons, 1754–1790* (3 vols., New York, 1964)
JAW   *Works of John Adams*, ed. by Charles Francis Adams (10 vols., Boston,
        1850–56)
JCC   *Journals of the Continental Congress*, ed. by W. C. Ford and Gaillard
        Hunt (34 vols., Washington, 1904–37)
JP   Papers of John Jay (Special Collections, Columbia University Libraries)
JPJ   *Correspondence and Public Papers of John Jay*, ed. by H. P. Johnston (4
        vols., New York, 1890–93)
KBGS   Königlich Bayerisches Geheimes Staatsarchiv (Munich—microfilm LC)
LC   Library of Congress
LMCC   *Letters of Members of the Continental Congress*, comp. by E. C. Burnett
        (8 vols., Washington, 1921–36)
LP   Shelburne (Marquess of Lansdowne) Papers (William L. Clements Li-
        brary)
LPB   Shelburne (Marquess of Lansdowne) Papers, Bowood, Calnes, Wiltshire
NA   National Archives
PCC   Papers of the Continental Congress (National Archives)
PCFG   *Politische Correspondenz Friedrich's des Grossen*, ed. by G. B. Volz (45
        vols., Berlin, 1918–37)
PH   *Parliamentary History*
PR   *Parliamentary Register*
R   Rockingham Papers, Wentworth Woodhouse Collection, Sheffield Public
        Libraries
RDC   *The Revolutionary Diplomatic Correspondence of the United States*, ed.
        by Francis Wharton (6 vols., Washington, 1889)
SF   B. F. Stevens, *Facsimiles of Manuscripts in European Archives Relating
        to America, 1773–83* (25 vols., London, 1889–98)
SGH   Archief Staten Generaal (Algemeen Rijksarchief, The Hague)
SKD   Staatskanzlei, Diplomatische Korrespondenz (Haus-, Hof-, und Staatsar-
        chiv, Vienna)
SP   State Papers (Public Record Office, London)
Sparks *Diplomatic Correspondence of the American Revolution*, ed. by Jared
        Sparks (12 vols., Boston, 1829–30)
SRIO   *Sbornik imperatorskago russkago istorichesgkago obshchestva* (St.
        Petersburg, 1867–1916)
WO   War Office Papers (Public Record Office, London)
YU   Juan F. Yela Utrilla, *España ante la Independencia de los Estados Unidos*
        (2d ed., 2 vols., Lérida, 1925)

PART 2
NEUTRALITY
IN JEOPARDY

INTRODUCTION

During the Confederation period, difficult in many ways for the fledgling American nation, international affairs were particularly trying. Encouraging the expansion of trade was a pressing problem, for, having given up the benefits of membership in the British Empire, America's merchants had to establish new commercial connections. Foreign powers, especially England, were almost totally indifferent to American proposals for reciprocal trade agreements, and the Confederation Congress was unable to convince the states to grant it the legislative authority necessary for the efficient regulation of commerce.

The question of national security too plagued the country. The alliance with France offered no real guarantees. On the contrary it was viewed as potentially dangerous, committing the United States as it did to the defense of France's holdings in the Western Hemisphere should she be attacked at some future time by another European power. Even before the peace was officially concluded in 1783, Americans were openly expressing regret over the Franco-American alliance and policy makers had set their minds to establishing genuine neutrality.

Through the remainder of the decade of the 1780's and into the 1790's American diplomatists weathered some crises without serious embarrassment. The French Revolution, however, which broke out in 1789 and was followed by nearly a quarter-century of general European war, created serious difficulties. As a major neutral carrier engaged in trade with virtually all the nations of Europe, America was, whether she liked it or not, a factor in the political and military calculations of the belligerents. It was soon apparent that the test of American diplomacy would be whether the United States could continue a trade important to her economic prosperity and simultaneously remain uninvolved in war.

Complicating matters was the fact that the French Revolution raised serious ideological questions in America, questions that had a telling effect both on the course of diplomacy abroad and on politics at home. At first France's struggle for liberty seemed a repetition of the earlier American experience, and in the United States scarcely a word was raised against it. As the revolution became more violent, however, some Americans began to express doubts about it. By 1793, after the execution of King Louis XVI and Britain's entry into the wars of the revolution as an enemy of France, the ideological cleavage in the United States was complete. Friends and enemies of the French Revolution took sides, disputing, sometimes violently, the relative virtues of the belligerents. Washington's administration, supported by the predominantly Anglophile Federalists, faced a growing phalanx of pro-French opponents who ultimately formed under the banner of the Jeffersonian Republican Party. Against this ideological backdrop the administrations of Washington and John Adams struggled to remain aloof from Europe's wars.

Anglo-American relations had been tense since the end of the American Revolution. After Shelburne's ministry fell, new British ministries adopted a harder line, refusing to negotiate a treaty of commerce with the United States and, until 1790, even refusing to send a minister to America. Moreover, in violation of the treaty of 1783, Britain retained seven military and trading posts on the American side of the northern border along the Great Lakes and on the Niagara frontier. From these posts her merchants dominated the valuable fur trade of the area, and her partisans incited the Indians against Americans living in the Ohio Valley.

Americans too fed the flames of bitterness, failing to live up to many stipulations of the treaty. For example, despite the fact that the agreement guaranteed British creditors the right to take legal action to collect more than five million pounds sterling in prerevolutionary debts from American borrowers, various state legislatures interceded, prohibiting litigation for the collection of these debts. Although the treaty recommended against the persecution of American loyalists returning home after the war, many were treated with extreme harshness and few succeeded in regaining their estates, sequestered during the revolution.

England's involvement in the European wars in 1793 increased tensions between the two nations both on the frontier and at sea. Fearing that a war with America would leave Canada undefended, British officials there sought to improve relations with the Indians who were then at war with the United States. In February 1794, Lord Dorchester, Governor General of Canada, even held a council with the Indians. He openly averred that soon England would be at war with America, a remark that encouraged the red men in their struggle against the American advance into the Ohio Valley. Two months after this, Dorchester made matters worse, authorizing the construction of a new British post deep in American territory near the rapids of the Maumee River south and west of Detroit.

At sea the Royal Navy proved a voracious enemy and, in late 1793 acting under orders-in-council issued earlier in the year, swooped down upon American merchantmen trading in the French West Indies. Without warning the British seized and their admiralty courts condemned more than three hundred American trading vessels on the ground that they were engaged in illegal trade. Legality in this case was defined by the British. By the end of 1793 the crisis in Anglo-American relations was acute. The clamor for retaliation against the British grew strong, and the Washington administration feared war. In an effort to avoid this the President dispatched John Jay to London in early 1794. Jay succeeded in negotiating a treaty but at considerable cost; it was a distinct setback for American foreign policy (selection 1). Its only redeeming features were that it guaranteed the return of the northwest posts to the United States and offered a possibility that the two countries might avoid war.

Though Federalists throughout the country disliked most of the stipulations of the agreement, they found the alternative—war with Great Britain—unacceptable. Such a war would not only have proven disastrous for American commerce, it would also have placed serious stress on the as yet delicate fabric of the new American government. Moreover, from an ideological point of view, it would have been a war against the wrong belligerent. For these reasons Federalists rallied to the treaty's support. Jeffersonian Republicans, however, were furious over what they considered an ignoble and unnecessary surrender (selection 2). Their reaction against Jay and his treaty was frenzied.

As many had predicted, the ratification of Jay's treaty did not solve America's foreign policy problems; it only redirected them. Before the end of 1796 a crisis with France had developed, the direct result of ratification of the Anglo-American agreement. French privateers swarming in the Caribbean seized almost as many American merchant ships as the British had. Moreover, French admiralty courts proved even more rapacious than their English counterparts. In Paris a new American minister, the South Carolina Federalist Charles Cotesworth Pinckney, was rebuffed. In Philadelphia the French envoy, Pierre Adet, worked to influence the outcome of the closely contested presidential election in favor of the Jeffersonians.

Despite the efforts of both the Jeffersonian party and the French Minister, John Adams won a narrow victory in the election and was inaugurated the second President of the United States in March 1797. Eager to avoid a total breakdown in relations with France, Adams dispatched a special diplomatic commission to Paris to negotiate a settlement. Carefully selecting his agents to represent different geographical sections and diverging political sentiments, Adams sent John Marshall, a staunch Virginia Federalist, and Elbridge Gerry, a personal friend and political ally from Massachusetts who was acceptable to the Jeffersonians, to join Pinckney in this effort to settle Franco-American differences. The refusal of the Directory to receive the mission and the cynical efforts of France's Foreign Minister Talleyrand to extract a bribe as well as other demeaning concessions from the envoys through the agency of three private and unofficial representatives (later known in America as X, Y, and Z) aroused American passions. In the summer of 1798 war seemed imminent.

For a time during the summer of 1798 Adams appeared determined to lead the nation to war. Indeed, he did conduct an undeclared naval war against the French during 1798 and 1799. By the autumn of 1798, however, as a result of changes in both the domestic political situation and abroad, Adams' passion for war had clearly abated. When Congress met in December of that year, his address to the opening session was, all things considered, conciliatory. The following February he surprised even his own cabinet by nominating William Vans Murray to attempt once more the settlement of differences with France. Although he later appointed Chief Justice Oliver Ellsworth of Connecticut and Governor William R. Davie of North Carolina to serve on a commission with Murray and did not dispatch these envoys until the following November, the decision was crucial. Adams thus reversed the trend of American foreign policy, deciding on yet another effort to make peace. His decision, fortuitous in many ways, resulted in the abrogation of the Franco-American alliance and restored to America a flexibility in the conduct of foreign relations only reluctantly surrendered in 1778 (selection 3).

1

TRUCE WITH BRITAIN
ARTHUR BURR DARLING

Jay arrived in England on June 12, 1794. He came to press the demands of the weaker party in dangerous controversies of long standing. He represented a small neutral dealing with a great belligerent who controlled the seas and possessed a commerce vital to his own country. Although he had scarcely anything to offer in return that Britain did not already enjoy, he was to seek concessions for American shipping in the West Indies where Britain had one quarter of her own commerce, and where two thirds of her enemy's commercial interests were centered upon San Domingo. He was to defend the position in regard to American debts which he had already compromised when conducting the foreign affairs of the old Confederation and the injustice of which he had virtually acknowledged as one of the signers of the Treaty of 1783. He had to negotiate with a man who was soon to learn Jay's chief handicap to success directly from the most influential person in the American Government next to the President.

In a way, his judicial temperament, his candor, his great personal pride—some called it self-esteem—unfitted John Jay for such undertakings. They may have made him an effective antagonist of Floridablanca at Madrid in 1780 and of Vergennes at Paris in 1782, but they could hardly make him a powerful advocate with Grenville at London in 1794. In another way, however, Jay's dignity, his judicial mien, even his susceptibility to compliment served the major purpose for which Washington had sent him abroad. It mattered not so much

From Arthur Burr Darling, *Our Rising Empire*, (New Haven, Conn.: Yale University Press, 1940), pp. 180–196. Used by permission of the author.

that he should obtain at once all his Government desired as that he should increase its prestige and make arrangements which would avoid war while the controversies between the two nations moved on to eventual settlement.

Lord Grenville, minister of foreign affairs, had not known until but a few days before the arrival of the American envoy that the situation in the United States had become so critical. The letters of the Canadian authorities and Hammond's despatches from Philadelphia telling of the Congressional debate over discrimination, the new army and the embargo, Dorchester's address to the Indians and Simcoe's new fort on the Maumee, had been delayed in crossing the Atlantic. Grenville had been absorbed in the war upon France, with maintaining the European coalition and preventing another league of armed neutrality such as had complicated the last struggle with France during the American Revolution. He had let American affairs slide, putting off final responses to Thomas Pinckney and trusting to Federalist sympathies with Britain to keep Republican irritation from reaching the explosive point. He had been justified in feeling somewhat secure as he observed that France also was violating American neutral rights on the sea. But there were anxious moments now as the British ministers wondered how far the effects of this outburst from America, in which even Federalists were raucous, would extend. The United States were Britain's best customer. The British Navy could not be divided for sea duty on both sides of the Atlantic for long without endangering its control of the sea. Britain could no more really afford war in America at this time than could the United States.

On second thought, however, Grenville must have realized that the coming of Jay in itself should allay as soon as risen any fear that the United States would go to war. Surely, the Jay mission bound President Washington to a policy of waiting. Congress might possibly get out of hand and declare war; but Congress could not actually make it; Washington was commander-in-chief. Grenville had more perception than Genet of the changes which the new Constitution had made in America. The President's personal agent, Gouverneur Morris, was saying to the Committee of Public Safety in Paris, that the American military preparations were to check the Indians and to put the Government in position not to fear an attack by Britain. There was reassurance for Grenville in that negative, the report of which came to him privately from a British agent in Italy.

A concession or so to the American Chief Justice, some of which had already been decided upon, would be in order. Dorchester should be set down for his remarks to the Indians. Appeals of the seizures in the Caribbean should be had from the admiralty courts in the West Indies to higher courts in England. And Britain would agree to evacuate the Northwest posts at a time to be decided, and upon conditions. The order-in-council of June 8, 1793, as it applied to the preëmption of neutral cargoes of grain bound to France, was withdrawn on August 6, 1794. With these points clear, negotiations could proceed in easy fashion.

As Grenville viewed the situation, the longer they took the better. A victory like Howe's over the fleet of Villaret on June 1, 1794, was hopeful, even though the convoy of supply ships from America had eluded the British patrol and reached the French port. Spain's restlessness in the coalition against France was disturbing, but Russia and Prussia this time could be counted upon the British side. So long as Jay could report home some progress, there was little chance of war with the United States—unless of course something unforeseen or unpremeditated should happen in the back country of America, or possibly this league of neutrals, talked among Danes, Swedes, and Americans at the instigation of Frenchmen, should develop into a real instrument of force. That Lord Grenville would much deplore.

Notwithstanding, therefore, the flurry caused by James Monroe's arrival in Paris with fervid greetings from the United States Senate, and his ostentatious acceptance of the fraternal kiss of the President of the French Convention, Grenville and Jay had accumulated in exchanges of opinion by September 13 a significant list of objects for a treaty. They agreed in principle that there should be: evacuation of the posts, a commission to settle the northeast boundary, compensation for damages to both parties, compensation for the British creditors, immunity for private debts and securities in time of war, admission into the British West Indies of limited American shipping, freedom of ports, sharp restrictions upon sales of prizes, regulations for the ownership and disposal of land, protection of vessels or property within respective jurisdictions, and a reciprocal prohibition of impressment.

But Jay had not been able to bring Grenville to final conclusions or to get him really down to the principles at issue concerning neutral rights of commerce. He therefore decided to submit the draft of a treaty which would comprehend the points in the interest of the

United States. This he did on September 30. By that time Grenville, however, had learned from Hammond what he was very pleased to know. The American Government, no matter what Secretary Randolph had put into the instructions of John Jay, would have nothing to do with the rumored league of armed neutrality toward which Denmark and Sweden were so feebly maneuvering.

Among Alexander Hamilton's "reveries" on March 8 had been the idea of concerted action by neutrals. No American statesman had forgotten the contribution of the European league in 1780 to the success of the American Revolution. With little more than that memory, and no knowledge that Russia was now on the other side, Secretary Randolph had instructed Jay to sound the ministers of Russia, Denmark, and Sweden upon the probability of an alliance to support the principles of armed neutrality—for, said he, they "would abundantly cover our neutral rights." But on July 8, 1794, the Secretary of the Treasury begged leave to inform the Secretary of State of his opinion: "Denmark and Sweden are too weak and too remote to render a co-operation useful; and the entanglements of a treaty with them might be found very inconvenient. The United States had better stand upon their own ground." Hamilton admitted that his impression had varied, but the foregoing, he announced to Randolph, was the "final result of full reflection."

Then, usurping the prerogative of the Secretary of State to negotiate with representatives of foreign states, the Secretary of the Treasury again indulged himself, as he had since 1789, and told the British minister the same thing, with elaborations: "It was the settled policy of this Government in every contingency, even in that of an open contest with Great Britain, to avoid entangling itself with European connexions, which could only tend to involve this country in disputes wherein it might have no possible interest, and commit it in a common cause with allies, from whom, in the moment of danger, it could derive no succour."

Jay himself was about to write to Washington—much as he had asserted to Montmorin at Madrid in 1780: "As to a political connection with any country, I hope it will never be judged necessary, for I very much doubt whether it would ultimately be found useful; it would, in my opinion, introduce foreign influence, which I consider as the worst of political plagues." Jay's behavior may easily have given a similar impression to Grenville at this time. But that is quite a different thing from deliberately stating the results of the discussions in the cabinet of the Administration to the minister of the opposing country. Hamilton's remarks to Hammond have been properly designated since then as statesmanship pioneering before the Monroe Doctrine of 1823. When they were made, they were nothing else than the betrayal of a state secret.

Hammond reported at once to Grenville, August 3, 1794. Grenville received the despatch on September 20. The draft of a treaty which Jay presented ten days later was subjected forthwith to ruthless excision, and he was left in the dilemma of sending home what it pleased Grenville to give him or virtually nothing at all. And yet, conclude the authorities on this period, and in historical perspective quite rightly, John Jay nevertheless signed on November 14, 1794, a treaty of great importance in his own time and of still greater value to the future of this nation.

TERMS OF THE JAY TREATY

This new contract to maintain peace with Britain is best appraised by its provisions concerning the West, the boundaries of the British domain, the claims of both parties for damages, their maritime commerce, the rights of neutrals, and the interests of France.

Britain agreed to evacuate her posts on American soil on or before June 1, 1796. The date was set ahead in order to allow time for her traders to withdraw from the Indian country or adjust themselves to the laws of the United States either as citizens or alien property holders. Safeguards were established for the continuance of British trading with the Indians below the international boundary, and reciprocal rights were given to American traders above that line. But the whole domain of the Hudson's Bay Company to the north and west was to remain closed to them. Their advantages in British territory, therefore, were not comparable to those of British traders in the Western part of the United States. Permanent freedom of transit over the waterways and portages interlacing the boundary was assured to both parties, but there were provisions to prevent the entry of prohibited goods into the territory of either. Tolls and duties were to be reciprocal and no higher than those charged of natives. The Indians were to pass and repass freely with their proper goods and effects of whatever nature.

There were no declarations in the treaty, however, such as Jay had included in his draft: that Indian parties might not pass back and forth when they were at war with either party to the treaty; that both parties would abstain from political connections with the Indians and would restrain their respective Indians from war; and that they would make common cause against every future Indian war so far as to prohibit supplying arms and ammunition and to refrain from encouraging any tribes to join in it. Nor were there in the treaty the suggestions which Hamilton had made and Jay presented in his draft; that neither party should maintain armed vessels on the lakes and waterways of the boundary, and that they should enter into arrangements for reducing and withdrawing all military force from the borders.

Grenville's refusal to admit these clauses into the treaty was deliberate. He was working toward the plan for an Indian buffer state largely on American soil south and west of Lakes Erie, Huron, and Superior. Britain's statesmen would not be ready to abandon that hope until after the War of 1812.

The treaty included a provision for postponing determination of the northwest line from the Lake of the Woods to the Mississippi River, without prejudice to the interests of either party, until they could have a joint survey. Having learned from Hammond that the line of 1783 was geographically in error—as in all probability the source of the Mississippi was not to the west but to the south of the Lake of the Woods—Grenville had pressed Jay to concede that the acknowledged right of Britain to navigation on the Mississippi implied the right to approach the river entirely through British territory. This would have been advantageous in constructing the Indian state. But Grenville had other reasons. Secret agents had not been reporting about the "Granary of America" in years past with no effect. Britons, although their seaboard colonies were gone, still thought of great things to come in the Mississippi Valley.

But John Jay, remembering the value which he and his fellow commissioners in 1782 had put upon the chance of American entry into the upper Mississippi Valley beyond Lake Michigan when they had given up pretension to the area from Lake Erie to Nipissing, had stuck to the argument of principle and intention. They had meant, he said, to draw the line due west to the Mississippi, not southward; the concept of free navigation did not necessarily include the possession of adjacent lands; otherwise, neither Britain nor America would have any basis for asserting, as they did, their right to use the Mississippi through Spanish territory to the Gulf.

Grenville did not see fit to press harder upon the point at that time. This did not mean, however, that Pitt and he had resigned themselves to the loss of that territory. It meant that they would await developments after they had done with the war in Europe. Neither British nor Americans then realized that the future value of the minerals in the Superior country was greater than the fur trade. Neither had any conception how important a part those resources were soon to play in making the United States of America self-reliant, even disdainful toward the rest of the world. But postponement of the decision in 1794 marked a distinct gain for them.

The dispute over the northeastern line between Maine and Quebec and New Brunswick, on the other hand, was referred to a board of commissioners at Halifax chosen by both parties. It was to determine the identity of the St. Croix River which had been designated in the Treaty of 1783. The creation of a mixed commission so to arbitrate and settle an international quarrel was a significant achievement, but this departure in international procedure was more easily obtained than the solution of the problem for which it had been made. The St. Croix River was identified in 1798, but the northeast boundary was not finally drawn until 1842.

The Jay Treaty also provided that British creditors who had found legal impediments, contrary to the Treaty of 1783, in the way of collecting debts contracted before the peace, might present their claims to another mixed commission sitting in Philadelphia. The United States undertook to guarantee the payment of such awards as this commission should determine. For the very reason that legal impediments had stood in the way of their obtaining satisfaction in American courts, the treaty gave these British claimants direct access to the commission without having first to take their cases through the tier of American courts.

The Federal Court in the district of Virginia (chief among the offending States) had already declared valid in 1793 those bona fide debts to British creditors which had not been confiscated by the State while conducting her war upon Britain. There was pending an appeal to the Supreme Court concerning those debts which had been confiscated, for they involved the treaty-making power of the new Federal Government under the Constitution. Jay had sat on the bench at the second hearing before the circuit court. He was still Chief Justice of the United States. He knew that the Constitution contained the statement: "All treaties made, or which shall be made, under the authority of the United States, shall be the supreme law of the land; and the judges in every State shall be bound thereby, anything in the Constitution or laws of any State to the contrary notwithstanding." He might have insisted, therefore, that in the end the British creditors would obtain from the Federal judiciary of the United States the satisfaction to which they were entitled under the Treaty of 1783.

But there was weakness in this procedure. The Constitution, although not adopted until 1788, was retrospective, to be sure, in that it declared all treaties which had been made under the authority of the United States to be the supreme law of the land. But Jay and his associates who had drafted the treaty with Britain in 1782 had written their pledge merely to read: "It is agreed that creditors on either side shall meet no lawful impediment to the recovery of the full value in sterling money, of all bona fide debts heretofore contracted." Was that, together with the retrospective force of the Constitution, strong enough to break down certain results of the revolution in the several States and to compel them to restore such debts as they had confiscated by right of their individual sovereignty?

It would seem so to us now, especially since the penetrating analysis and reasoning of the Justices on the Supreme Bench who in 1796 decided the case on appeal in favor of the British creditors against the State of Virginia. As Justice Wilson summed up the matter then, no State should have the power to confiscate debts: it was a disreputable proceeding, discountenanced in the law of nations; but even if Virginia had possessed the power to confiscate, the Treaty of 1783 had annulled her confiscation.

Instead, however, of relying on that position, in advance of the decision of the Supreme Court, and using the issue to enhance the prestige of the Court while he was in London, Chief Justice Jay had chosen rather to dispose of the question there under the strongest light which was then playing upon it. It was not then a judicial question so much as a matter of international politics. Jay committed the United States to settlement by an instrument of international arbitration.

If the Senate were to ratify his treaty and the mixed commission successfully to dispose of the claims of the British creditors, public respect for the Federal Government which he had sponsored in close association with Hamilton would be increased as effectively and far more rapidly than by the obscurer process of judicial decision. John Jay's use of the treaty-making power at this time is to be included with Alexander Hamilton's contemporaneous demonstration of the taxing power among the inhabitants of western Pennsylvania in any discussion of the rise of Federal authority above the sovereignty of the States.

Passing by the decision of the Supreme Court in 1796, the two parties then proceeded with the organization of the mixed commission in May, 1797, as provided in Jay's Treaty. The first member was chosen by lot, with the result that the commission was composed of three British and two American representatives. The American minority, however, would not listen to British opinion that interest on the debts should have continued during the Revolution and that the property of Loyalists confiscated through attainder should be restored. The work of the commission came to a stop, and in retort the British Government withdrew its members from the commission in London which was dealing with American claims. This deadlock had finally to be broken by diplomacy.

In 1802, Rufus King negotiated a convention between the two countries which determined that in the future no creditors on either side should meet with any lawful impediments to the collection of debts and fixed the amount due British creditors on bona fide debts contracted prior to the American Revolution at $2,664,000. It was appropriated by Congress and paid.

The third mixed commission, organized in similar fashion and seated in London, had taken charge of American claims resulting from interference with neutral commerce "under Colour of authority or Commissions from His Majesty," and also of British losses from the depredations of those French privateers which had been sent out from American ports at the time of Genet. In the case of this commission, however, the American claimants had first to seek justice in the British courts before they could appeal to the commission.

Nowhere in Jay's Treaty was there any provision for compensating those Americans whose slaves had been carried away with the British armies. For reasons of sympathy with freedmen as well as of diplomacy, Jay had let the interest of American slaveowners go by the board. He justified this on the ground that the United States had gained compensation for the loss from the commercial clauses elsewhere in the treaty. Virginians, however, could hardly appreciate this benefit. Shipmasters might have some chance of reimbursement for damages to their commerce in the West Indies; but planters were now obliged both to satisfy their old creditors and to give up their claims for the loss of their property in slaves. Jay's Treaty was criticized in the mansions of the South as bitterly as in the counting-houses of the Northeast.

The commission in London was organized on August 25, 1796, with three American and two British members. Their procedure was marred by disputes over technicalities in regard to their jurisdiction and the quarrels of the debt commission at Philadelphia. But after resuming its sessions in 1802, the commission at London completed awards of $143,428 to meet the British claims and of $5,849,082 to compensate Americans for the spoliations "under Colour" of the King's orders. Britain thus had not been directly confronted with any decision that its orders-in-council were invalid. Rather, it had been formally obligated by an international tribunal, in which it took part, to pay specific damages for what had been decided to be contrary to international law. It was a narrow but effective distinction.

The Jay Treaty endeavored to reduce the controversy which had persisted since the failure of John Adams' mission to London in 1788 over rival shipping and the trade between the United States and the British Empire. One article gave reciprocal rights of trade between the "Dominions of his Majesty in Europe, and the Territories of the United States." For a period of twelve years, the merchants and goods of both parties were to suffer no discrimination in tonnage and port dues or customs duties. This was a definite concession to American shipowners, even though existing laws in England made it extremely difficult to compete with the British there. Another article allowed American vessels of small tonnage to enter the British West Indies during the war with France and two years thereafter, but under the strict proviso that the United States would restrain American vessels from carrying molasses, sugar, coffee, cocoa, or cotton "to any part of the World, except the United States," either from those islands or from the United States. A third article gave the United States privileges of direct trading with British territories in the East Indies, under the restriction that American vessels should not engage in the coastwise trade there. But American vessels could sail from port to port in the British East Indies to leave goods in the transoceanic traffic, and it was agreed to have further negotiations after the close of Britain's war with France.

Thus the envoy extraordinary for President Washington eliminated the Acts of Congress of 1789 and 1790 as means of favoring France, and destroyed the Jeffersonian program of economic reprisal upon Britain. In return, Grenville had conceded reciprocal rights of trade between British dominions in Europe and the United States, and had agreed to open the Oriental trade for the benefit of American shipping. The opportunity which he offered in the British West Indies, however, amounted to little, and the restriction which he maintained upon the export of cotton would impede a growing domestic enterprise of the American people.

Their cotton crop was expanding from a million pounds in 1789 to eight millions in 1795. Over six millions were shipped abroad that year. And by 1800 the production of raw cotton had reached thirty-five million pounds, its export nearly eighteen millions. The shipments from South Carolina alone had increased from $2,693,268 in 1791 to $5,998,492 in 1795. Cotton was chiefly responsible for this and most of it went to British mills. How much was carried in American vessels is hard to determine, but it is certain that the agreement between Grenville and Jay to confine the traffic to British shipping angered American shipmasters. And it hardly pleased the cotton planters to have such restraint upon their foreign trade. The Senate struck out this clause of the treaty.

Jay had included in his draft a provision similar to that in the commercial treaty of 1778 with France giving the protection of the nationality of a ship to its cargo regardless of the ownership of the goods. "Free ships," he hoped, were to make "free goods." But Grenville would have none of it. The treaty continued the British practice; vessels suspected of carrying an enemy's property could be seized and detained, the goods confiscated. Jay's ideas upon contraband were rejected as well. He had attempted to establish a list of commodities such as textiles, metals, grain, flour, meats and other foodstuffs which should be noncontraband. He had to accept instead a clause permitting articles not generally considered contraband to be made so, provided only that they should not be confiscated but should be bought at full value "with a reasonable mercantile Profit thereon, together with the Freight, and also the Demurrage incident to such Detension."

In short, although the United States reserved their general principles concerning neutral commerce and gained also a pledge for subsequent discussion and adjustment of views, they conceded to Britain that she must continue specific practices so long as she should be at war with France. Her cruisers would visit and search, detain neutral shipping, seize contraband, preëmpt noncontraband according to her own ideas on those matters—until that terrifying menace to herself and, in her opinion, to all correct principles of liberty and government, should be removed from the other side of the Channel. And more notable, perhaps, because Grenville had been willing in September to discuss the subject, the Jay Treaty was silent altogether upon the impressment of American sailors into the British Navy.

THE INTERESTS OF FRANCE—FAUCHET'S APPRAISAL

As for American relations with France, Jay's Treaty asserted in so many words that nothing in it should be "construed or operate contrary to former and existing Public Treaties with other Sovereigns or States." He had been given only two rigid instructions: they were to get admission of some sort into the British West Indies for American shipping and to make no agreements infringing upon American obligations to France. The inference is that he had not done so. And yet, this stipulation was not made in a separate article of the Jay Treaty, manifesting by its very position of equality with all other articles that its contents were comprehensive in their meaning and effect. It was made within the article which dealt with the reception of ships of war, privateers, and their prizes into the ports of the contracting parties. Did this imply, contrary to Jay's instructions, that there were to be no restrictions upon Britain in regard to any other matters which involved American commitments to France? It seems placed at least in such a way as to create ambiguity.

The United States could declare, and did consistently, that they had violated no pledges in their treaties of 1778 with France. Their position was technically correct. The Jay Treaty left them still legally free to deny Britain the right to fit her privateers or to dispose of her prizes in American ports, as they had contracted with France in 1778. They were still obligated, if they should become belligerents, to respect the neutrality of French vessels, and cargoes excepting contraband, even if those vessels were carrying the goods of an American enemy. They were still bound, in case they went to war with France herself, to refrain from taking French goods from a neutral vessel.

They were not bound, however, and they never had been, as neutrals, to protect French goods aboard their own vessels by the use of force against an enemy of France. There was nothing in the treaties of 1778 obligating them, in case they were neutrals, to assume anything like the status of armed neutrality. They had a legal right still to the neutral ground of 1793 that they were under no obligation to participate on the side of France, unless France called upon them to guarantee her West Indian possessions; and they were therefore entirely free, so long as they did not violate any of their prior engagements with France, to make a treaty even with the enemy of France if that would make their own position as neutrals more secure.

On the other hand, no candid person could have had any doubt then, or since, but that the Jay Treaty directly injured French interests to which the United States had been virtually, if not precisely, committed by the Alliance of 1778 against Britain in world politics. It restricted the application of the principle *free ships free goods* as general international law. The United States repudiated to a degree as neutrals what they had proclaimed as belligerents, and they did so to the disadvantage of their old ally in war. The inference from the contracts of 1778 with France, though not the legal requirement, had been that the United States would maintain their neutrality with force if necessary.

The Jay Treaty furthermore permitted Britain to resume her interference with the vital commerce of the French West Indies, without having to confine her cruisers to the narrow limits of accepted principles of contraband and blockade. It admitted British warships into American ports and gave their officers and men privileges ashore. This, of course, the United States had a right to do, but it afforded the British Navy practical advantages on the western side of the Atlantic close to the possessions of France. Such advantages might properly have been withheld at that time by a Government which was professing its friendship for France as well as its neutrality in the wars of Europe. This may readily be admitted without suppressing Alexander Hamilton's point that the United States had no obligation to guarantee the French West Indies inasmuch as France had taken the offensive against Britain. Jay's Treaty offended France, moreover, by submitting British claims for damages from the French privateers which had been fitted in American ports to an international body in which the British Government itself was represented. But above all, it flouted the old ally of the United States by including commercial agreements for the future with the common enemy of the past.

From the French point of view it appeared that, for a trivial concession in the West Indies, nominal privileges in English ports, and a share in the carrying trade to the Orient, the United States had bound themselves to admit British shipping into their home ports over a period of years upon the same basis as the most favored nation; that is, upon equality with France. They had deserted the common cause of all those who were struggling to free the world from the monopolistic control of the British naval and mercantile system. They had dropped the strongest weapon for that purpose—their power to injure Britain heavily by discrimination—in order to gain a slight although immediate advantage for themselves. This, they had done covertly—hiding it, apparently, even from their own minister in Paris. How could it be anything to Frenchmen but a deliberate slap in the face of France? That neither Jay nor Hamilton was reluctant to give it seemed clear from the reports of the French representatives in Philadelphia.

In such an attitude as this, a mixture of disappointment and genuine grievance, Frenchmen and their friends in America turned over the incidents which had accumulated during Washington's administration to the climax in Jay's Treaty with Britain against the interest of France. They did not expend so much reflection upon the actions of the Government in France which in violation of the treaties of 1778 had been seizing American vessels laden with goods that were not contraband, had been reversing the colonial policy of the Girondists and nationalizing the direct trade between France and the West Indies at the expense of American shipping. Nor were they thinking much upon the activities of French agents within the United States other than Genet. There was plenty astir throughout this country, however, despite Fauchet's proclamation and the neutrality law of 1794, to give the American President not only cause for grievance but intense anxiety concerning the survival of the Federal Union and its territorial domain beyond the Alleghenies.

Washington did not know it, of course, but Fauchet himself was appraising the likely contents of the Jay Treaty with notable accuracy, even before it reached America, and advising the French foreign office upon a policy to meet the new state of things in America. Prior to this he had conceived that the "system of conduct" dictated by the interests of France was simply to keep the United States in "a prolonged inertia" with respect to their relations with her powerful enemies until she should be freed from the major needs which she felt concerning her existence. Then, she could "attain a rank and establish an active system among the Foreign Governments." This he epitomized as a course of "wise delays and useful procrastinations." Of such a nature had been his renunciation of Genet's expeditions from Georgia and Kentucky into Spanish territory.

But now, Jay's Treaty was destroying the *status quo,* and Fauchet proposed a "permanent system" for France to employ against the United States. Jefferson, he reported, had remarked: "The force of things surrenders the French colonies to us, France enjoys the sovereignty, we the profit." Her possessions in the West Indies were dependent upon the United States for their food supply. But to Fauchet, they did not have to remain so. There was Louisiana holding out her arms; control of New Orleans would give France control of provisioning her West Indies. Far more important than that, it could be the citadel of an empire in the heart of America—as Moustier had written—which would soon include those Western States and territories of America where there were so many friends of the Revolution. Possessing New Orleans, what could France not do at pleasure to quicken or to suspend the growth of those Western settlements!

The revolutionary leaven in that part of the United States, asserted Fauchet, had been further strengthened since the repression of the latest movement. (He was thinking of the Whisky Rebellion.) And the decision as to dismemberment of the United States would so rest with France, said he, that France would surely be respected and courted by the Federal Government as soon as it had the French for neighbors. So, Fauchet urged that his Government take back Louisiana. This should be done by negotiation with Spain, but he did not neglect to suggest also that "a small force sent in the greatest secrecy from Europe or the Colonies, will land without much resistance and will see itself forthwith enlarged by western Americans won by the prospect of the advantages promised to them."

What if George Washington had read this despatch in 1795 as he studied the Jay Treaty and wondered what next should be done? Secretary Pickering was to see a copy of it, intercepted by the British and submitted to him several years later when reports first appeared that Spain had returned Louisiana to France. But again as in 1793, Washington did not need particular evidence of a European design. He

sensed the situation as it was. He faced the severest test of his statesmanship, and it was a highly personal matter.

He, and he alone, sooner or later, had to make the decision whether
or not this country should accept the results of Jay's endeavors in
London. How widely and how deeply adverse influences had penetrated public opinion and divided its loyalty was the most alarming
uncertainty. The conditions upon which Britain had agreed that peace
was to continue irritated him as much as anyone, but he knew that his
country must not have war with Britain. That would be self-destruction. And yet, would the people submit to such a truce as Jay had sent
home? Or, would they rage to the utter ruin of a national character so
promising in its youth?

2

THE DAMNATION OF MR. JAY

FRANK MONAGHAN

The Democratic societies had howled when they learned of Jay's nomination as envoy to Great Britain. They well remembered that he and King had assisted notably in dishing Genêt. Their opposition to his appointment was futile. When the Senate ratified it "the whole Union began to ring with their vociferations." As he sailed from New York the Philadelphia Democratic Society, which Cobbett declared was "never last in the pursuit of mischief," fired a parting volley of invective. The partisans of France wanted a war, not a peace, with George III and "his satanic imp, William Pitt."

Nor were the Democratic societies and the newspapers idle during Jay's absence in London. Every scrap of news that could be picked up concerning his conduct at the British Court was made the object of sarcasm or twisted into a prognostication of his concluding a dishonorable treaty. Even the formality of his presentation to the Queen sent them into fits of indignation. When James Monroe was kissed by the president of the National Convention they celebrated. When Jay kissed the hand of the Queen of England they declared he was "prostrating at the feet of Majesty the sovereignty of a great people," for which he deserved to have "his lips blistered to the bone." To this Cobbett retorted: "Had I been in *Mr. Jay's* place, perhaps I should have preferred the hand of one of the Queen's daughters; but his taste was, at any rate, as good as that of the *Patriot's*; for, who would not

From Frank Monaghan, *John Jay, Defender of Liberty* (New York: Bobbs-Merrill Co., 1935), pp. 389–390; 399–401. Used by permission of Mrs. Sylvia H. Monaghan.

rather kiss the shrivelled hand of the Queen of England than the monstruous beef-stake lips of an African *Patriot* (the greatest part of the negroes are most excellent *Patriots*, and firm friends of the modern French), or the snuffy chops of a regenerated Baboon?"

Early in June, 1794, the Republicans of Philadelphia provided a vivid demonstration of what the reception of any treaty with England would be. They made an effigy of Jay and stuffed it with powder. In its right hand was placed an iron rod; in the left, a copy of Swift's detested speech on British depredations. Suspended from the neck by a cord was a copy of John Adams' *Defence of the Constitutions*. The figure was placed on the platform of the pillory while a crowd hooted and jeered. After several hours of exposure they took it down, solemnly guillotined it and set the clothes afire. An explosion scattered the remnants and ended the ceremony. After this, said Cobbett, "the drunkards went home, snorted themselves sober and returned to their employments." In New York an effigy of Jay bearing the inscription "No man e'er reached the heights of vice at first" was disposed of in the same fashion while the crowds danced the "Carmagnole." These activities of the Republicans led Washington to remark dryly to Gouverneur Morris that "The affairs of this country *cannot go amiss.* There are *so many watchful guardians of them,* and such *infallible guides*, that one is at no loss for a director at every turn."

David Blaney was the courier who brought the treaty from London to Philadelphia. Storms, head winds and French cruisers lengthened the voyage from November till late in February. Landing at the Virginia Capes he raced to Philadelphia with such speed that his hands and feet were frozen when he reached the capital on March sixth, three days after the adjournment of the Senate. Randolph turned the treaty over to Washington; they guarded it closely until the Senate was convened on June eighth to consider it. In secret session it was debated, each senator having solemnly pledged himself not to divulge the contents. Yet Pierce Butler of South Carolina, who had once dreamed of the envoyship himself, was sending the treaty to James Madison before the session was four days old.

Washington's exact opinion of the treaty is difficult to ascertain, but it is certain he was far from enthusiastic about it. Hamilton, who knew the provisions of the treaty long before it reached the Senate, is said to have dubbed it "an execrable one" on the part of "an old woman." Since this alleged remark passed through three Francophiles—Talleyrand to Volney to Jefferson—it is impossible to know what Hamilton did say. He was determined that it be ratified, but with a suspension of Article XII which related to the trading restrictions. He was bound to support it. It was a treaty of the Federalists, concluded by an envoy of their choosing, whose instructions had been drawn by them. Although he probably would not have admitted it, he had been partly responsible for Jay's lack of success in London.

Debate in the Senate was bitter. For eight days the discussion was general; then the Federalists submitted a form of ratification which called for the suspension of that part of Article XII enumerating the articles American ships could not carry to or from the British West Indies. Senator Aaron Burr moved to postpone ratification and to begin new negotiations, but was voted down. Senator Henry Tazewell moved that the President be advised not to sign the treaty and advanced seven reasons. But this, with other hostile motions, was defeated. On June twenty-fourth, in a strictly party vote, the treaty was approved by twenty to ten, just the requisite number for ratification. Two days later the Senate imposed upon its members a prohibition against publication of any parts of the treaty and adjourned. Hamilton justly lamented that this injunction would give "scope to misrepresentation and misapprehension."

.   .   .

When it was learned that Washington had signed the treaty the Republican press broke forth in a fresh fury. Again there came the roll of drums, marching mobs, torchlight processions by night, speeches, banquets, food, whisky and fraternal huggings. Forth came the dung carts once more, more effigies of Jay, more hangings, more burnings of the treaty. One editor announced the ratification to his readers with a coarse parody on the birth of Jesus. The treaty was the child, "the long-expected embassorial, diplomatic, farci-comical savior of fifteen states." The mother was named Chief Justice, who had been "overshadowed by the prolific spirit of Gracious Majesty at the Court of St. James." In Boston the walls surrounding the house of a prominent Federalist were chalked in large letters: "Damn John Jay! Damn every one that won't damn John Jay!! Damn every one that won't put lights in his windows and sit up all night damning John Jay!!!" The author of *An Emetic for Aristocrats* presented the temptation of Jay by the Devil in Biblical style: "One John, surnamed Jay, journeyed into a far country, even unto Great Britain. 2. And the word of Satan came unto him saying, Make thou a covenant with this people, whereby they may be enabled to bring the *Americans* into bondage, as heretofore: 3. And John answered unto Satan, of a truth . . . let me find grace in thy sight, that I may secretly betray my country and the place of my nativity. . . ."

On September eleventh riots broke out in Boston. The windows of those who favored the treaty were broken by shots. Effigies of Jay were hauled about; one was a watermelon shell cut out to resemble a man's face, the whole decorated with scurrilous labels. They marched up to Governor Adams' house where the staunch old Whig smiled a benediction from the window. When the Federalists appealed to him to restore order he characterized the riot as "a mere watermelon frolic." The mob stoned the home of the author of the *Federal Orrery*, whose barbed wit had long been gall to the Republicans. Ten days later when the friends of France banqueted in celebration of the anniversary of the founding of the French Republic the *Federal Orrery* published a "Song of Liberty and Equality which ought to have been sung," including the following stanzas:

> From the State-house in order the Sansculottes move
> Like cattle or swine in a drove—a drove
> Composed of all colors and figures and shapes,
> Two and two as the patriarch Noah of old
> Drove into the Ark, the unclean of the fold,
> Skunks, woodchucks and apes,
> Toads, adders and lizzards
> And vultures and buzzards.
> Now striving amain for a fortunate chance
> To taste of the Freedom of France, of France,
> Stealing softly through alleys and winding through lanes,
> Our mob-loving Governor wanders in haste,
> His eyes up to heaven—his heart with the feast;
> In anarchy's strains
> Psalm-singing and praying
> He smiles at man-slaying.
> Farewell, ye Sansculottes—I leave ye to dine
> With your hoofs in your dishes like swine—like swine.

The wrath of the Republicans was boundless. Without neglecting "that damned arch-traitor, John Jay," they heaped abuse on Washington as the man who "had completed the destruction of American freedom." The *Aurora* declared that the President had thundered contempt upon the people "with as much arrogance as if he sat upon the throne of Indostan." Since he has abandoned the people let the people no longer regard him as a saint. Indeed, "A Calm Observer," said to have been John Beckley, Clerk of the House, was already preparing a series of newspaper articles to prove that the President was a thief. Another writer declared that to be an opposer of the President would soon be a passport to popular esteem. In Virginia "A speedy Death to General Washington" was toasted; in New York the Thanksgiving Proclamation of Governor Jay was denounced because it ventured to include the preservation "of the valuable life and usefulness of the President of the United States" as one of the subjects worthy of a prayer of thanks.

Bache filled the columns of the *Aurora* with abuse of Washington. Every scribbler who wished to denounce Jay or Washington knew that Bache would give his effusions the greatest publicity. But the most venomous shafts were his own. Each day he delighted in sending the President two copies of his newspaper; each day Washington, with increasing anger, read them. In the course of his diatribes Bache declared that "If ever a nation was debauched by a man, the American nation has been by Washington." He republished an edition of the forged letters of Washington that had been printed by the British during the Revolution. He published the pamphlet in which Tom Paine declared that Washington had joined with Robespierre in an attempt to assassinate him. When Washington retired Bache called upon the nation to rejoice mightily "that the name of Washington ceases from this day to give a currency to political iniquity and to legalize corruption." Little wonder that Washington complained to Jefferson that he had never dreamed "that every act of my administration would be tortured and the grossest and most insidious misrepresentations of them be made . . . and that too in such exaggerated and indecent terms as could scarcely be applied to a Nero—a notorious defaulter—or even to a common pickpocket."

3

THE FRENCH MISSION OF 1799–1800: CONCLUDING CHAPTER IN THE STATECRAFT OF JOHN ADAMS

STEPHEN G. KURTZ

President Adams split the Federalists into openly hostile factions when he named William Vans Murray to treat with France in February 1799. The peace mission of 1799–1800 seriously weakened the structure of the party, but it led ultimately to the termination of an alliance that had proven dangerous to American interests, and it was Adams' own conviction that it had prevented a test of American federalism that might well have ended in disunion. In later life he repeatedly claimed that his conduct of foreign relations as President had been his greatest public service, "the most splendid diamond in my crown," as he put it in 1815. That Adams should pass over his constitutional writings, his parliamentary leadership in the struggle for independence, and his foreign diplomatic service during the seventeen-eighties, indicates that he regarded his conduct of peace negotiations in 1799 and 1800 as a master-stroke of statecraft, one of his own creation and execution.

An examination of the domestic as well as foreign pressures which influenced his conduct and careful consideration of the timing of his actions leads to deeper appreciation of his assessment. It is maintained here that Adams viewed the foreign and domestic crises of his administration as inseparable, that his peace decision was dictated largely by concern over internal unrest, that in responding positively to Talleyrand's overtures Adams continued to regard war as a likely possibility, and that the eight-months' delay between Murray's nomination and the sailing of the other two members of the mission was deliberate

Reprinted with permission from the *Political Science Quarterly*, 80 (December 1965), pp. 543–557.

on Adams' part and owed nothing to the backstairs intrigues of cabinet officers. Adams waited until October to order the departure of Ellsworth and Davie because of unexpected delays encountered in completing the three squadrons of the Caribbean fleet. He did not lose direction of the negotiation to the Hamiltonian faction or its partisans within the cabinet.

ONE

In his message to Congress of December 1798 Adams declared that the administration would be prepared to settle differences with France when official assurances of her willingness to treat with any minister selected by the United States government had been received. Until that time, he concluded, defense measures would be pressed: "An efficient preparation for war can alone insure peace." When a few weeks later Adams decided that Talleyrand had provided such assurance through an exchange of letters between Pichon, the French chargé, and Murray, the American Minister, at The Hague, he named Murray to the Senate as minister plenipotentiary; but Adams did not rule out the possibility of declaring war or slacken efforts to float a battle fleet at any time during the course of negotiations. "Our operations by sea and land are not to be relaxed in the slightest," he told Secretary of State Pickering in August 1799. "On the contrary, I want them animated with fresh energy." As late as the summer of 1800 Adams requested that John Marshall, Pickering's successor, place the question of declaring war upon France before the cabinet for discussion prior to his return to the capital.

By the time that Talleyrand turned the initiative back to the United States, Adams had taken advantage of his position to direct the building of the nation's defenses and to inflame public opinion against the French government. The powers granted the President under the Constitution were found sufficiently flexible to achieve the administration's goal of peace with honor in spite of division within the Federalist party, the threat of sectional cleavage represented by the Virginia and Kentucky Resolutions, and the threat to the independence of the executive which Secretary Pickering posed in bringing Washington, Hamilton, and C. C. Pinckney into cabinet discussions in the fall of 1799. In spite of his subsequent reputation as a weak President, Adams proved bold in his conduct of foreign relations. He had developed a doctrine of executive power since 1776 which was as close to monarchical as American conditions would allow. In the third volume of his *Defence of the Constitutions of Government of the United States of America* (1787) Adams had written:

> The parties of rich and poor, of gentlemen and simplemen, unbalanced by some third power, will always look to foreign aid . . . Whig and Tory, Constitutionalist and Republican, Anglomane and Francomane . . . will serve as well as Guelf and Ghibelline. The great desideratum in a government is a distinct executive power of sufficient strength and weight to compel both these parties in turn to submit to the laws.

Nor was Jefferson wrong in viewing Adams as the leader of what he termed the "monocrats" and the basic cause of party division as disagreement over executive power.

It is clear that from the beginning of his administration Adams was aware of the loyalty which Pickering, Wolcott, and McHenry felt toward Alexander Hamilton. If he had not known of it, which seems inconceivable, he had well-meaning friends to warn him. A few weeks after his inauguration he replied to such a notice from Elbridge Gerry: "Pickering and his colleagues are as much attached to me as I desire. I have no jealousies from that quarter." Adams showed by the private instructions which he gave to John Quincy Adams at the time of the latter's appointment as Minister to Prussia, however, that he was not prepared completely to trust Pickering: "Continue your practice of writing freely to me, more cautiously to the officer of State." Secretary of the Treasury Wolcott was told by Adams that there existed a natural antagonism on the part of Congress that would attempt to weaken the President's powers by encouraging cabinet officers to operate independently of his control. He pointed to a tax bill which, in his opinion, had granted entirely too much latitude to Wolcott as a case in point. "That policy will be pursued," Adams stated, "until we have a Quintuple or Centuple Executive Directory."

TWO

Whether Adams was wise in retaining Washington's secretaries is another question; his belief in the necessity of developing a permanent or semi-permanent civil service dictated it, and the difficulties which his illustrious predecessor had met in attemptng to fill low-paying cabinet posts were clear enough. That a "three-vote President" might hesitate to face the same humiliating search is worth considering. Adams operated much more independently of the cabinet than had Washington. He followed precedent in asking for their written advice upon important questions, but there is no indication that he paid much attention to the opinions of his secretaries when his own opinions were contrary. Adams expected little more of them than that they write the routine dispatches and reports of their departments. Study, as well as experience, had shown him that an executive must make his own decisions, and most important to an understanding of his relations with his advisers, Adams had taken from his reading in Cicero, Tacitus, Machiavelli, Bolingbroke, and his other mentors a rule of operating with maximum secrecy. "The unity, consistency, promptitude, secrecy, and activity of the whole executive authority," he commented to Gerry in 1797, "are so essential to my system of republican government, that without them there can be no peace, order, liberty, or property in society." He explained to John Marshall, who replaced Pickering in the Spring of 1800, that in pretending to no firm opinion himself on a matter under discussion, he was able to extract honest opinions from subordinates. Although Adams had made it clear in his December 1798 message that a second mission might be dispatched should French policies change, his secretaries were given no intimation that he had decided to take the step prior to the eighteenth of February when Murray's name was submitted to the Senate. The President admitted to his wife, who was as surprised as others, that he had deliberately kept the decision to himself.

THREE

Most high-ranking Federalists regarded the decision as idiotic, a result of his solitary deliberation. "If any good results from it," Chief Justice Francis Dana of the Massachusetts Supreme Court commented to an English correspondent, "he will be entitled to the honour exclusively. His friends foresee none and deprecate nothing more seriously than a revival of diplomatic connections with France while under the influence of revolutionary principles." Dana frankly admitted his hope that the embassy would fail. If so, he concluded, ". . . it would create

neither surprise or regret among the Federalists, who deem every procrastination a public blessing." Pickering, who dated his falling out
with Adams from the moment of Murray's nomination, surmised that
the President had kept his own counsels because of a bargain with the
Jeffersonians, a promise of support in 1800 in return for the necks of
McHenry and himself and a new French mission. Others saw in the
peace move the insidious influence of Elbridge Gerry, who was known
to have been in private conclave with the Adamses at Quincy. Although initially angered by Gerry's conduct during the first peace
mission, Adams did not repudiate him or reject the report which
Gerry gave of a change of policy at Paris, a nagging problem that
ripened gradually into a major source of friction between the President
and the Secretary of State.

Adams showed no confidence in the ability of his secretaries to deal
with foreign affairs. His vanity and his habit of lecturing on the immense value of personal experience in foreign embassies only exacer-
bated feelings which his secrecy in important questions both reflected
and created. That Talleyrand's use of Murray and Pichon as interme-
diaries was acceptable diplomatic form, Adams knew from his experience at Paris in 1781; Pickering could not accept it any more than
McHenry could the President's insistence that recruiting a large standing army would prove an unnecessary danger and expense. Beneath
the surface frictions, however, lay a fundamental divergence of viewpoint on the nature of the crisis itself. To Adams, the undeclared war
with France was but one episode in the chronic situation which Americans had faced since the Revolution—that of avoiding dependence
upon either of the great powers. As he expressed it to former Governor Thomas Johnson of Maryland, the basic aim of American foreign
policy was "to avoid becoming a mere satellite to a mighty power," a
danger that was as great from Britain as from France.

Washington, writing to Lafayette on Christmas day 1798, expressed
the same apprehension:

> That there are many among us, who wish to see this country em-
> broiled on the side of Great Britain, and others who are anxious that
> we should take part with France against her, admits of no doubt. But
> . . . the Governing powers of the country, and a large part of the
> people are truly Americans . . . unwilling under any circumstances . . .
> to participate in the politics or contests of Europe.

FOUR

By 1798 many leading Federalists, including the Secretary of State, had forgotten the lessons of the American Revolution in their antagonism toward the French Revolution and its American champions. The defense measures, tax increases, and security acts adopted in 1798 had produced a major crisis in American federalism and a threatening division which was reflected in the Virginia and Kentucky Resolutions. Although historical investigation has uncovered little that suggests preparation for armed rebellion on the part of Republican leaders in 1798 or 1799, Federalist eschatology insisted upon it. In the eyes of many Federalists, it has been remarked, the Republic seemed to have reached senility while still in its infancy.

Hamilton was convinced that Virginians contemplated armed revolt, and to all intents and purposes he commanded the United States Army. In January and February 1799 Hamilton's apprehension was so great that he pointed to reports of military preparations by the Virginia government and proposed strengthening the Alien and Sedition Acts, enlarging the jurisdiction of federal courts, the division of the southern states into smaller territorial units, and a movement of federal troops southwestward in order, as he put it, "to put Virginia to the test of resistance."

Characteristically, Fisher Ames, even as New England was reacting most violently against the French, saw the spirit of "Jacobinism" increasing on all fronts and called upon the executive to take steps to combat it. Jonathan Mason, also of Massachusetts, lamented that the Fifth Congress had failed to declare war, a step which, as he saw it, would be the most effective way of dealing with internal security; while the most pessimistic utterances were made by Francis Dana: "I pray Heaven I may be mistaken when I declare it as my expectation that if we do not have a foreign war, a civil war will be the lot of Americans and possibly both." Even the sanguine Jefferson harbored fears of violence and cautioned his political lieutenants against doing anything that could give the national government reason for moving troops into the South.

Tensions were increased precisely because France was believed to be incapable of transporting troops to American shores by virtue of Nelson's remarkable victory at Aboukir Bay, news of which reached

Philadelphia in November 1798. "We are not afraid of a French invasion this winter," Adams wrote in reply to one of many congratulatory letters he had received. To exultant Federalists the way now seemed open to an even closer understanding with Britain than had developed since the conclusion of the Jay-Grenville negotiations of 1794. Evidence of cooperation undreamed of during Washington's administration had recently crossed the President's desk in the form of a convention concluded by British and American agents and Toussaint L'Ouverture, the ex-slave whose rebel forces had broken France's hold on the Island of Santo Domingo. A dispatch from Rufus King, American Minister in London, reached Adams on January 17 in which it was announced that Toussaint had agreed to open ports under his control to British and American vessels while closing them to French privateers. A subsequent dispatch announced that the British ministry had ordered its chief agent in Santo Domingo, General Maitland, to Philadelphia with full powers "to adjust a plan concerning St. Domingo." The American Minister added that George III had been generous in his praise of Adams' statesmanship and had asked repeatedly when the United States could be expected to declare war upon France.

The Federalist majority in Congress, over bitter Republican protests, responded warmly by authorizing trade with any former French possession whose local authorities promised to refrain from attacks upon American shipping. Simultaneously, Congress also suspended commerce between the United States and the French Republic. President Adams signed the new legislation six days before naming Murray to resume diplomatic relations with France.

The situation in the early weeks of 1799 had become dangerous in Adams' judgment: the dominant faction in Congress welcomed closer cooperation with England despite the danger represented by her naval ascendancy, and, while admitting their concern over a clash between state and national authority, supported a large army officered by Federalists with no prospect of an invader in sight. The guarantee from the French government that he had insisted upon arrived in January 1799, a promise by Talleyrand that an American envoy would be received with dignity and honor. The reports of Gerry, Murray, John Quincy Adams, George Logan, and Joel Barlow from Europe indicated a change at Paris favorable to peace. Washington's brief note accompanying the Barlow letter testified to his belief in a general longing for peace. But in his own accounts of the mission, Adams insisted that in his conduct of foreign relations in 1799 and 1800 domestic unrest had been uppermost in his mind.

In a letter to John Jay written in November 1800 Adams pointed out that only among what he termed "a faction who have been laboring and intriguing for an army of fifty-thousand" had the peace decision been an unforgivable lapse. The peace mission and the reduction of the army, he stated, were intimately bound together. Adams wrote an explanation of his decision in 1801, a reply to Hamilton's attack upon him of the previous year, that was not published until 1809 in the *Boston Patriot*. He declared that had the French crisis not been relieved,

> . . . it was my opinion then, and has been since, that the two parties in the United States would have broken into civil war; a majority of all the states to the southward of the Hudson River, united with nearly half New England, would have raised an army under Aaron Burr; a majority of New England another under Hamilton.

To John Taylor in their exchange of letters in 1814, he wrote: ". . . we have had Shays's, Fries's, and I know not whose rebellion in the western counties of Pennsylvania. How near did Virginia and Kentucky approach in the last years of the last century?" Finally, in 1815 he pointed once more to the pressure of potential civil war:

> To dispatch all in a few words, a civil war was expected. The party committed suicide; they killed themselves and the national president (not their president) at one shot, and then, foolishly or maliciously, indicted me for the murder. . . . My own mission to France . . . I esteem the most splendid diamond in my crown. . . .

FIVE

In acting to break the domestic tension, Adams responded to a fear of states'-rights sentiment that he had harbored for years. "If the superiority of the national government is not more clearly acknowledged," he wrote in 1791, "we shall soon be in a confusion which we shall not get out of for twenty years."

Adams' solution to the problem of rising tensions, however, was not that of the Hamiltonian Federalists, who made no effort to conceal their anger. At the insistence of a Senate deputation the mission was enlarged with the addition of Chief Justice Oliver Ellsworth and Patrick Henry. A few week later, Governor William R. Davie of North Carolina was named in place of Henry, who declined. The President then packed his bags for a trip to Braintree where he remained from March until October. The failure of Ellsworth and Davie to depart until November has been repeatedly explained as the result of intrigues on the part of Secretaries Pickering, Wolcott, and McHenry, the Hamiltonian stalwarts in the cabinet. To explain the mission in terms of conspiracy is to suggest that while Adams remained at the side of his stricken wife, a cabal of Federalists, who wished to prolong hostilities or bring on a declaration of war, worked through Secretary Pickering to frustrate the President's policy. It is pointed out that mail was held up, orders questioned, and confidential information widely disseminated. According to such a construction, it was only when Navy Secretary Stoddert warned him that Adams awoke and, hurrying to the temporary capital at Trenton, broke with Pickering and ordered the departure in mid-October. If this interpretation is accepted, it is necessary to take a view of Adams that suggests dereliction of duty, premature senility, or worse. It also rests upon untenable assumptions: that Adams was unaware of attempts to delay the mission, that these attempts caused the eight-months' delay, and that Adams himself wished negotiations to commence as promptly as possible.

Britain's supremacy on the sea presented the prospect of being drawn tightly into her orbit, a situation that Adams, like Washington before him, believed dangerous to American interests. Nelson's victory on the Nile had released a mechanism whose movement threatened to result in what would have amounted to an Anglo-American alliance, a joint-expedition against Spain's American empire, and the fulfillment of Hamilton's military and imperialist dreams. A declaration of war early in 1799 pointed toward the ascendancy of "the feudalists," as Elbridge Gerry called them; a gesture of peace toward France promised the relaxation of internal unrest and the frustration of military adventures.

Adams' behavior between February and October 1799 indicates strongly that he considered the nomination of Murray premature in terms of diplomacy and that he had no intention of hastily beginning to negotiate. Patrick Henry was certainly a strange choice if speed was a consideration: he had twice before refused federal appointments pleading advancing age, and, as could be anticipated, the exchange of letters alone consumed several weeks. Governor Davie was not notified of his appointment until June and was instructed to remain silent about departure plans until the Directory had sent a specific guarantee to treat with the three men named. The exchange of letters between Murray in the Netherlands and the Paris government covering this point was not completed until the middle of May and not sanctioned by Adams until August. On September 10 Davie took leave of the North Carolina legislature and did not reach Trenton, the yellow-fever season capital, until early October. The correspondence between Adams and Pickering during this period reflects neither urgency nor anger on the President's part.

Furthermore, the reasons for holding up the mission which were advanced by Pickering were respected by Adams. Benjamin Stoddert, about whose loyalty there has never been question, pointed out to Adams that the Murray nomination had hurt relations with England and that the Anglo-American commission making awards to former Loyalists and British merchants under Article VI of the Jay treaty was at loggerheads:

> No doubt their commissioners have for a long time been soured, and have in some instances acted as if it were their desire to plunge the two nations into war. If England insists on a quarrel, however we may lament the calamity, we need not fear the result if our own people are satisfied that the Government has acted in all instances right.

Secretary Pickering pressed for delay on the basis of discord at Paris and the rise to power of Napoleon which Federalists saw as the first step toward a Bourbon restoration. Adams dismissed the restoration possibility but agreed with Pickering that it would be wise to delay: "The revolution in the Directory, the revival of the clubs and private societies in France, and the strong appearance of another reign of democratic fury seem to justify relaxation of our zeal for the sudden departure of the envoys." Two weeks later he wrote Stoddert: "I have no reason nor motive to precipitate the departure of the envoys." As late as September he informed Pickering that when he arrived at Trenton there would be ample time to decide what should finally be done about the mission. He added that from his own experience he knew late October to be a safe time for ocean travel. Stephen Higginson, federal naval agent and shipbuilder at Boston, reported that there were rumors among Adams' friends who had visited him at Quincy that the President had doubts about dispatching the mission at all.

Finally, what lay behind the long delay was the President's conviction that the defense of American rights must rest upon naval power, the keystone of Adams' *realpolitik*. He had been the warmest advocate of American naval power since the seventeen-seventies. "Floating batteries and wooden walls have been my favorite system of warfare for three and twenty years," he wrote to the Boston Marine Society in the fall of 1798. But, he added, "I have had little success in making proselytes." The principal theater of war between the United States and France was the Caribbean and, after Nelson had eliminated the possibility of transporting a French army to America, could have been nowhere else. Although a nation of limited resources the United States was capable of building a fleet that could deal France's trade with the West Indies a crippling blow in the judgment of both Adams and Stoddert. "The sixty or eighty French privateers out of Guadaloupe must be very small and trifling," Adams commented to Stoddert in August. "We shall be very indiscreet if we depend upon the British to defend our commerce and destroy French privateers. We must depend on God and our rights as well as the English."

The foreign policy of neutrality was fragile without the means of protecting America's rapidly expanding ocean commerce. Adams acted upon the assumption that the only chance of ending French attacks upon United States shipping rested upon her fears of the power to retaliate. What was needed in 1799 was time, time to complete the three squadrons authorized for operations in West Indian waters. The leisurely manner in which Adams dealt with his correspondence with Pickering in 1799 stands in marked contrast to the haste and careful attention to detail which he gave to his communications with Secretary Stoddert. Copies of their letters found in the "Letterbooks" in the Adams Family Papers as well as those printed in the fourth volume of *Naval Documents Related to the Quasi-War between the United States and France* abundantly testify to the deep concern which Adams and Stoddert shared for the completion of naval vessels. Unexpected construction problems and severe epidemics of yellow-fever in the summers of 1798 and 1799 had slowed efforts in government yards and in Stoddert's office which had to be moved twice from Philadelphia to Trenton.

It was not until September 1799 that the Secretary could report the squadrons fit for sea duty. The first, under the command of Captain Silas Talbot of the U.S.S. Constitution, was ordered to rendezvous off Santo Domingo; the second, under Daniel McNeill, to Surinam off the Guiana coast; and the third, commanded by Richard V. Morris, to Guadaloupe. Each was to have consisted of a frigate and five brigs, but Stoddert's final orders of September 9 show that both the Surinam and Guadaloupe flotillas would be incomplete for several weeks. The date for each group to rendezvous at its station was October 10, the day of Adams' arrival at Trenton where he at last issued orders for the departure of Ellsworth and Davie. He did so over the protests of Pickering, Hamilton, and Ellsworth, all of whom argued that news from Europe indicated an impending victory for the Coalition and the restoration of the monarchy in France.

In the months that followed, Napoleon and Talleyrand gave scant attention to the relatively inconsequential problem of American relations. Adams awaited the result anxiously, convinced that France would be guided largely by considerations beyond his control, by the outcome of European battles and diplomacy but also by advice which he was certain American Republicans would supply with their eyes upon Jefferson's election. Renewal of hostilities was possible, he told his secretaries in the summer of 1800, for he feared that France would attempt to maneuver the envoys into repudiating the terms of the Jay Treaty with England. Defense preparations would not be relaxed until an acceptable treaty had been signed and ratified as long as he remained President. All that the American government could do to influence the outcome was being done.

The Americans at Paris met with a three-man commission headed by Joseph Bonaparte and pressed for reparations amounting to twenty million dollars as well as recognition of the legality of the abrogation of the treaties of 1778 and 1788. By the Treaty of Morte-fontaine, however, the United States assumed the claims of its own citizens as the price of severing the French alliance. While Adams waited, he doubted. "These Federalists may yet have their fill at fighting," he commented to John Trumbull in September 1800. "They may see our envoys without peace, and if they do, what is lost? Certainly nothing, unless it be the influence of some of the Federalists by their own imprudent and disorganizing opposition and clamor. Much time has been gained."

PART 3
WAR AND
PEACE WITH
BRITAIN

INTRODUCTION

In March 1801, Thomas Jefferson was inaugurated President of the United States. He believed his election was a revolution, for John Adams and the "Monocrats" had been driven from the temple, and power now rested in the hands of able and trustworthy defenders of republicanism. For almost five years, aided by James Madison, his Secretary of State, Jefferson steered a successful course in world affairs. He conducted a vigorous war against the Barbary States in defense of America's right to trade in the Mediterranean and managed to purchase the Louisiana Territory from France. Thus did the United States secure her agrarian future. Moreover, she gained unchallenged control of the Mississippi River, with its outlet to the world market-place at New Orleans. This was the fulfillment of an American ambition dating back to revolutionary times and the abortive mission of John Jay to Spain in 1779.

The revival of the European wars, however, created difficulties and ultimately threatened to involve the Jefferson administration. On the Continent, the Emperor Napoleon of France crushed the third coalition assembled against him by William Pitt. In a series of smashing victories beginning with Austerlitz in 1805 and ending at Friedland in June 1807, Napoleon made himself the master of Western Europe without an enemy in the field to oppose him. At sea, England stood alone, retaining her predominance as a result of Lord Nelson's stunning victory over the combined fleets of France and Spain at Trafalgar. The ensuing life and death struggle between England and France was deeply felt in the United States. A neutral attempting to trade peacefully with all nations, America's maritime rights were violated with impunity by both belligerents as each struggled to effect the economic strangulation of the other. The issues that arose between America and England, particularly the questions of neutral rights and the impressment of American seamen into the Royal Navy, were, however, the most serious (selection 1).

In June 1807, the impressment question reached crisis intensity as a result of the *Chesapeake* incident. The U.S.S. *Chesapeake*, an American vessel of war sailing for the Mediterranean was off the Virginia Capes when fired upon by the British frigate *Leopard*. Three were killed and eighteen wounded before Commodore James Barron, the *Chesapeake's* commander, struck his colors. The incident occurred after Barron had refused a request made by the British captain, in violation of all international precedent, to search the ship for deserters. Angered at this act of British arrogance, Jefferson responded by ordering all British vessels enjoying the hospitality of American harbors to leave forthwith. His bitterness notwithstanding, the President believed that in a diplomatic sense the incident would prove beneficial, for he was convinced that he had as a result of it suddenly acquired considerable leverage. The nation seemed ready for war, and Jefferson believed that he might be able to use American public outrage and the threat of war to bludgeon the British into surrendering their claimed right of impressment. He erred twice. In the first place he committed a prime diplomatic sin by resorting to a threat he had no intention of fulfilling, thus jeopardizing his credibility. More significantly, because he failed to understand the Anglo-French conflict, he completely misconceived the importance of impressment to Britain. The antagonists viewed the war as a struggle for survival; Jefferson saw it as another in a series of similar contests that had plagued Europe for centuries. Consequently, he regarded impressment as simply a manifestation of British arrogance and hostility to the United States instead of as a matter of fundamental military significance. The unfortunate result of this error in judgment was that the President mishandled the situation.

The talks that followed the *Chesapeake* incident took place in London and were handled there by the regular American Minister to the Court of St. James, James Monroe, and a special envoy, William Pinckney. Both were evidently aware of the intensely passionate nature of the European conflict and the significance of impressment to the British war effort, for in violation of their instructions they negotiated a treaty that made no mention of impressment but, like the Jay

Treaty before it, promised peace and some commercial advantage. There is a good deal of irony in this, for James Monroe had been the American Minister in Paris when the Jay Treaty was leaked to the public in 1795. At that time he had been livid at what he considered Federalist treason. Now, however, bearing the responsibility that comes with power, he made concessions similar to those Jay had made more than a decade before.

President Jefferson could have had peace and a commercial agreement to replace the expiring Jay Treaty, but at the price of a surrender on the question of impressment. Unwilling to accept this, he refused to submit the Monroe-Pinckney treaty to the Senate, preferring instead to continue the crisis in hope of gaining greater concessions.

The failure of the negotiations following the *Chesapeake* affair together with increased belligerent pressures on American commerce, the result of new and more restrictive British and French regulations, elicited countermeasures from the administration. An embargo on all trade with the outside world was instituted (selection 2). American ships were restricted to coastal trade, and the export of American products was totally prohibited. Though this measure was applicable to all trade and therefore was, from a legal standpoint, strictly neutral, it was aimed primarily at Britain.

The embargo failed for numerous reasons, and it is difficult to know exactly where to lay greatest emphasis. One of its singular weaknesses stemmed from the totally materialistic assumptions on which it was based. Jefferson and Madison reasoned that in the face of serious economic pressures, England would make concessions. Either because they were unconcerned with or unaware of the passionate commitment of most Englishmen to the struggle against Napoleon, neither the President nor the Secretary of State gave any serious thought to the prospect that in the face of American economic pressure patriotic Englishmen might simply increase their determination to resist. Ironically, the administration failed also to carefully consider the economic impact of a total embargo on the United States, especially on New England, where prosperous commerce was crippled. There, during the whole time the embargo was in force, talk of secession and formation of a New England confederation grew steadily more strident while canny traders found means of violating the law.

Even in economic terms the embargo failed, for it had neither the material nor political effect on England that Jefferson wished. Some sectors of the British economy were indeed hurt, yet the Tory ministry of Spencer Perceval proved unresponsive to pleas from these sources. Moreover, in one sense the embargo played directly into British hands by guaranteeing Britain a virtual monopoly on world trade.

In March 1809, his foreign policy a shambles, Jefferson gratefully retired to Monticello and left his former Secretary of State, now President James Madison, to deal with the still unresolved crisis. Just prior to Madison's inauguration the embargo had been repealed and was replaced by a policy of nonintercourse with England and France. The new law, in the spirit of the embargo, removed some of the domestic pressure on the new administration by continuing a prohibition on trade with the belligerents but allowing trade with other parts of the world.

In the year following, with no indication that either Britain or France would in any way modify their maritime practices, Congress and the administration reached their ultimate degradation, by replacing nonintercourse with Macon's Bill Number Two. This law restored trade on a normal basis with all parts of the world, even with areas under the control of the belligerents. It contained, however, a stipulation that if either of the major combatant powers should agree to rescind its decrees against neutral trade, the United States, after a three-month period, would reinstate nonintercourse against the other.

In a cleverly worded response to Macon's Bill, Napoleon's Foreign Minister, the Duc de Cadore, announced the immediate repeal of French decrees infringing on America's neutral rights, *providing* England first revoked her orders-in-council or America established complete nonintercourse against England. It was a crude trap. Napoleon had reversed the order of priorities stipulated in Macon's Bill, promising revocation of his offensive decrees if either England or America acted first. Despite the obvious intention of the French to exacerbate Anglo-American relations without altering their own repressive trade practices, Madison cooperated. Contending that the French had substantially complied with the stipulations of Macon's Bill, he announced that nonintercourse would be applied against Great Britain on February 2, 1811, unless she repealed her orders-in-council.

Historians differ over whether the President understood Napoleon's duplicitous intentions. It seems likely, however, that he did. After years of humiliation and drift it is probable that Madison simply decided to use the situation as a way out of an unfortunate dilemma. There was ample cause for war with either England or France, yet it would have been insane to have declared war against both. Moreover, England was the principal offender and, from a military standpoint, because of her exposed flank in Canada, the more vulnerable enemy. Thus Madison used a convenient fiction to eliminate France from the picture and focus his attention on England. He was determined apparently either to force concessions from the mistress of the seas or to fight.

Although it is a relatively simple matter to reconstruct the sequence of events leading up to Madison's declaration of war, historians have never agreed about the meaning of those events, and numerous conflicting interpretations of them have appeared over the years. According to the traditional view, which still has the most adherents, maritime questions were of primary importance in Madison's calculations. Other historians, however, have been struck by the sectional breakdown of the congressional vote for war in 1812 and by the fact that western Congressmen were vehement in their fervor for war while New Englanders hung back. Why, scholars wonder, did politicians representing western districts become militant over maritime questions, while others representing maritime states held back in opposition? The answer some have suggested is that frontier questions were of greater significance than maritime matters in determining national policy. War would serve western purposes well, offering an opportunity for expansion into Canada and the Floridas. Then too, such a war seemed the only way to fulfill the long-cherished western desire to establish once and for all American control over the Indians. To the men of the West it seemed evident that as long as the British provided the red men with weapons and supplies there could be no peace along the frontiers. Removal of the British from North America became a prerequisite to control of the Indians.

This frontier interpretation of the causes of the war has been challenged from a number of directions. George Rogers Taylor, for example, accepts the view that the West was a prime mover in forcing the nation into war. He suggests, however, that this section was in no way isolated from the commerce of the world. On the contrary, he believes that westerners had perhaps more economic reason than other Americans to be concerned about the struggle over a free sea (selection 3). More recently, scholars have questioned whether the congressional vote for war really was sectional. They maintain that the vote was instead intensely partisan, and an analysis of the vote along party lines does show that the great majority of Republicans voted in favor of war while the overwhelming majority of Federalists opposed it. One of the most interesting of these recent political interpretations is that of Roger Brown, who blends politics and ideology to offer a challenging new view (selection 4).

On Christmas Eve in 1814 American and British negotiators, assembled since August in the Belgian town of Ghent, signed a peace treaty bringing to an end the War of 1812. The talks had been long, argumentative, and at times had seemed hopeless. Each side had been forced to retreat a long way from its initial demands before the war could be concluded, and finally neither side achieved any of its war aims. The old issues, impressment and the rights of neutrals, remained unsettled. Questions raised by the war itself, such as America's continued use of the North Atlantic fisheries, the future of the Canadian-American boundary, and the naval armaments race on the Great Lakes, were left unsolved.

In one sense the treaty, which restored the *status quo ante bellum*, was for America a kind of negative victory. The easy invasion of Canada envisioned by some in 1812 had failed disastrously. By the end of 1813 America's military fortunes on land seemed almost irretrievable and looked only slightly more promising a year later. At sea, although American war vessels accounted for themselves with distinction in several single ship actions, the overwhelming might of the British Navy was unchallengeable. Under the circumstances, and considering the fact that the European wars were rapidly drawing to a close, freeing Britain's vast naval and military power to concentrate on the United States, the country was fortunate to be able to arrange such a settlement.

Had the British ministry been willing to persevere in the war against the United States for another year, it might have won a major military and diplomatic victory in North America. Britain's leaders simply did not choose to do so. Ultimately their failure to win a smashing victory in America in 1814, the burden of the national debt, domestic unhappiness over continued high taxation, and a dangerously unstable situation in Europe had convinced the ministry that its interests were not well served by continuing the American war.

The Treaty of Ghent is less significant as the ending of a war than as the beginning of a new cordiality in Anglo-American relations. Between 1815 and 1818 John Quincy Adams, first as America's minister to the Court of St. James and then as Secretary of State in the Monroe administration, worked closely with Britain's Foreign Secretary, Lord Castlereagh, to settle differences between the two nations. Not since Shelburne had a minister in England been so attuned to the idea of Anglo-American amity as Castlereagh was. Believing that Canada was a hostage to American arms, that Europe and Asia were of far greater importance to Britain's future than was North America, and that the wisest course to follow in Anglo-American relations was to eliminate frictions wherever they might develop, even at the cost of major concessions, he adopted a persistently conciliatory attitude toward the United States. Exceptions were made in his policy on some issues which were not of immediate importance and where failure meant little to either side; among these were the limitation of Britain's right of impressment and the rights of neutrals to trade during time of war. In 1817 the famous Rush-Baghot agreement, demilitarizing the boundary between the United States and Canada and restraining the naval armaments race on the Great Lakes, was concluded. In the following year the Convention of 1818 solved in America's favor other irritating matters, including a dispute over fishing privileges in the Newfoundland-Labrador area, the question of the northern boundary of the Louisiana Purchase, and the issue of right of occupancy in the Oregon country.

The result of these four years of diplomacy was impressive. Assuredly, a vast reservoir of popular hostility remained between the two countries, and some political issues were still unsettled. Nevertheless, relations between the two powers were, by the end of the decade, fundamentally stable and officially friendly.

The culmination of this growing amity between Britain and the United States came in 1822 and was triggered by a wave of political reaction which swept Europe in the wake of Napoleon's final defeat. Under the leadership of Czar Alexander I and Prince Metternich of Austria, five major continental powers—Austria, Prussia, Russia, France, and Spain—dedicated themselves to the eradication of liberal movements wherever they appeared. A revolution in Italy was quickly put down by Austrian troops; the Republic of Spain, established in 1820, was crushed by a French army in 1823 and Ferdinand VII restored to his throne. Wild rumors spread of an impending congress to be held in Paris to discuss a projected Franco-Spanish military expedition to restore Spain's power in the Western Hemisphere where new republics had sprung from the ashes of her defunct empire. At this time George Canning, who had succeeded Castlereagh as Britain's Foreign Secretary, proposed that the United States and Britain join together to warn the continental powers that any attempt to restore Spain's power in Latin America would be resisted by force. In doing so he set the United States on a course of action which resulted, in December of 1823, in the enunciation of President Monroe's famous doctrine (selection 5). Although ultimately the Monroe Administration acted unilaterally and the Canning proposal did not result in cooperation, it does mark a high point in the friendly relations between Washington and London. What British ministry before that time would even have considered making such a proposal?

1

MARITIME ISSUES AND THE
WAR OF 1812
A. L. BURT

. . . It may be well to clarify the issues in the quarrel between the United States and Britain arising out of the latter's conflict with France. To accomplish this purpose, it will first be advisable to make some comments upon international law; for the quarrel was embedded in it, each side seeking to uphold its own "rights" under that law.

The nature of international law is perhaps the most important thing of all to remember in this connection. As a human institution, law implies some legislator and some tribunal capable of interpreting it and commanding its enforcement; but the sovereignty of the state has denied these conditions for international law, and therefore many careful authorities have insisted that it is not law at all. Strictly speaking, it has been a body of rules derived from common custom and consent. Private individuals, such as Grotius and Vattel, analyzed and expounded it in scholarly texts which became classics but nothing more. The principles thus set forth, being based on precedents which were by no means uniform, were necessarily very general and always open to conflicting interpretations to cover conflicting interests. Then the only solution was the superior force of one side. The whole structure was made more uncertain still by one principle, that of reprisal, which might undo any other principle, and by the insoluble problem of change. Consent is necessary for change, but consent becomes most impossible when change becomes most imperative—when war reveals

From A. L. Burt, *The United States, Great Britain and British North America* (New Haven, Conn.: Yale University Press, 1940) pp. 210–224. Used by permission of The Carnegie Endowment for International Peace.

new circumstances that undermine and destroy the old law governing the conduct of hostilities.

The relation between the "common law of nations" and specific treaties has also been fruitful of much trouble. Britain maintained that the former allowed her to do to the United States certain things which, under the latter, she could not do to certain European powers. The United States therefore insisted that Britain, by signing the latter, had inferentially abandoned her position under the former. Britain, on the other hand, insisted that she had inferentially strengthened it by concluding these treaties. They regulated only the relations between the signatories. By making an exception to the general rule as it applied among themselves, they confirmed its application elsewhere. The law of the world still governed the relations between Britain and America, and it would continue to do so until they agreed to change it. Finally it should not be forgotten that the law has undergone an evolution, and that the principles recognized at one time do not necessarily apply earlier or even later. The failure to recognize this evolution has often befuddled those who would explain old quarrels.

Impressment was the most baffling issue between the two countries. Though thrust forward by the war, it was not a question of the laws of war which define the balance between belligerent and neutral rights. It concerned something more permanent, more deep-seated—sovereignty. It was raised by the attraction of British seamen to the American service. They deserted the navy, where life was too much like a floating hell; and they left the British mercantile marine, whence they were liable at any time to be impressed into the navy. There was only one place where they could go, and it was an inviting heaven where they would be at home right away. The merchant marine of the United States was hungry for sailors. Under the stimulus of the war, it was expanding so rapidly that it required four or five thousand additional hands every year. The increased demand tripled American wages afloat. This salvation of the British tar, however, threatened the destruction of Britain by draining the lifeblood of her sea power, the one thing that stood between her and downfall. To check this vital loss, British warships searched American vessels and removed British fugitives.

Necessity overrides law, and Britain was impelled by necessity. But she insisted that her action was not illegal. Though this may seem strange now, it was not then, for important developments in international law and usage have since taken place. One is in our concept of nationality. We have become accustomed to think of people changing their national status almost as readily as they change their shirts. Then nationality was commonly considered to be about as impossible to change as one's skin. It is the phenomenal growth of the United States by immigration that has made the difference, and even yet the new American-born principle has not gained universal acceptance. This principle, however, played no part in the quarrel over impressment. The American government did not pretend to throw the protecting cloak of American naturalization around the bodies of these British fugitives. The quarrel over impressment turned on the right of search for deserters, and on the abuses which inevitably accompanied the practice.

The right of search was the main point in the dispute, and here the clash between the past and the future stands out clearly. The British position rested on the prerogative of sovereignty to pursue fugitive nationals anywhere up to a line where another sovereignty barred the pursuit. The United States claimed no right to protect American vessels from search in British territorial waters; nor, on the other hand, did Britain claim the right of search within territorial waters of the United States. It was a question of jurisdiction on the high seas, over which there was of course no sovereignty, and there the difference was not over the immunity of government vessels. Though the *Chesapeake* incident has at times led people to suppose the contrary, Britain never asserted the right to search units of the United States Navy. What she did assert, and the United States deny, was the right to search private vessels because this involved no invasion of another sovereignty. Both sides were right, Britain by the old usage, and the United States by a new doctrine then only beginning to take shape: that a country's ships at sea are detached portions of its soil and therefore covered by its sovereignty. Though already admitted for public vessels, it was not yet really established for private ones. Even today this sovereignty is not as complete as that which exists on land or within the limits of territorial waters, and the United States admitted qualification then. The American government recognized, for example, the British right to stop and search private American ships for contraband in time of war.

It was the abuses which accompanied the practice of searching for deserters that inflamed the quarrel, and these abuses occurred on both sides. The British never claimed the right to impress American seamen, but they did impress them as British subjects. It was often impossible to tell the difference between the American and the British members of a crew, for there was no national distinction of language, physical appearance, dress, or manners. British deserters sailing under the Stars and Stripes would insist that they belonged to that flag; and the officers under whom they were serving, loath to lose valuable hands, would support their contention. A boarding officer in search of men whom he badly needed was judge in his own cause, and there was no real check upon his arbitrary decisions. No officer who seized goods as contraband could touch his share of the prize until it was brought into port and there condemned after a legal trial of the seizure, but there was no such procedure to protect human beings seized on the wide ocean. The only way to rescue an American thus carried off was to prove to the Admiralty that he was an American, and then an order for his release would be issued; but this was a difficult business and painfully slow. Early in the first period of the war the American government thought to check the abuse by what were known as "protections." These were certificates of American citizenship issued by magistrates at home and consuls abroad. But the granting of these papers was not hedged about by proper restrictions. It was all too easy for a British tar to get one. They were often given out indiscriminately; sailors lost them and sold them; they were cheap. So notorious did the traffic become that the device made things worse instead of better. British officers naturally came to have nothing but scorn for these official documents of the United States. As the years passed, the number of kidnaped Americans serving in the Royal Navy mounted until it was several thousand. This right of search and practice of impressment was the British counterpart of the unrestricted submarine campaign conducted by Germany a century later, for it touched American lives, and lives are more precious than goods.

Interference with American trade, the other great issue which the French war raised between the United States and Britain, was a complicated question. . . . The trouble springs from the very nature of war. It is a triangular affair. In addition to the clash of arms between belligerents, it precipitates a clash of interest between belligerent and neutral over intercourse with the enemy. The one would like to stop it completely and the other to continue it without any interruption. Long experience has tended to work out a rough compromise between them, for both have felt the restraint of prudence, the belligerent fearing to push the neutral to the point of open hostility, and the neutral shrinking from resistance that would mean fighting. Hence it came to be generally recognized that a belligerent could seize and condemn as legal prize any neutral vessel and cargo containing contraband being sent to the enemy country; and also, under the same penalty, could prohibit any neutral vessel, no matter what her cargo, from entering or leaving a blockaded port of the enemy.

All governments admitted that arms and accouterments of war constituted contraband but there was no common agreement upon the further definition of the term. The textbook writers offered confusing advice. From the conflicting precedents which they recorded, they could deduce only the general principle that other things which might be used by the fighting forces could be treated as contraband when particular circumstances warranted such procedure. A few treaties gave greater precision to the meaning of the word; but there was conflict between them, and each had only a limited application. Thus the original clash of interest survived. Belligerents sought to expand the definition of the term, and neutrals to contract it. Both dressed up selfish interests as legal rights, and the decision between them was left as before to force tempered by prudence. Because the British soon chased the French from the sea, it was the interest of the latter to uphold the narrowest neutral view, and of the former to maintain the opposite, so that over this question the United States became embroiled with Britain and not with France. As we have already seen, however, prudential considerations moved Britain to qualify her seizure of provisions as contraband by purchasing them and paying demurrage. But this was only a mitigation of a principle which Americans regarded as evil; and when France and the United States made up their quarrel in 1800, Bonaparte apparently tried to revive the Anglo-American quarrel over the principle by inserting in his treaty with the United States a definition of contraband as warlike material only.

More exasperating difficulties grew out of the application of the other principle mentioned above. When was a blockade not a blockade? It was commonly conceded that a blockade had to be officially declared and had to be effective, but there was absolutely no consensus of opinion on what was "effective." Here treaties and classical authorities were of much less assistance than in the definition of contraband. Here Nature intervened to render impossible the formulation of any but a very general rule when it was at last adopted by the principal powers, with the exception of the United States, in the Declaration of Paris in 1856. So variable was the combination of such essential conditions as channels, currents, coasts, and weather, that each application of a blockade was a special problem. Here also Bonaparte tried to feed the starved Anglo-American quarrel by inserting into his treaty of 1800 a narrow definition of blockade. As long as the problem of blockade was confined to single ports, it was relatively simple; but, as will be noticed presently, that limitation soon disappeared in the titanic struggle between Britain and the Napoleonic Empire, and it has never returned.

From the ancient and undoubted right of a belligerent to capture private ships and goods of the enemy at sea, sprang other issues between the United States and Britain. One was the principle of "free ships, free goods," which would limit this right by giving immunity to enemy goods, other than contraband, on board neutral vessels. The limitation was so severe that, if enforced, it would have largely destroyed the value of the right, for an enemy could then trade with impunity under the protection of neutral flags. It was a doctrine made by neutrals in the interest of neutrals, to whom it would hand over the carrying trade of belligerents. Its advocates gave it a specious appearance of justice by coupling it with the converse, "enemy ships, enemy goods," which would likewise benefit neutrals by discouraging neutral use of belligerent bottoms. Free ships, free goods, was another of the principles laid down in the Declaration of Paris in 1856. At the time of the French Revolutionary wars, it was a subject of rather violent disagreement. It was already well on the way to establishment, for it had been written into a number of specific treaties. Even Britain had signed an odd treaty embodying it, but she had never admitted its general application, and she could not do so then without playing into the hands of France. For this very reason, France had lined up with the neutral powers; and she tried to use them, particularly her American protégé and ally, in forcing it upon Britain. It was the official doctrine of the United States government, but opinion in the country was far from being unanimous in support of it. When Jefferson was Secretary of State, he wrote to Genet: "It cannot be doubted, but that, by the general law of nations, the goods of a friend found in the vessel of an enemy are free, and the goods of an enemy found in the vessel of a friend are lawful prize." Jay's failure to insert the principle in his treaty was to the French a violation of their treaty with the

United States signed in 1778, and therefore one of the grounds of the subsequent Franco-American breach. In repairing this, Bonaparte revived the subtle French game. One of the maritime principles which he put into his treaty of September, 1800, with the United States was "free ships, free goods."

Of more serious consequence was the disputed right of neutrals in time of war to enter a trade that was shut to them in time of peace. This likewise threatened to destroy the value of the belligerent right to capture enemy property at sea. No compromise principle of any kind had arisen to regulate this issue. It involved two important branches of trade—coasting and colonial. Both were almost universally preserved as strict national monopolies in the period with which we are concerned. If a belligerent, exercising the clear right of capturing enemy ships and cargoes, could drive the enemy from the sea, the enemy would naturally seek relief by temporarily opening its monopoly to neutrals. If they took advantage of this indulgence they would certainly be bringing succor to the distressed enemy. Could neutrals do it and yet remain neutrals?

It was the colonial side of the question which first thrust itself forward, and therefore the first to get any answer. That was in the Seven Years' War, during which the British Empire devoured most of the French Empire overseas. Hard pressed by British maritime superiority, France was unable to supply her West Indies or to bring their produce to Europe under her own flag; and therefore she resorted to the expedient of relaxing her colonial monopoly in favor of neutrals. To counter this novel action, the British prize courts promulgated the novel doctrine which came to be known as "the Rule of the War of 1756," and later simply "the Rule of 1756." . . . It was naturally a categorical negative to the question just stated. Made in Britain to support the interest of Britain, it was another illustration of law being the declared will of superior force. But there was justice in the contention that a trade prohibited by municipal law during peace should be prohibited by international law during war. It deprived neutrals of no right which they enjoyed prior to the outbreak of war, and it was necessary to preserve the value of an unquestioned belligerent right. It was a new rule called forth by new conditions, and it was promulgated in the only way possible. Yet, however just it might be, it ran counter to the interests of neutrals and of belligerents that suffered from naval impotence; and they would not recognize the validity of this fiat of a single power.

The first American collision with this rule . . . nearly precipitated the United States into a declaration of war in the spring of 1794. Indeed Britain had overstepped her own mark by ordering the indiscriminate capture of American vessels trafficking in the French West Indies, for a limited trade in American vessels of small burthen had been legalized before the war; and she drew back just in time. She then contented herself with only a partial application of the rule, ordering the capture of vessels laden in the French West Indies with produce of those islands and sailing thence for Europe. The fruits of the naval superiority of the belligerent were being shared with a neutral.

The nature of this compromise is worth noting. It was confined to a single neutral, the United States, and it was wholly practical. Britain did not renounce any part of her full right under the Rule of 1756. What she did was done voluntarily, under no pressure from America, for the restrained practice was inaugurated long before people in the United States knew that the unrestrained practice had begun. When Jay went to London he found it impossible to extract a renunciation of the principle, as desired by his government. So intent were the British on retaining it that they persuaded him to accept a provision which, without formally according any recognition of the principle, would throw a legal cloak over the practical compromise until two years after the war ended. This was the price exacted for the opening of the much coveted British West Indian trade to American shipping during the same period. The bargain was made in Article XII of the treaty, which bound the American government to make it illegal for American bottoms to carry molasses, sugar, coffee, cocoa, or cotton anywhere except to the United States. These, of course, were the staples of the island colonies; and the object of this provision was to limit American intercourse with the West Indies, both British and French, to a direct trade. American ships were to be forbidden to supply Europe with any such produce even if it had first been landed in the United States. This article would have given an American guarantee, not only to the British monopoly of the transatlantic trade with British colonies, but also to the British prohibition of the same trade with French colonies under the Rule of 1756. The Senate rejected this article because it would outlaw a lawful and profitable American commerce between the French West Indies and France via the United States, recent decisions of British prize courts having legitimized it under the doctrine of the "broken voyage." The Senate's action saved the United States from winking at the Rule of 1756, so that the nature of the compromise remained untouched. It continued to be a matter solely of British grace inspired by prudence.

The liberality of this compromise, and its adoption by unilateral action, may seem to imply a tacit admission on the part of Britain that the principle she had enunciated to meet new conditions in the Seven Years' War did not apply to the yet newer conditions created by American independence, and therefore should not be applied against the United States. The late Admiral Mahan was inclined to draw this deduction, but it is not quite just. This particular British moderation was simply part and parcel of the regular British policy to keep the interference of belligerent rights with neutral rights down to the minimum necessitated by the exigencies of war. In this instance the interference was considerably less than landlubbers might imagine, for the trade winds blew away much of the hardship imposed on American vessels. They did not have to go very far out of their regular course to call at an American port when sailing from the West Indies to Europe. Yet the situation was fraught with danger. In the American treaty of reconciliation with France in 1800, Bonaparte committed the United States to a definition of commercial rights which condemned the British principle without naming it. But he could not rouse the American government over this issue. Only Britain could do that. The danger lay in the nature of the compromise. At any time the British prize courts might shift the basis of their rulings, substituting the "continuous" for the "broken" voyage, and the British government might decide to apply the Rule of 1756 in all its rigor. This decision was never made, but the shift did occur, upsetting the compromise and precipitating trouble.

American action, both public and private, was responsible for destroying the foundation of the British prize-court decisions favorable to the American interest. The doctrine of the broken voyage rested on the assumption that the goods in question were legally imported for use in the United States before they were reëxported. Importation meant the payment of customs duties, and the performance of such operations as unloading, checking, weighing, and storing, all of which involved time and expense. The corresponding operations attendant upon exportation of course added more to the cost. Here were hardships which the trade winds could not blow away, but American ingenuity might remove.

In 1799, Congress passed an act authorizing drawbacks which reduced to a nominal rate the duties paid on certain articles. These, it was observed, were "the ordinary and peculiar subjects of trade between Europe and the West-India colonies." This piece of legislation, which would go far to mend what had been broken, remained unnoticed in England for some time, probably because the hostile relations then subsisting between the United States and France blocked its effect upon the operation of the Rule of 1756. But it could not escape attention after the rupture of the Peace of Amiens, when its effect was bound to be felt because Franco-American relations were once more friendly. This effect was enhanced by another mending process which, by contrast, was quite illegal and therefore conducted less openly. There was a constant temptation to cut corners with cargoes in port. Why go through all the motions of importing and reëxporting, when the same freight was put back in the same hold? Why should Americans suffer this absurd handicap for the benefit of British competitors? Patriotism pulled with profits, private shippers conspired with public officials, and proper papers covered improper performance. Some vessels even cleared with untouched cargoes. What was pious fraud in American ports became plain fraud under British questioning elsewhere. Thus, by congressional enactment and by official connivance, the Rule of 1756 was circumvented in the United States. But it was impossible to mend the broken voyage without ending it. That this was what Americans were doing, the British began to see when the war with France was resumed in the spring of 1803. Almost immediately the modern doctrine of the continuous voyage raised its head in the British prize courts, though it was not until the spring of 1805 that it was finally established by a judgment on appeal. Its establishment doomed American ships and cargoes to capture and condemnation, thereby ruining a lucrative American trade.

Whether neutrals could engage in the coasting trade of an enemy—the other part of the question which had evoked the Rule of 1756—remained in the background much longer than the problem of colonial trade. Though it had not yet pressed for an answer, Bonaparte's treaty with the United States in 1800 supplied one inferentially. The definition of commercial rights mentioned above stipulated the freedom of a neutral to navigate between enemy ports. Not until some little time after the renewal of hostilities in 1803 did this issue thrust itself forward, and then it was soon obscured by other issues. As Napoleon's power spread on land and Britain's grew on the sea, he was relieved and she was frustrated by neutrals' taking over the coasting trade of his empire. Sooner or later she was bound to strike at their interference in this new sphere as she had struck at their interference in colonial trade during the Seven Years' War. She held her hand until January, 1807, when, finding a plausible excuse in Napoleon's recent Berlin Decree which was still little more than an empty threat, she outlawed all commerce between ports under his control. Apparently this extension of the Rule of 1756 was directed at northern Europeans, chiefly the Danes, rather than the Americans, but it was plainly recognized that they would feel the blow too. The American government promptly protested that the British action was illegal unless based on "actual blockades," and pointed out that it would ruin a trade which Britain herself recognized as wholly legitimate. The profits of a voyage commonly depended on dropping some cargo here and some there, and on picking up a return cargo in the same way. If an American merchantman had to make the whole exchange in one place, it might as well not go to France at all.

Thus did the issue over the enemy's coasting trade come into the open when the issue over the enemy's colonial trade was finally chased out of its hole by the doctrine of the continuous voyage. Together they were capable of doing great damage to Anglo-American relations, and therefore it is easy to imagine the havoc wrought by the quarrel which soon swallowed them up along with all the other particular issues concerning trade—the quarrel over Napoleon's Berlin and Milan decrees and Britain's equally famous orders-in-council.

To understand these decrees and orders, we should remember that they accompanied the approach of the supreme crisis in the life-and-death struggle between the two powers which were then by far the greatest on earth. Napoleon had come to realize that his position in Europe would never be secure until he subdued Britain, and she that her freedom depended on his downfall. Having had to abandon his projected invasion of the island kingdom because British sea power effectively barred the way, he perforce fell back upon the use of his land power to accomplish by slow strangulation what was impossible by quick assault. Taking advantage of the fact that Britain had stretched her declaration of blockade to cover a considerable length of his northern coast line, he stretched his declaration still farther and justified his action as a proper reprisal. He proclaimed the blockade of the whole of the British Isles.

This was a sort of fantastic and inverted blockade. Napoleon had no navy to enforce it, and his object was not so much to keep goods from reaching Britain as it was to prevent them from leaving. Because of this inversion, however, and also because of the wide extent of his power upon the Continent, he could undertake to enforce the blockade without a navy. This was what he was doing when he ordered the confiscation of all British goods and also, under pain of confiscation, the exclusion of every ship that touched at a British port. By depriving Britain of access to the European market upon which her economic life depended, he calculated that he could soon reduce the nation of traders and manufacturers to cry for mercy. Such, in short, was his Continental System which he began to enforce vigorously in the late summer of 1807. Britain saw that, if he carried it through, she was done. The orders-in-council were her desperate reply. She extended her blockade to every port from which he excluded her ships; and she turned back upon him the provisions of his own decrees, declaring that she would treat as an enemy any ship which, without first going to Britain, sought to enter any port controlled by him.

The position of neutrals became impossible. It would have been much easier for them if they could have chosen to trade either with Britain or with the Napoleonic empire, but this was not the alternative that was forced upon them. The real issue was the Continental System. Would they coöperate with Napoleon in upholding it, or with Britain in undermining it? The question presented a perfect dilemma. A neutral vessel could not approach any European port that was under Napoleon's sway without being liable to seizure, either outside by a ship of the Royal Navy or inside by Napoleon's officials; inside, if it had touched at a British port, or had procured British papers; outside, if it had not. It was a choice between the devil and the deep sea.

Each belligerent was coercing neutrals to serve its own end; and as neutral rights disappeared under the combined pressure, each belligerent defended its departures from the traditional law of nations by accusing the other of prior violations and by blaming neutrals for their nonresistance to these violations. Neutrals, however, could not accept the self-justification of either without shedding their neutrality, nor could they offer resistance to either without running the same risk.

Resistance to both was unthinkable. It was then more terribly true than ever that law is what those who can and will enforce it say that it is; and that the principle of reprisal, once let loose, may destroy the other principles of the laws of war. Indeed, the "laws of war" is a contradiction in terms.

Both belligerents this time flouted the United States, and both professed eagerness to resume conformity to traditional law; but each insisted that the other should do it first, or that the Americans should resist with force the coercion of the other. Theoretically, the two belligerents were equally oppressive; but practically, legally, and psychologically they were not. Britain's control of the sea, being greater than Napoleon's control of the land, gave her greater power of enforcement. Much more important was the legal difference. Her seizures were made at sea and therefore, according to her own admission, were a violation of neutral rights under international law, her justification being that it was a necessary reprisal against Napoleon. His seizures, except an occasional capture by a fugitive French frigate or privateer at sea, were all made in port and therefore within the undoubted jurisdiction of his own or a subordinate government. Strictly speaking, his only violation of neutral rights under international law was confined to the occasional captures just mentioned. Napoleon also struck a responsive chord in the United States when he denounced the orders-in-council as designed to establish the economic supremacy of England upon the ruins of the industry and commerce of European countries. Here we approach another fundamental factor in the growing Anglo-American bitterness.

Between Britain and the United States there was a mutual suspicion mounting to a settled conviction that each was using the war to cheat the other out of its rights. The British were exasperated by the paradox of their position. Never had they possessed such complete control of the sea, yet more than ever the sea-borne trade of the enemy was escaping from their grasp. As already suggested, neutrals were running off with it and giving it their protection. They were climbing up on the back of the British navy, whose supremacy persuaded the enemy to hand over this trade; and they were throwing dust in the eyes of British judges, causing them to release as neutral what was really enemy property. By such means not only were they expanding their merchant marine while that of Britain shrank; they were actually robbing her of the profitable prizes of war and also of the crowning prize of a victorious end to the war. In other words, their cupidity had leagued them with the enemy and drawn them into an underhand war against Britain. The tricks by which they performed the daily miracle of transforming enemy into neutral commerce were publicly exposed, and a new British policy was demanded, by James Stephen in his *War in Disguise, or the Frauds of the Neutral Flags*, a pamphlet of more than two hundred pages which appeared in the fall of 1805. The author knew whereof he spoke, for he was perhaps the leading practitioner in the prize appeal court and he had earlier followed his profession in the West Indies. He probably shared the responsibility for the adoption of the principle of the continuous voyage, but this did not satisfy him. He was positive that there was only one cure for the evil, and that was a rigorous application of the Rule of 1756. Even if it drove neutrals into open hostilities, that would be preferable to this covert war. Britain would then be free to use her strength to strike down those who were injuring her.

Stephen gave forceful expression to a latent but growing feeling of hostility against neutrals in general and Americans in particular. It was directed against Americans in particular because they were gathering by far the greatest harvest at British expense, their mercantile marine having rapidly become the only great rival of Britain's. The pamphlet was very popular, running through three editions in four months. It undoubtedly had a great effect upon public opinion and may even have had some part, as has been supposed, in suggesting the famous orders-in-council. Be this as it may, the chief significance of Stephen's outburst would appear to have been symptomatic rather than causal. The logic of events was teaching Britain that she could not much longer allow neutrals to reap where she had sown.

As British people believed that Americans were abusing their neutral rights to the vital injury of Britain, so were Americans convinced that Britain was abusing her temporary belligerent rights to serve her permanent economic interests and that in doing so she was furtively dealing a dangerous blow at their country. They saw her trying, under cover of the war, to monopolize the commerce of the world. This may seem absurd when we remember that their mercantile marine had enjoyed a phenomenal expansion through the war while hers had suffered a contraction; but we should not overlook some other important considerations. Britain was in a position to do this very thing, international law being what it was and the Royal Navy being virtually

supreme upon the sea; and there was no gainsaying the fact that measures which she took to win the war also tended to benefit her own
carrying trade and commerce at the expense of others. In the United
States this further effect was bound to be regarded as intentional and
not just incidental. The adoption of the doctrine of the continuous
voyage contained the suggestion that Britain would destroy what she
could not appropriate; and the orders-in-council seemed to prove it.

The American reaction appears all the more natural when viewed in
the light of the past. Britain had laid herself open to this suspicion by
a policy which she, and she alone, had followed for generations. It was
the policy of her navigation laws, by which she excluded foreigners
from all but a corner of her carrying trade. This application of the
monopolistic principle was purposely made to stimulate the growth of
the country's merchant marine, and was commonly credited, both at
home and abroad, with having made it what it was—the greatest in
the world. Another object of the exclusion of foreigners was to deprive
them, particularly the Dutch, of their function as middlemen in international trade, and to transfer this function and its profits to England.
Not unconsciously had she become the chief storehouse and clearing-
house of the world's commerce, or, to use the language of the day,
the great entrepot. She had attained a position where she held the
world in fee. It is not surprising, therefore, that non-British eyes saw
in the orders-in-council a new and ruthless projection of the old and
selfish design. To Americans, of all people, these orders-in-council
were particularly offensive. The reason for their peculiar sensitiveness
lay in their own history: they were being forced back into the dependence of colonial days. Once more Britain was insisting that they
should have no trade of their own, that all their foreign commerce
must be under her control. American Independence was at stake!

2

THE EMBARGO ACT: DECEMBER 22, 1807

AN ACT LAYING AN EMBARGO ON ALL SHIPS AND VESSELS IN THE PORTS AND HARBORS OF THE UNITED STATES

Be It enacted by the Senate and House of Representatives of the United States of America in Congress assembled, That an embargo be, and hereby is laid on all ships and vessels in the ports and places within the limits or jurisdiction of the United States, cleared or not cleared, bound to any foreign port or place; and that no clearance be furnished to any ship or vessel bound to such foreign port or place, except vessels under the immediate direction of the President of the United States: and that the President be authorized to give such instructions to the officers of the revenue, and of the navy and revenue cutters of the United States, as shall appear best adapted for carrying the same into full effect: *Provided,* that nothing herein contained shall be construed to prevent the departure of any foreign ship or vessel, either in ballast, or with the goods, wares and merchandise on board of such foreign ship or vessel, when notified of this act.

Sec. 2. And be it further enacted, That during the continuance of this act, no registered, or sea letter vessel, having on board goods, wares and merchandise, shall be allowed to depart from one port of the United States to any other within the same, unless the master, owner, consignee or factor of such vessel shall first give bond, with one or more sureties to the collector of the district from which she is bound to depart, in a sum of double the value of the vessel and cargo, that the said goods, wares, or merchandise shall be relanded in some port of the United States, dangers of the seas excepted, which bond,

---

From *Public Statutes at Large of the United States*, Vol. 11, pp. 451–453.

105

and also a certificate from the collector where the same may be re-landed, shall by the collector respectively be transmitted to the Secretary of the Treasury. All armed vessels possessing public commissions from any foreign power, are not to be considered as liable to the embargo laid by this act.

3

AGRARIAN DISCONTENT IN THE MISSISSIPPI VALLEY

GEORGE ROGERS TAYLOR

No one of the drawbacks described above nor all of them together were necessarily fatal to western hopes, for, though difficulties are great and costs high, if prices are still higher, prosperity may yet be obtained. Still these difficulties surely tended to make the West of this period a sort of marginal area in relation to world-markets. When world-prices ruled high, Monongahela and Kentucky flour could be disposed of in competition with that from Virginia and Maryland. Likewise, when cotton and tobacco brought good prices, the Kentucky and Tennessee product could be sold along with that of the Atlantic states and still yield a profit to distant western farmers. But when markets were dull and prices falling, western producers not only saw the fading of their roseate hopes but often enough found themselves in desperate straits to secure necessary imported commodities or to meet obligations for land bought on credit when hopes ran high with prices.

Free navigation of the Mississippi, unprecedented immigration, and unusually high prices had brought a great wave of optimism to the West following 1803. . . . The peak year proved to be 1805, but times were relatively good in 1806 and 1807 except for those parts of the West which were adversely affected by glutted markets and lower prices for west-country provisions. Acute depression did not come until 1808. The price situation of that year speaks for itself. Since 1805

From George R. Taylor, "Agrarian Discontent in the Mississippi Valley . . . ,", *Journal of Political Economy*, Vol. XXXIX, August 1931, pp. 484–505. Used by permission of the University of Chicago Press.

the index of wholesale prices of western products at New Orleans had fallen over 20 per cent. Except for hemp growers in Kentucky and infant manufacturing interests at Pittsburgh and Lexington, practically the whole West was prostrated.

Immigration into Ohio seems virtually to have ceased, and land sales north of the Ohio River were greatly reduced. Those who had previously purchased lands now found it impossible to meet their obligations. In a petition to Congress the legislature of Ohio stated:

> . . . the unprovoked aggressions of both England and France, which could neither be foreseen or evaded, has so materially affected the whole commerce of the United States, that it has almost put a stop to our circulating medium, and rendered the payment of the installments of the purchase money for the . . . lands almost impracticable; forfeitures of interest for two, three and four years, are daily accruing.

Stay-laws and relief for debtors were the rule in Kentucky, Tennessee, and Mississippi Territory, and depressed conditions were reported at New Orleans as early as April, 1807.

Two main remedies for the situation received increasingly enthusiastic support from the frontiersmen in the period of falling prices and hard times, which began for parts of the West as early as 1806, became general by 1808, and continued down to the War of 1812 with but partial and temporary relief in 1809–10. One was the development of manufactures; the other was forcing the European powers to repeal their restrictions on our foreign commerce. Of course, still other remedies were advocated from time to time. Occasionally, some one saw clearly enough that fundamental difficulties of marketing, of transportation, and of business and financial organization must be overcome. Some violent partisans believed all would be well if only the Federalists might be returned to power and the national government thereby saved "from the incapacity . . . of our own rules, and the want of that pure patriotism" which distinguished the time of Washington. Even the moralists were present to attribute economic ills to the laxity of the laws and the absence of a feeling of moral responsibility on the part of the people. These, and other solutions were suggested, but the two most popular measures of relief were those intended to stimulate manufactures and those designed to force Great Britain to modify her commercial system.

The enthusiasm for manufacturing cannot be dwelt on here. The following statement from the *Western Spy and Miami Gazette* may be regarded as typical of this western attitude:

> Raise articles of produce, which can be manufactured, rather than such as require a foreign market; Rye to distill; Barley to brew; Flax and Wool to spin, rather than Wheat to ship.
>
> Above all *observe* the household manufactures of your neighbors. *Observe* the accounts of them in the newspapers. Imitate what you see manufactured. . . . Shew our foreign spoliators we can live in comfort without their finery.

Our attention in this paper is centered primarily upon western attempts to mend their failing fortunes through supporting commercial coercion and war. An understanding of the course of frontier opinion in respect to these measures involves, first, a realization of the degree of support which the West gave to the Embargo Act of December, 1807, and, second, an appreciation of the importance of economic motives in prompting the West to support a measure accompanied, as this one was, by widespread depression. An examination of the situation reveals that in his policy of commercial coercion President Jefferson received no more faithful support than that which came from western congressmen. Almost to a man, they voted for the original act of December, 1807, which placed a general embargo on foreign trade; and they supported him loyally in the numerous measures which followed to make its operation effective. When, in November, 1808, the House of Representatives by the very close count of fifty-six to fifty-eight voted to continue the measure in effect, the western members were solidly with the majority. And the next spring, when others weakened, western congressmen stood out for the continuance of the embargo, or, failing that, for the adoption of a non-intercourse act. A westerner, George W. Campbell, of Tennessee, was one of the Senate leaders who held out most firmly against any loosening of commercial restrictions.

On the whole, the citizens of the western states were just as enthusiastic for commercial restrictions as their representatives in Congress. Yet some frontier opposition did appear. At Pittsburgh and Presque Isle (Erie) in Pennsylvania, and in parts of Ohio where some Federalism still survived (e.g., Dayton and Chillicothe), newspaper writers vigorously attacked the measure. In Kentucky, the *Western World* of Frankfort, a paper with an extremely small following, was the only one in the state antagonistic to the embargo. As might be expected from the presence of commercial and shipping interests, some active disapproval appeared at New Orleans, where at least two of the newspapers attacked the measure. Even here probably the group opposed to the embargo formed but a small minority. Its size, however, may have been minimized by the intensely partisan Governor Claiborne, who wrote to Madison: "Two or three British Factors, and some violent Federalists censure the Embargo, but the better informed, and worthy part of Society, appears highly to approve the measure."

Despite the opposition noted above, the frontier was, as a whole, no less favorable to the embargo than its representatives in Congress. The commercial boycott had been successfully used against England in our earlier struggles, and it now seemed to westerners a natural and powerful weapon. State legislatures, local political leaders, and public meetings expressed their enthusiastic approval. Most western newspapers printed articles which ardently championed the embargo. Opinion was so united in its favor in Tennessee as to call forth the following statement: "We never witnessed a greater unanimity to prevail in any considerable district of country, and relative to any important question, than now prevails throughout the state of Tennessee respecting the measures of the General Government. The voice of approbation is universal." Two months after the measure had been superseded by the Non-Intercourse Act, they were still drinking toasts to it in Vincennes. Perhaps at that distant frontier outpost they had not yet learned of its repeal.

Two American students, Professor L. M. Sears and Professor W. W. Jennings, have given special attention to the embargo of 1808. Both emphasize the traditional hatred for England, and the former specifically denies the significance of economic factors. Approval of the embargo, he tells us, was the result of the "simple trust" in Jefferson which filled the hearts of southern Democrats. As for the approval which was given the embargo in Mississippi Territory, Sears regards it as the pure flower of disinterested logic.

It cannot be denied that traditional attitudes and party loyalty played some part in determining western support for the embargo. To some extent the westerner was playing the role of a good Democrat and supporting his president. In part he was acting as a good patriot and a high-spirited frontiersman who resented insults to the national honor either by France or England. The traditional friendship of Democrats for France doubtless made the westerner quick to resent untoward acts by Britain and slow to see evil in the French aggressions. But these explanations are, at most, not the whole story, for an examination of western opinion clearly indicates that the support which was given the embargo on the frontier had in it a considerable element of economic self-interest.

The western farmer was quite willing to admit his lack of interest in the carrying trade. Even impressment of seamen, though to be deplored, did not seem to him very important. But he did want adequate markets and good prices for his produce, and these he believed impossible so long as Great Britain restricted the West Indian market, forbade direct trade with the Continent, and placed exceedingly burdensome duties upon American imports into Great Britain. In the eyes of the western farmer, the depression of 1808 was primarily the result of the belligerents' decrees and orders in council, not of the embargo which he regarded as a highly desirable act, designed as a measure of retaliation to force the abandonment by foreign nations of their destructive interference with the marketing of our surplus products. "Who now blames the embargo?" demanded a Cincinnati editor. "Who considers it a matter of French interest or procurement? Who does not allow it to be a *saving measure?* . . . The embargo was produced by the foreign belligerent powers. They made it wise, just and necessary. They made its continuance necessary."

In Congress western representatives made no effort to conceal their economic interest in the embargo. Said Senator Pope of Kentucky, in stating the very core of the argument in defense of this measure:

> What, Mr. President, is our situation? . . . The dispute between us and the belligerents is not about the carrying trade, but whether we shall be permitted to carry our surplus produce to foreign markets? The privilege of carrying our cotton to market, is one in which, not only the growers themselves are interested, but one which concerns every part of the nation.

He then went on to show that if the embargo were taken off while the orders in council remained in force, cotton would be confined alone to the British market and the price would fall to a ruinously low level. "The necessity," he continued, ". . . of resisting the British orders and forcing our way to those markets where there is a demand for the article, must be evident to every one who will consider the subject."

In conclusion he added that if England did not change her course war might be necessary.

When the question of continuing the embargo was again debated in the spring of 1809, much was said of markets and prices by those favoring a continuance of restrictive measures. In arguing in the House of Representatives against the proposed repeal of the Embargo Act, George W. Campbell, of Tennessee, declared:

> . . . though you relieve your enemy, you do not furnish any substantial relief to your own people. No, sir, I am convinced that, in less than three months from this day, should this measure succeed, produce will sink below the price which it now bears, or has borne for the last year. There are but few places to which you can go, and those will naturally become glutted for want of competition; and, in a short time, the prices will not pay the original cost. It will, therefore, afford no substantial relief. The relief, too, which it may afford will be partial, confined to certain portions of the Union, and not equally beneficial to the whole. Tobacco will find no market; cotton a temporary market only—for, although Great Britain will receive it, yet, as we have more on hand than she will immediately want, or can make use of, and as we cannot go to France, and our trade to the Continent will undoubtedly be interrupted by Great Britain, she has nothing to do but wait a few days, weeks, or months, and buy it at her own price.

If the inhabitants of Mississippi Territory gave, as has been held, a completely disinterested support to the embargo, one must conclude that their delegate in Congress failed somehow to understand the position of his constituents. George Poindexter, the delegate in Congress from Mississippi Territory, wrote the editor of the *Natchez Chronicle* that nothing could be gained by removing the embargo, for British taxes and trade restrictions would so limit the market for cotton as greatly to depress the price.

By the Non-Intercourse Act, which superseded the Embargo Act in the spring of 1809, direct trade with England and France and their colonies was prohibited. Although there was nothing now to stop an indirect trade with England, the British orders in council still kept American produce from reaching the Continent. On the whole the West did not like the change, and their representatives were right in predicting that such partial opening of trade would glut markets with our products and bring prices still lower. Poindexter denounced England's attempt to monopolize world-trade and "tax the product of our farms when exported to foreign markets." He even advocated war against her if necessary, and did not hesitate to recommend to his constituents that cotton be shipped immediately to England via a neutral port so as to get a fair price before markets were glutted.

The course of events during the summer of 1809 was well calculated still further to inflame western hatred for Great Britain and convince the frontier farmers that their surplus could never be exported at a profit until England was somehow forced to permit free trade upon the seas. Prices, although somewhat improved, continued low as compared with pre-embargo years. The Spanish West Indies were now open to American trade; but as early as June 5, 1809, Havana, the most important Spanish port, was reported surfeited with exportations from New Orleans. Erskine's treaty (April 19, 1809) by which direct trade was to be reopened with England was, at least in some quarters, regarded with suspicion. If it should not result in opening trade with the Continent, it was held that there would be loss for us and gain for England. The editor of the *Lexington Reporter* wrote:

> What will be the price of our produce confined and concentrated totally in British warehouses?
>
> Where will be our carrying trade? Why, British merchants and British manufacturers will purchase our productions for the mere expense of shipping and the duties and commissions to London and Liverpool merchants! *Our manufactures will be annihilated.* Britain will have gained a most glorious victory. . . .
>
> What is become of the 100,000 hogsheads of Tobacco exported from the United States?
>
> Will Britain consume and manufacture all our cotton?
>
> No, not one tenth of our Tobacco—not one half of our Cotton; and our flour, our grain, our ashes, our staves, and every other property must center there, and be held as a *pledge for our allegiance.*

In July news reached the West of the extension of the British continental blockade and of the new duties to be levied upon cotton. The *Reporter*, while bitterly attacking England, held that her insults were the results of our weak policy. "Submission only encourages oppression," wrote the editor, "and Britain will follow up her blow, 'till our chains are fully rivetted." Probably this writer's attitude was extreme. Some westerners were inclined to look with considerable hope upon the Erskine arrangements. But when, in the late summer of 1809, word was carried over the Appalachians that England had repudiated the acts of her minister, the frontier was thoroughly aroused. Public gatherings were called for the denunciation of British perfidy. Editors joined in the clamor, and state legislatures sent communications to the president denouncing England and declaring their willingness to resort to arms.

The editor of the Lexington *Reporter* was not slow to drive home the moral. In a long analysis of the situation he said in part:

> The *Farmer* who is complaining of the low price of Cotton, of Tobacco, of any other produce cannot now be deceived of the real cause, he will not attribute it to embargo systems, or to French decrees, for French decrees were in full force when we so anxiously made the experiment of *confining* our trade to Britain, the farmers will see clearly that the orders in council prohibiting and interrupting all commerce to the continent is the only cause for his embarrassments.
>
> . . . The farmer who wishes a market for his produce, must therefore charge his representative in Congress to cast off all temporising. . . .

The winter of 1809–10 found hard times on frontier farms and western sentiment more bitter than ever against the British as the chief cause of the farmers' troubles. The attempt at commercial coercion had failed, but Congress was not yet ready to declare war. Beginning May 1, 1810, commerce was freed from the restrictive measures of our own government. On the whole, conditions seemed on the mend in the following summer, and western farmers were busy harvesting crops which they hoped might be floated down the river to good markets in 1811. Some thought they perceived a promise of better times, while others saw no assurance of prosperity until foreign restrictions should be withdrawn.

But, instead of improving, conditions actually grew seriously worse during the next two years. Wholesale prices of western products were below even those of 1808 in the year before the war. In this new period of general depression on the frontier, the northern part of the Ohio River Valley appears to have suffered less than other parts of the West. Frequent newspaper notices of the building of flour mills in

Ohio and increased advertising by those wishing to buy wheat and flour indicates at least some optimistic sentiment. Also, advantage must have resulted from a considerable increase which now took place in the number of cattle and hogs driven eastward over the mountains. Although some settlers still came via Kentucky or by the river route, the fact which now called forth newspaper comment was the large number of wagons bringing immigrants to Ohio which were to be met on the Pennsylvania turnpikes and on the Zanesville Road in Ohio. Along with this new wave of immigration, land sales rose, though not to their pre-embargo peak. So, at least a temporary market must have been afforded for considerable quantities of country produce.

In so far as contemporary appraisals of the economic situation in this northern area are available, they show little or no reflection of the favorable factors just noted. Dullness of business, scarcity of money, "poverty, disappointment, embarrassment," "the present disasterous state of our affairs"—these are typical of contemporary statements. Taken along with what we know of the price situation, the disorganization of the Mississippi commerce in the winter of 1811–12, and the fact that settlers on public lands were still petitioning for relief, the indications are that, although there was some promise of better times, the region north of the Ohio River was certainly not enjoying general prosperity in the year or two immediately preceding the war.

Judging from the extremely low prices brought by tobacco, hemp, and cotton, one might suppose that the frontier south of the Ohio River suffered from a more serious depression than that to the north. The records clearly show this to have been the case. The Kentucky farmers, who had turned so enthusiastically to hemp culture in 1809 and 1810 that hemp had become the most important staple of the state, now complained even more loudly than those who produced wheat, cotton, or tobacco. There is hardly an issue of the Frankfort and Lexington papers which does not give voice to the despair and resentment of these unfortunate frontiersmen. In spite of public resolutions and even co-operative action to keep up the price by refusing to sell (probably one of the first efforts of this kind among American farmers), ruin was not averted and prices continued their disastrous decline.

In western Tennessee and Mississippi Territory where cotton was almost the only sale crop, the plight of the frontier farmers was most desperate of all. Tennessee cotton planters were reported in the fall of 1810 as so discouraged that to a considerable extent they had ceased the cultivation of their staple. An able contributor to Nashville papers wrote:

> Ask a Tennessee planter why he does not raise some kind of crop besides corn! His answer is—if he were to do it he could get nothing for it—that he could not sell it for money, unless he carried it to Natchez or Orleans—and that was out of his power—therefore he was content to make just what would do him, (as the saying is.) Hence it is undeniable that the want of encouragement forms the principal cause of the indolence of our inhabitants.

This was written in 1810. In the next year conditions were, if changed at all, worse; and "hardness of times and scarcity of money" continued to be the farmer's story.

As for Mississippi Territory, conditions there were also "very dull." Planters were heavily in debt for slaves as well as for land, and in the autumn of 1811 they petitioned Congress to permit them to defer payments due on public lands because of "the severe pressure of the times" and the "reduced price of cotton."

In Orleans Territory the picture was much the same except that cattle raisers in the central and western part of the territory and sugar planters along the river received fair prices for their produce. But cotton growers were as hard pressed as elsewhere. And business at New Orleans experienced a severe crisis in 1811. The editor of the *Louisiana Gazette* declared:

> The numerous failures lately in this city, has not alone been distressing to the adventurous merchant, but it has in a great measure paralized commerce, by destroying that confidence which is the grand key stone that keeps the commercial world together. This city is young in business, we have but few capitalists in trade amongst us, and a shock of adversity is severely felt.

Increased bitterness toward Great Britain and a renewed determination to force her to repeal her commercial restrictions accompanied the depression of 1811–12. But frontiersmen showed no desire to repeat the attempt at commercial coercion; past failures had shaken their faith in pacific measures. The new attitude is epitomized in the following toast offered at a Fourth of July celebration held at Frankfort in 1811: "Embargoes, nonintercourse, and negotiations, are but illy calculated to secure our rights. . . . Let us now try old Roman policy, and maintain them with the sword."

Although it cannot be questioned that this toast expressed the predominant feeling of the West, the existence of an opposition must not be overlooked. Two western senators, one from Ohio and the other from Kentucky, cast ballots against the declaration of war. Letters to newspapers and editorial comments opposing a definite break with England are not uncommon in the Ohio and western Pennsylvania press. In Allegheny County, which included Pittsburgh, the peace party was actually in the majority. Elsewhere in the Mississippi Valley, with the possible exception of New Orleans, where, as during the embargo, the *Louisiana Gazette* was outspoken in its attack on all administration policies, the opposition was of very little consequence.

Taking the frontier as a whole, the predominance of the war spirit cannot be doubted. All of the congressmen from western states voted for war, and the delegate to Congress from Mississippi Territory repeatedly showed himself an enthusiastic advocate of hostile measures toward Great Britain. Both the governor and the state legislature of Ohio took occasion publicly to approve the aggressive stand taken by the Twelfth Congress. In a vote regarded as a test of the peace sentiment the rural elements in Pennsylvania showed themselves strongly for war.

In no part of the Union was the demand for war more clamorous or determined than in Kentucky. The *Reporter*, which had long called for war, now demanded it more insistently than ever, and the other papers of the state followed its lead. Before Congress met in the autumn of 1811 the Georgetown *Telegraph* declared: "We have now but one course to pursue—a resort to arms. This is the only way to bring a tyranical people to a sense of justice." And the next spring the editor of the *Kentucky Gazette* expressed the impatience of the frontier when he wrote: ". . . we trust no further delay will now take place, in making vigorous preparations for War. Indeed those who believed Congress in earnest, expected a declaration of war long ago. . . ." The Kentucky state legislature, which had declared itself ready for war at least as early as December, 1808, now insisted upon a break with England and condemned further "temporising."

To one familiar with the situation on the frontier in 1808–10 it can hardly come as a surprise that, in the same breath in which the farmers deplored their ruined agriculture, they urged war against England.

Both on the frontier and in the halls of Congress westerners now demanded war as a necessary measure for economic relief.

When word of President Madison's warlike message to the Twelfth Congress reached western Pennsylvania, the editor of the Pittsburgh *Mercury* declared himself attached to peace but if necessary ready to fight for commerce. And at the other end of the frontier, Governor W. C. C. Claiborne, in his inaugural address before the Louisiana state legislature, declared: "The wrongs of England have been long and seriously felt; they are visible in the decline of our sea towns, in the ruin of our commerce and the languor of agriculture." Perhaps the statements of the somewhat bombastic governor must not be taken too seriously. But the following by a Louisiana cotton planter seems to come directly, if not from the heart, at least from the pocketbook:

> Upon the subject of cotton we are not such fools, but we know that there is not competition in the European market for that article, and that the British are giving us what they please for it—and, if we are compelled to give it away, it matters not to us, who receives it. But we happen to know that we should get a much greater price for it, for we have some idea of the extent of the Continent, and the demand there for it; and we also know that the British navy is not so terrible as you would make us believe; and, therefore, upon the score of lucre, as well as national honor, we are ready.

In Kentucky even the editor of the lone Federalist paper the *American Republic* denounced foreign restrictions as the cause for the depressed prices for western produce. He differed from the Democrats only in that he blamed not England but France, and also, of course, the Democratic administration for the hard times. But this editor had almost no popular following. His paper, which went out of existence in the spring of 1812, represented little more than his own personal opinions.

When aggressive action toward England seemed imminent late in 1811, the *Reporter*, which had advocated war to secure markets as early as 1809, printed an editorial saying: "It appears likely that our government will at last make war, to produce a market for our Tobacco, Flour and Cotton." And as Congress hesitated over the fatal step, the *Reporter* continued to clamor for war. In April a communication printed in that paper violently attacked England as the source of western difficulties and declared that western hemp raisers would be completely ruined by English measures. And the editor himself wrote in similar vein:

> We are . . . aware that many circumstances combined to reduce the price of produce. The *British Orders in Council,* which still prevent the exportation of cotton, tobacco, &c. to the continent of Europe, *are the chief*—(at the same time confining every thing to their own glutted market) whilst those continue, the carrying trade will be very limited, and bear down considerably the consumption and price of hemp, yarns, &c.

In what was perhaps the most curious and at the same time most revealing article to appear in the West, this same editor wrote:

> Should those *quid* representatives and *quid* members of the administration support war measures after Britain has forced us into war, they support it only for *popularity,* and fear of *public* opinion. Not that their hearts are with their country—But with the British agents and U. States aristocracy.—But the scalping knife and tomahawk of *British savages, is now, again devastating our frontiers.*
>
> *Hemp* at three dollars,
>
> *Cotton* at twelve dollars.
>
> *Tobacco* at nine shillings.
>
> Thus will our farmers, and wives and children, continue to be *ruined* and *murdered,* whilst those half-way, *quid,* execrable measures and delays preponderate.
>
> Either *federal* or democratical energy would preserve all.

When it is remembered that the streets of Lexington were safely distant from the nearest conceivable point of Indian depredation, the editor's reference to economic ruin and the depressed price of commodities appears somehow more sincere than his dramatic reference to danger of tomahawk and scalping knife.

Nor did the economic aspect of the situation fail to find emphasis in the debates at Washington. In the discussions there on declaring war, western congressmen repeatedly emphasized the economic argument. Said Felix Grundy, of Tennessee, a leader of the western War Hawks second only to Henry Clay: ". . . inquire of the Western people why their crops are not equal to what they were in former years, they will answer that industry has no stimulus left, since their surplus products have no markets." And Samuel McKee, of Kentucky, expressed frontier exasperation with those who counseled delay, in the following words:

> How long shall we live at this poor dying rate, before this non-importation law will effect the repeal of the Orders in Council? Will it be two years or twenty years? The answer is in the bosom of futurity. But, in the meantime, our prosperity is gone; our resources are wasting; and the present state of things is sapping the foundations of our political institutions by the demoralization of the people.

So much has been made of the youthful enthusiasm of the War Hawks, of their national feeling and keen resentment of foreign insults, that it may possibly appear to some that these western leaders were great hypocrites who talked of national honor but acted secretly from economic motives. By way of extenuation it may be suggested that national honor and national interest seldom fail to coincide. Furthermore, the western leaders made no secret of their "interests" even though they did have much to say of "honor." Clay demanded vigorous measures against England, declaring that through failure to fight we lost both commerce and character. "If pecuniary considerations alone are to govern," he said, "there is sufficient motive for the war." Three months later, when writing to the editor of the *Kentucky Gazette* assuring him that war would yet be declared, Clay did not hesitate to state in a letter which was probably intended for publication: "In the event of war, I am inclined to think that article [hemp] will command a better price than it now does."

Confusion has sometimes arisen from the failure to realize that commercial privileges were as essential to those who produced goods for foreign exportation as for the merchants who gained by performing the middleman service. John Randolph did accuse the Democratic majority in Congress of being the dupes of eastern merchants. But one has only to read the words of the southern and western advocates of war to find that their position was clear and straightforward enough. Said Felix Grundy:

> It is not the carrying trade, properly so called, about which this nation and Great Britain are at present contending. Were this the only question now under consideration, I should feel great unwillingness . . . to involve the nation in war, for the assertion of a right, in the enjoyment of which the community at large are not more deeply con-

cerned. The true question in controversy, is of a very different character; it involves the interest of the whole nation. It is the right of exporting the productions of our own soil and industry to foreign markets.

Repeatedly this matter came up, and as often western representatives clearly stated their position. Henry Clay left the speaker's chair to explain:

> We were but yesterday contending for the indirect trade—the right to export to Europe the coffee and sugar of the West Indies. Today we are asserting our claim to the direct trade—the right to export our cotton, tobacco, and other domestic produce to market.

Too much has been made of Randolph's charge against the War Hawks that they sought the conquest of Canada, and not enough of his declarations that western representatives were much influenced by consideration of their own advantage. It is true that pro-war Democrats of the coast states hurried to deny that their western colleagues were actuated by "selfish motives." But Calhoun's reply to Randolph is worth quoting, for, although apparently intended as a denial, it is actually an admission of the charge. He is reported as saying:

> . . . the gentleman from Virginia attributes preparation for war to everything but its true cause. He endeavored to find it in the probable rise of the price of hemp. He represents the people of the Western States as willing to plunge our country into war for such base and precarious motives. I will not reason on this point. I see the cause of their ardor, not in such base motives, but in their known patriotism and disinterestedness. No less mercenary is the reason which he attributes to the Southern States. He says, that the non-importation act has reduced cotton to nothing, which has produced feverish impatience. Sir, I acknowledge the cotton of our farms is worth but little; but not for the cause assigned by the gentleman from Virginia. The people of that section do not reason as he does; they do not attribute it to the efforts of their Government to maintain peace and independence of their country; they see in the low price of the produce, the hand of foreign injustice; they know well, without the market to the Continent, the deep and steady current of supply will glut that of Great Britain; they are not prepared for the colonial state to which again that Power is endeavoring to reduce us.

Not only were westerners accused of seeking war for their own economic advantage, but many held they were mistaken in believing that war with England would bring them the results they sought. Federalists and anti-war Democrats repeatedly declared in Congress that war would not open markets or restore the price of hemp, tobacco, or cotton. These speeches, cogent as they often were, failed in their purpose of dissuading the frontiersmen from demanding war, but they are convincing evidence to us that the anti-war minority, no less than the majority which favored the conflict, recognized clearly enough the important relation of economic motives to the war spirit.

As noted at the outset, factors other than those emphasized in this study undoubtedly played a part in bringing on the war. The expansionist sentiment, which Professor Julius W. Pratt has emphasized, was surely present. English incitement to Indian depredations and Spanish interference with American trade through Florida should be noted, as should also the fact that the frontiersmen sought every possible pretext to seize the coveted Indian lands. Restrictions on the carrying trade, even impressment of seamen, may have had some effect in influencing western opinion. No doubt the traditional hostility of the Republican party toward England played a part. Many veterans of the Revolutionary War had settled upon western lands, and time had not failed to magnify the glory of their achievements or to add to the aggressive ardor of their patriotism.

But important as these factors may have been, the attitude of the western settler can hardly be evaluated without an understanding of his economic position. He was, after all, typically an ambitious farmer who moved to the Mississippi Valley in order to make a better living. In the boom times following the Louisiana Purchase he had regarded the western frontier as a veritable promised land. Moreover, the fertile river valleys rewarded his toil with luxuriant harvests. But somehow prosperity eluded him. When, in spite of tremendous difficulties, he brought his produce to market, prices were often so low as to make his venture a failure.

We know now that the farmers' troubles were, in no small degree, fundamentally matters of transportation, of communication, and of imperfect marketing and financial organization. But is it unexpected that in their disappointment (and not unlike their descendants of today who still are inclined to magnify political factors) they put the blame for their economic ills upon foreign restriction of their markets and supported the Embargo and Non-Intercourse acts as weapons to coerce the European belligerents to give them what they regarded as their rights? And when peaceful methods failed and prices fell to even lower levels, is it surprising that the hopeful settlers of earlier years became the War Hawks of 1812?

4

THE REPUBLIC IN PERIL
ROGER H. BROWN

Congressman Jonathan Roberts of Pennsylvania had expressed belief that "every body would be exceeding glad to remain at peace." Congressman Nathaniel Macon of North Carolina had implied the same when he asked rhetorically whether any man would wish to fight if war could be avoided. The statement of Congressman John Harper of New Hampshire: "I pray to God, that he may open the eyes of the British Government to the interests of their renowned nation, and save us, them, and the world, from the evils of the impending conflict," struck a keynote for the party as a whole. The repeated expressions "we are driven to war," "we must fight," "we have no choice," reflect these feelings. Up to the very moment war began the party would have welcomed, with great relief, news of British repeal of the Orders in Council.

Understandably, Republicans had not found it easy to decide for war. William W. Bibb of Georgia spoke for many colleagues when he confessed to "great difficulty in bringing my mind to the 'sticking place.'" He deprecated a war "at the present time, and under the existing circumstances of Europe," as an aid to Napoleonic ambition to conquer the world. He may have considered, as did colleagues, a number of other evils. The nation would suffer from losses in men and materials; the country was young and could ill afford loss of population and wealth. Casualties would occur, however brilliant the strategy

---

From Roger Brown, *The Republic in Peril* (New York: Columbia University Press, 1964), pp. 67–87. Used by permission of Columbia University Press and the author.

or skillful the conduct of battle. A stoppage in all trade, a fall in revenue, a decline in agricultural prices, and destruction of shipping and war materials would probably occur. All these adversities, undesirable in themselves, might well culminate in alienation of public opinion and a Federalist victory. "Is there not some ground to fear a reverse of public opinion?" asked Charles Tait of Georgia, "I think there is." In Republican minds a "change of men," as Secretary of the Treasury Gallatin put it, might "lead to a disgraceful peace, to absolute subserviency hereafter to G. B., and even to substantial alterations in our institutions."

War might possibly have other pernicious effects. A swollen national debt, the probable outcome of prolonged hostilities, in addition to the check it would give to national growth, would threaten republican government. Creation of a large standing army cast another gloomy prospect. War would corrupt "our habits, manners, and republican simplicity," thought Hugh Nelson of Virginia. There was a chance of being driven into the arms of Napoleon during the course of the contest.

There was also concern over the outcome of the war. The nation's military and naval establishments were weak. Harbor defenses and fortifications stood in disrepair. Few men had experience in meeting problems of supply, recruitment, strategy, and tactics. There was concern as to whether Americans would volunteer in sufficient numbers to allow effective military operations, and whether they would pay taxes or subscribe to the loan. What if Great Britain bombarded coastal cities or invaded at some weakly defended point? What if the expedition against Canada should fail? Would not this lead to the "change of men" that all Republicans so greatly feared?

Obviously, there were major dangers. Logically, submission must have involved still greater evils if Republicans considered war preferable. In the phrase of Bibb of Georgia, he considered war "unavoidable, (unless the steps of our adversary be retraced) without a sacrafice greater in its extent, than will be the calamities of war." A "sacrafice" greater than the "calamities of war" would prove great indeed. Other Republicans showed less restraint. Joseph Desha of Kentucky declared that "it would be folly in the extreme to depend upon negociation any longer." Israel Pickens of North Carolina averred that "evils incalculable must visit our country, if we continue to slumber." David R. Williams of South Carolina asserted that "indifference is criminal" and that submission would be "a ruinous and disgraceful course." Jesse Franklin of North Carolina wrote after the declaration that peace any longer would have been "Criminal." The President himself reportedly said that "anything was better than remaining in such a state" of ruinous peace.

Not until June, 1812, eight months after the session began, did Congress take up the question of actually voting a declaration of war. Meanwhile, Republican leaders showed anxiety lest the nation fail to resist the Orders in Council by force. Their feelings indicated the extreme peril in submission. Felix Grundy of Tennessee, concerned over the decision, wrote that he was "hoping for the best & fearing the worst that can befall our Country." William Blackledge of North Carolina exclaimed on the matter of congressional energy: "God forbid they should prove to be the 2d edition of the 10th [Congress]." During the fortnight of debate on the war resolution, Roberts wrote emotionally that "the suspense we are in is worse than hell!!!!" Even the sanguine-tempered Clay of Kentucky betrayed strong feeling in his avowal that "*all* is at hazzard."

Republican leaders outside of Congress also felt anxiety. Elbridge Gerry, Governor of Massachusetts, thus wrote on learning in June of House approval of the war resolution: "God grant to the Senate the same Wisdom & fortitude. Our anxiety is great, in a state of such awful suspense; but we have great confidence in a majority of its members." Henry Dearborn, a Massachusetts Republican leader and commander of the northern army, confirmed that the "Republicans of New England, with few, if any, exceptions, as far as I have the means of knowing, are extremely anxious for the ultimate discision of Congress on the question of war." Thomas Rodgers, a Pennsylvania Republican editor and party leader, deemed the American people now "ripe for the contest, and to delay would be jeopardizing all." John Binns, another Pennsylvania Republican editor, confided that "I wait in confidence but not without my fears & forebodings, to which I give no tongue." Richard Rush, newly appointed Comptroller of the Treasury and close observer of congressional affairs, had perhaps the most expressive words. On May 16: "I think *all* is at stake on our holding on." On May 24: "We are gone" if we hesitate. On June 9: "What a time of anxious, most anxious, suspense it is? what fears, what doubts, what bodings, what hopes, for our common our beloved country, now fill the bosoms, and throb the bosoms of all?"

It is natural to wonder at such expressions. What kind of prospect haunted Republicans as they considered the consequences of submission? What dark perils lay in store for the nation from a continuation of peace?

The prospect of continuing economic adversity had influence on members. Some southern Republicans thought the British blockade had caused price decline in cotton and tobacco which in normal times had been able to reach buyers in France, the Low Countries, and Italy. John C. Calhoun of South Carolina saw in the low price of cotton "the hand of foreign injustice." David R. Williams of the same state directed a "curse" at the one who had "meddled" with the cotton and tobacco export; the most recent crop was rotting at home in the hands of the grower, "waiting the repeal of the Orders in Council." Langdon Cheves of South Carolina asserted that the blockade of Continental markets explained the depression in cotton and tobacco. But it would be a mistake to put great weight on sectional interests. These men also stressed the economic implications for the entire nation. Calhoun wrote of the contest as involving important national rights and national interests, and in speeches called attention to losses not only in agriculture but in commerce too. Williams averred that the British system was "levelled at your most valuable interests," and "in a pecuniary point of view" carried "poverty and wretchedness everywhere." Cheves called for war for the protection of commerce, "the second great interest of the nation" and vital to the prosperity of agriculture.

The economic consequences of submission worried Republicans from other areas of the country. Men foresaw continuing depression in agriculture and commerce. They predicted a large loss in tariff revenue as the result of continuing economic stagnation. William King of North Carolina asserted that we must fight for the right to export our produce—"the deprivation of which strikes at the very foundation of our prosperity." Roberts of Pennsylvania declared that to give up "our fair export trade" was to affect adversely "the great resources of national strength." Henry Clay of Kentucky declared that "if pecuniary considerations alone are to govern, there is sufficient motive for war."

Despite this evidence, however, one should not overemphasize the economic motive. The private correspondence of individual members does not stress economic considerations. Leaders such as Calhoun gave

From Roger Brown, *The Republic in Peril*, (New York: Columbia University Press, equal emphasis to both "national honor and interest" in letters explaining the need to protect American maritime rights. David R. Williams of South Carolina remarked that the British system "in a pecuniary view" was harmful, but added that "in every other [point of view] it ought to be spurned with detestation." Some Republicans even denied the importance of assuring American trade with the Continent. Jesse Franklin of North Carolina complained that overseas commerce should have been left from the very beginning to fend for itself without government protection.

> I have always been of opinion that the united states true interest was as it respected our Commerce—after Laying on proper Discriminating duties upon Tunage &c to have left its Regulation pretty much to the Custom House and insurance office. Particularly in such a state of things as has existed in Europe for years passd. But such has been the thirst of our Citizens for foreign Commerce and such their unbridled avarice in pusuit of Commerce and extravegant profit that they have run into great extream, and perhaps rather exsesably Carried the government a Long already too far.

Men also weighed in the balance against submission the question of America's sovereignty. Many Republicans believed that surrender to the Orders in Council would be to yield a portion of national independence. The right to regulate one's own commerce on the high seas was the exclusive prerogative of every truly independent nation. "Practically considered," said Williams of South Carolina, the operation of the Orders in Council "is the exercise of supreme legislation over us, involving not only all the attributes of legitimate sovereignty but despotism direct." When it is considered, said Pickens of North Carolina, that the right of carrying our products to foreign markets belongs to the independence won by the patriots of the Revolution, "the duty on us becomes indispensable, to protect it unemcumbered for posterity, who have a fair claim to the valuable inheritance." Grundy of Tennessee wrote that "Our Fathers fought for and bequeathed liberty & Independence to *us* their children," and that a firm and manly effort "will enable us to transmit to *our children* the rich inheritance unimpaired."

Furthermore, to yield a portion of sovereignty would only encourage further infringements. "Further forbearance," argued Tait of Georgia, "would but invite further aggression and . . . no nation ever did preserve its independance and its Rights which did not repel with spirit the first incroachments on them." Clay made this point in debate. Yield to the Orders "and to-morrow intercourse between New Orleans and New York—between the planters on James River and Richmond, will be interdicted." The "career of encroachment is never arrested by submission. It will advance while there remains a single privilege on which it can operate." Pickens of North Carolina declared:

> History affords no instance of a nation securing, or successfully resist- ing encroachments on its sovereignty, when this resistance has been weak and timid. On the contrary, does not all experience show, that in proportion as a nation is found regardless of injuries, even of minor consequence, in that proportion have exactions been made upon it.

The same thought led John Sevier of Tennessee to write that the time had again come "to contend for our Independency."

A concern for national honor also led Republicans towards war. Many anticipated that failure to resist would degrade and demoralize Americans. They could reason from their own sense of honor. Senator Thomas Worthington of Ohio considered "the Point of Honour" as the crux of the controversy and told Augustus J. Foster, the British minister, that "he would rather live on a Crust in the Interior than live degraded." William Eustis, the Secretary of War, gave eloquent testimony of the humiliation he would feel if the country failed to fight. Answering George Logan, the famous Quaker pacifist who had written opposing war, Eustis avowed that this could only mean "submission with disgrace." On what honorable basis could a new negotiation be initiated? "Describe what you imagine might be said. Look at it after it is written—and see if a check of disgrace does not follow every word. Lay aside every sense of honor & national pride in your men. Imagine them perfect courtiers who will speak with out a blush—but remember they are to speak the language of an honest decent long abused na- tion." Therefore, Republicans could easily project how fellow citizens would react to submission. "[S]omething must be done" avowed Grundy of Tennessee in November, 1811, or we shall "cease to respect ourselves." General Henry Dearborn described the shame Americans would feel, writing during the June debates: "[I]f the Senate should ultimately negative a vote of the House for war, we may hang our harps on the willow, and hide our heads in the dust, for we shall have no character left, worth contending for."

Even so, when Clay warned that "*all* is at hazzard," when Grundy feared "the worst that can befall our Country," when President Madison exclaimed that "anything was better than remaining in such a state," concerns larger than assured commerce, national sovereignty, and national honor were at stake. Republicans thought of themselves as defenders of republicanism against enemies both at home and abroad. Certainly the economic consequences of submission concerned many. Certainly the threat to national independence caused worry; certainly, too, did the matter of personal and public self-respect. But Republicans in 1812 feared above all else that submission would threaten their control of the nation's political life and draw odium down upon republican government. No other possibility could have so overweighed the predicted dangers and evils of war, or evoked such dire forecasts at the thought of submission.

Republicans anticipated peril to the Republic from party disgrace and the loss of political power to the Federalists—from "a change of men." Having taken upon themselves the task of defending the nation's commerce, independence, and honor against foreign aggression, Republicans could foresee that their own party would bear the brunt of public scorn if they now gave up the struggle. Thus John Binns, the Philadelphia editor, wrote on the eve of war: "The honor of the Nation and that of the party are bound up together and both will be sacrificed if war be not declared." Now that all measures short of war had failed, the administration and its Republican supporters in Congress must embrace war, or court disaster at the polls. James G. Jackson of Virginia, a former congressman writing from retirement, warned President Madison, his brother-in-law, of this danger: "I am rejoiced that the crisis has produced a corresponding attitude because I fully believe the national spirit & the national honor demand it and if the Government were now to succumb—what with the pressure from abroad & at home—it would be crushed to annihilation." William Crawford, a Pennsylvania congressman, feared the downfall of the administration. Writing the President he urged more vigorous direction in leading Republicans to war—"the only safe & honorable alternative which offers to preserve [the nation's] independence." For "even among those who profess to have *only* the same objects in view, so much diversity of sentiment prevails; that some means to unite their views & their efforts, appears essential to the immediate preservation of the government." From John Sevier, the famous Indian fighter and Tennessee congressman, came in May, 1812, another forthright statement of the danger: "The Government have exhausted every measure to support peace, and an honest and impartial neutrality, but all in vain, and in my opinion nothing but a war can possibly save the *Government*, and the *Nation*." One may imagine Sevier's thoughts on the subject of submission: surrender of "our Independency," a change of men, Federalist betrayal of the Republic.

Federalist taunts during the session fed these fears of political disaster. Barring a last-minute British concession, actions and words had firmly committed the Republican majority to war. Federalists in Congress and throughout the country responded with scoffs and derision: the ruling party had neither the intention, the courage, nor the ability to make war, and would never do so. Under such an attack, Republicans felt the precariousness of their position still more keenly. Governor Gerry expressed a common view in describing opinion in Massachusetts: "The anxiety here is great for the final decision. The opposition increases with delay, & predicts that it will terminate in vapour. This would produce on the one part a compleat triumph, & on the other an overthrow." In April a movement got under way in Congress for a brief adjournment previous to the final decision. Some Republicans feared this might divert the march towards war. John A. Harper, the New Hampshire congressman, wrote in a private letter: "In my opinion, if we have a recess, we shall have no war, but complete disgrace"; and again on the same subject of a recess: "[Y]ou may well consider that the friends of the government feel anxious."

Roberts, the Pennsylvania congressman, predicted disaster from an adjournment which seemed to him "as settling the question of peace and war in favor of peace." When it became likely that the measure would pass, the Pennsylvanian moved to disallow compensation to members during their absence from the capital. "Every consideration of a personal & public nature engaged me to oppose it—When it seemd that no hope was left but thro the weakness or the error of our friends we were to be thrown prostrate before our enemies—I movd to disallow any compensation during the recess." Not only did he think adjournment would leave the President alone at a dangerous time—"worse than all it would have been taken as evidence of the indecision of Congress & of an anti warlike spirit in the public councils." It is understandable that Roberts should have greeted the final decision for war with satisfaction. His party had given the lie to Fed-

eralist propaganda. The declaration of war was "a great point gain'd.
. . . The Feds & their Foster are both at last deceiv'd. They persuaded
themselves that war could not nor dare not be resorted to & with all
the warning they at Last are by surprise."

If Republicans foresaw party dishonor in submission, would not
disgrace also fasten itself to the form of government that permitted
such weakness? Ever since the Revolution American leaders had been
conscious of the unproven capacity of their republic to function effectively in the jungle of international life. The question was still unan-
swered whether a government made up entirely of elected members
possessed enough unity of purpose and firmness of will to give full
protection to vital national interests—by force if necessary. Years of
temporizing and postponement in the face of European maritime aggression—negotiation after negotiation, restriction after commercial
restriction—had deepened doubts as to the competence of the present
American form of government. Perhaps, after all, republicanism was
(as Washington once put it) "ideal & fallacious." Thus, Henry Clay,
deploring the fear of British power in the "councils of the nation" and
its influence on the retreat from the embargo in 1809, referred to "that
dishonorable repeal which has so much tarnished the character of our
Government." It was of the utmost importance to dispel all doubt as
to the capacity of republican government and to avoid giving any
further proof of weakness.

Republicans warned that submission would disgrace not only their
party but also the government. Some tentatively made their predictions. Gideon Granger of Connecticut, the postmaster general, in December, 1811, confessed: "I cannot perceive the grounds on which we
can remain at peace without a change of measures which will dishonor
the Administration and possibly the government." Others voiced more
certain opinions. Joseph Gales, Republican editor of the nation's leading newspaper, the semiofficial *National Intelligencer*, avowed that the
standing of republican government had become involved in the issue
of war versus submission. "Not only the rights of the nation, but the
character of the government, are involved in the issue," he wrote.
"The deliberations of Congress 'at this momentous era,' will, perhaps,
do more to stamp the character of genuine republican governments,
than has been effected in this respect since the creation of the world."
Congressman James Pleasants of Virginia believed firmness imperative
for the reputation of the government. Pleasants wrote in 1812 that he

failed to see "how it can be any thing else" than war. Remarks made during debate explain his rejection of submission. He pointed to a growing feeling at home and abroad that the American government was unable to stand firm on its own resolves and urged the importance of dispelling this impression. "A very general impression has been produced on foreign Governments, and indeed on this people also, that our councils are so vibratory, so oscillating, that we are incapable of carrying into effect our own resolves." It was "of the utmost importance to us that that impression should be done away, almost at any hazard." It was "the interest of no party, but of the whole people, that our own character should be fixed; that we should no longer be the sport of foreigners, nor an object of distrust to our own citizens." Congressman Hugh Nelson of Virginia stated the great importance of refuting impressions of weakness. Great Britain and France believed (he told constituents in July, 1812, explaining his vote for war) that our republican government was "inefficient and incompetent to exert the power and energy of the nation, and to assume the attitude and posture of war."

> [To] repel these unfounded imputations, to demonstrate to the world and especially to the belligerents, that the people of these states were united, one and indivisible in all cases of concern with foreign nations, to shew that our republican government was competent to assert its rights, to maintain the interests of the people, and to repel all foreign aggression, were objects with me of primary importance. My conduct as your representative has been regulated entirely by these great and important considerations.

Talk of war and military legislation led to more such expressions. To retreat from these pledges to fight would be sure proof of weakness. John McKim, Jr., a Maryland merchant and party leader, lamented "so much unsteadyness in the Councils of the Nation," and exclaimed: "If the Stand that is now Taken is departed from, Without bringing England to Justice, we may as well give up our Republican Government & have a Despot to rule over us." Calhoun of South Carolina warned of the harmful effects of submission on the prestige of the government: "I think the friends of the country of whatever politicks, must see, that it is impossible for us to receede without the greatest injury to the character of the government." Congressman Burwell Bassett of Virginia warned that there was "nothing so much to be guarded against in this government as vacillation," and that there was "more now at stake than the mere question of war or peace"; if we failed to fight now "the people never would believe that Congress or the Government possessed energy enough to support their rights."

Such expressions reveal how Republicans linked the prestige of republicanism to the issue of war versus submission. Submission would demonstrate that republican government lacked energy, staying power, the ability to organize and bring to bear the will and strength of the nation. In the event of submission, would republicanism survive? It seemed possible that it would not. Proven inability to ensure such vital concerns as the economic interests of citizens, national sovereignty, and national honor might destroy the faith of all America in the republican form of government.

A government must afford protection to the personal economic interests of its citizens if it wishes to keep their loyalty, urged John Roberts, a Pennsylvania Republican, in April, 1812. Otherwise, citizens will not give the government their confidence and support.

> [T]he Circle I am acquainted with have pretty much made up their minds to meet a War—Town & Country say our condition cant be worse than it has been and it is to the Representatives of the Nation we now look—and I think with [Edward] Gibbon [the historian] "that that Government which is found too weak for the protection of its Citizens, will be found to[o] weak and unworthy [of] their protection."

Calhoun repeatedly expressed such a view. The Carolinian believed it to be a prime duty of a government to give protection to its citizens. Unless it did so, he implied, it could not long exist. Speaking to the House during the war debates, Calhoun declared that the government must "protect every citizen in the lawful pursuit of his business"; that the citizen "will then feel that he is backed by the Government; that its arm is his arms; and will rejoice in its increased strength and prosperity." Calhoun told Augustus J. Foster, the British minister, at a Washington state dinner, "that the Merchants would put up with any wrong and only thought of Gain, but a Government should give Protection." Calhoun's personal correspondence shows that he believed American opinion to be dissatisfied with the protection afforded by the government. The South Carolina congressman felt that a long period of negotiations and commercial restrictions had caused disillusion at home and contempt abroad. All efforts had failed to maintain respect for "national honor and interest." Negotiation and restrictions "might suit an inconsiderable nation, or one that had not such important rights at stake. Experience has proved it improper for us. Its effects have been distrust at home and contempt abroad." He therefore hoped that Congress would stick to its "salutary resolve" of military preparations.

Following the declaration of war Calhoun returned to this point. Great Britain had repealed her Orders in Council on a conditional basis, but now the issue was impressment—the protection of American seamen against compulsory service in the British navy. In a scathing attack on continued Federalist obstructionism, Calhoun warned that such opposition could paralyze the war effort. When governments failed to protect citizens, they failed in their most essential function and forfeited public confidence. Indeed, those responsible for obstructing the operations of republican governments had commonly been among the first to exploit ensuing public discontent to their destruction—an obvious allusion to suspected Federalist purposes.

> The evil [of partisan opposition] is deeply rooted in the constitution of all free governments, and is the principal cause of their weakness and destruction. It has but one remedy, the virtue and intelligence of the people—it behooves them as they value the blessings of their freedom, not to permit themselves to be drawn into the vortex of party rage. For if by such opposition the firmest government should prove incompetent to maintain the rights of the nation against foreign aggression, they will find realized the truth of the assertion that government is protection, and that it cannot exist where it fails of this great and primary object. The authors of the weakness are commonly the first to take the advantage of it, and turn it to the destruction of liberty.

A government must also assure national independence. If British infringement of American sovereignty went unchallenged, would not this weaken the attachment of the people to a government found unable to protect so vital an interest? Richard Leech, a Pennsylvania leader, made this point to a party colleague: I confess I feel the most painful anticipations. How is it possible that a Govt. can have the respect & Confidence either of its own Citizens or of Foreign Nations which is afraid to do any thing more than *talk* about its Independence

& its rights?" John Campbell, a Virginia leader and state representative, wrote his brother late in 1812 that he had been for war in order to demonstrate "the stability of the government" and prove its capacity "to support our independence," concluding: "Time will soon test the durability of republican governments and shew the truth or falicy of the maxim that man is incapable of self-government." Among members of Congress Nathaniel Macon of North Carolina declared that the nation must now fight to protect its sovereignty or place its destiny in the care of some authority other than the present government. "If we cannot fight by paper restrictions, we must meet force by force. If we cannot do this, it is time we put ourselves under the protection of some other Power."

Finally, there were Republicans who foresaw that Americans would not undergo dishonorable and degrading submission without reacting against the cause of their shame. Submission would depress national honor to so low a level that citizens would seek another kind of government to restore their sense of self-respect. National pride—"the national spirit" as contemporaries called it—had to be supported if Americans were to remain loyal to republicanism. James Jackson of Virginia, the former congressman, expressed this point of view. At the time of the *Chesapeake* affair he had written to Madison, who was then Secretary of State:

> [A] tame submission to such outrages will disgrace the Government & its Friends: it will be the signal for every species of insults, until the national spirit, broken, sunk, & degraded: will return with loathing & abhorrence from the Republican system we now so fondly cherish & take refuge against such wrongs in a military despotism, where another Buonaparte, or a Burr will give Law to the Republic.

What was true in 1807 was no less so in 1812. Among members of Congress, Roberts of Pennsylvania stated this view in debate. Submission, he declared, "must not only affect us, in the great resources of national strength; but it must break the spirit of our citizens, and make them infidels in the principle of self-government."

Thus Republicans saw in submission great danger to republicanism. A government found unable to protect such important concerns as the personal economic interest of citizens, national sovereignty, and national honor might well forfeit public support. But these dark warnings of waning confidence remain tantalizingly obscure as to ultimate processes. Precisely how the Republic would fall is rarely discussed in available source material. Perhaps men were not entirely clear in their own minds how the castastrophe would occur. A few hints point to concrete possibilities. Jackson of Virginia clearly predicted that a man on horseback would come to rescue Americans from the depths of humiliation, "another Buonaparte, or a Burr." David Campbell, a Virginia Republican, also anticipated the rise of a military dictator. Demoralized by submission, wrote Campbell, Americans will "crouch to the oppressor like the slaves of Europe, and then, a violent, unprincipled & misguided rabble become fit instruments for some designing and desperate leaders to commit acts, the cruelty of which the world has not yet seen an equal." Edward Fox, a Pennsylvania Republican, foresaw demoralization, increasing factional squabbles, the disgust and despair of "well disposed men," and ultimately such disorder that "any change will be readily agreed to that will promise quiet and tranquility." Wilson Cary Nicholas of Virginia, writing in 1813 when the American war effort had stalled, warned that domestic enemies of republicanism might persuade the American people to adopt a different government.

> [O]ur feebleness and imbecility now will invite agressive attempts to conquer us hereafter. Perhaps the greatest & most pressing danger to us is that it may lead to a change in our government which will lose the confidence and attachment of the people. It may not be difficult to induc[e] them to believe that a government that can neither defend the persons nor the property of the Citizens nor preserve the national character and honor is not worthy of their support. Altho as in this case the failure may justly be ascribed to the wickedness of some and the folly of others.

Other Republicans feared a Federalist return to power. In the event of submission, so these men believed, the Federalist party, whose leaders presumably championed monarchy and aristocracy, would gain popular favor. William Plumer of New Hampshire, a former Federalist turned Republican, predicted Federalist gains among disillusioned citizens. Congress must remain in session one month longer, he wrote to Congressman Harper at the end of April. "By that time the Admin will have information on which they can rely from England, whether that haughty nation will do us justice, without an appeal to arms. If she refuses, one of two things will follow, Congress will declare war, or the government of our Country will be *degraded*—degraded so that *hosts of tories will* emphatically *be* found *in private life*." Indeed, thought Plumer, a war declaration "must necessarily produce a great change in public opinion & the state of parties— British partizans must then either close their lips in silence or abscond." Again, in May, he deplored the spectacle of so many members obtaining leave of absence, feared a quorum might not be raised on the war question, and exclaimed: "But we must not despair of the Republic—a steady firm undeviating prudent spirit will save us from our fears." The danger seemed real enough. Even if Federalists gained control only in the northeast, they could secede from the Union and rejoin the British empire.

Finally, there are the views of President James Madison and his chief adviser on foreign policy matters, Secretary of State James Monroe. The President was opposed to submission because of its ruinous economic effects. He felt that surrender to British blockade of the Continent would hurt all classes of people in America. The British market would continue to be overcharged with American exports, causing low prices for farmers and planters. Disproportionate imports from Great Britain "would drain from us the precious metals, endanger our monied Institutions; arrest our internal improvements, and would strangle in the cradle, the manufactures which promise so vigorous a growth." The "Ship owners & Shipbuilders and mariners" must be equal sufferers in the cramping effect of British blockades on commerce. The President saw other evils in submission: national dishonor and the betrayal of independence. "It would be," he wrote, "a voluntary surrender of the persons and property of our Citizens sailing under the neutral guaranty of an Independent flag." Furthermore, it "would recolonize our commerce by subjecting it to a foreign Authority; with the sole difference that the regulations of it formerly were made by Acts of Parliament and now, by orders in Council."

At the Constitutional Convention in 1787 Madison had labored to save republicanism. His efforts to organize opposition to the Federalists in the 1790s had been to save this precious form of government. In 1812 he was again concerned. Richard Rush, a Pennsylvania Republican, famous in later years as a diplomat and cabinet member, was the newly appointed Comptroller of the Treasury. Rush believed that further submission to British Orders in Council would destroy republicanism as a system of government for all time and that Americans must therefore resort to war. "Being the only republick, the destinies of that sort of government are in our keeping. Should we stand by and see it longer debased by submission, or sordid avarice, its cause is gone forever." Moreover, being "the first republick," that is, "genuine popular democratical government" at war since antiquity, Rush believed there to be "proportional considerations to animate us to great deeds, and hold out to us prospects of glory." In a drawing-room conversation with the President, Rush had propounded these two ideas. Madison, reported Rush to a correspondent in April, 1812, "fell in with them, particularly the last, which he thought should animate." Here the President, in agreement with the concern behind Rush's first proposition, stressed the second, possibly to suggest means of arousing national enthusiasm. But the future of republicanism was not far from his thoughts, as other evidence reveals. It was Madison's concern that dictated a passage in the Annual Message of November, 1812, where he reviewed the course of British aggression.

> To have shrunk under such circumstances from manly resistance would have been a degradation blasting our best and proudest hopes; it would have struck us from the high rank where the virtuous struggles of our fathers had placed us, and have betrayed the magnificent legacy which we hold in trust for future generations.

There was also the Second Inaugural Address in which the President stated that war had not been declared by the United States until all hope of accommodation had been exhausted, "nor until this last appeal could not longer be delayed without breaking down the spirit of the nation, destroying all confidence in itself and in its political institutions, and either perpetuating a state of disgraceful suffering or regaining by more costly sacrifices and more severe struggles our lost rank and respect among independent powers."

There was also, we may infer, fear of Federalist resurgence in the President's mind. His wife, Dolley Madison, seems to say so in a letter to her sister, Mrs. Anna Cutts, wife of Congressman Richard Cutts of Saco, Maine. Congressman Cutts had been on leave during much of the session, and Mrs. Madison was urging her sister to persuade Richard to return to Washington. The President's brother-in-law was needed to help the party in the coming vote on war. "You may rely upon it, if Mr. Cutts does not come it will be a disadvantage to him as well as to his party—some of them have reproached him already, but he will be here, we hope, just in time—not a moment too soon, it is supposed, to give his vote for War."

Madison's Virginia compatriot and chief adviser was James Monroe. The prestige and security of republicanism depended on successful defense of maritime rights, wrote Monroe during the war debates. The Federalists demanded repeal of all commercial restrictions and surrender of our commerce to British regulation. "But where," asked Monroe, would this act of submission "have left the U States? & what effect would it have had on the character—, & destiny of our republican system of govt? My idea was that such a step would have put it in great danger if it had not subverted it eventually." Likewise, to rely further on measures which had failed to accomplish their object, "while war is carried on, on the other side, is equally unworthy the character & inconsistent with the true interests of the U States." In an interview with the British minister in the month before war Monroe expressed a belief that America must now fight, or he would despair of the present republican form of government. As Foster recorded:

> Mr. Monroe confidentially spoke of the impossibility there was for this Government now to recede without a change of any kind on the part of England. He even said that he should feel like a man disgraced and ashamed to shew his face, if after the steps which were taken they were now to submit; that they had no ground on which to stand but upon continuing their present course; that should they submit now it would be impossible ever again to speak about neutrality or neutral rights; that they might as well be without a Government at once and that he for his part would rather quit the United States at once and go somewhere else where there was a Government that could make itself respected.

The enthusiasm of the Republican response to news of the war declaration is a measure of men's anxiety over possible submission. One might have expected hostilities against the world's most formidable naval power to have aroused somber thoughts of coming difficulties and dangers. Initial responses were, on the contrary, exultant. An unconfirmed report of the congressional declaration of war prompted Thomas Rodgers, the Pennsylvania editor, to exclaim: "The news last night cheered me; for I was, I confess, very much afraid of the Senate. If the news is true we hear, the Republic is safe, and all must now rally round the standard of our country." Celebrations, parades, illuminations, resolutions, and salutes testify to the emotions released by the congressional action. Governor Gerry of Massachusetts expressed the feelings of many. He wrote to President Madison soon after receiving news of the declaration: "War is declared, God be praised, our country is safe." A stranger, observing these events, could easily have concluded that war was just over, not just beginning.

It remained for Henry Clay to sound a more realistic judgment. Clay in 1810 had referred to repeal of the embargo as "that dishonorable repeal which has so much tarnished the character of our Government." Clay in 1810 had written a party colleague in the Madison administration of his "great solicitude for our Country & for our cause." Now Clay in 1812 believed that "*all*" was "at hazzard." Submission was a "potion of British poison actually presented to our lips." But war could be fatal also. The simple fact of a declaration by no means assured the fate of republican government. A long, difficult, and perilous road lay ahead. Once the government had shown itself capable of declaring war, it must show itself capable of waging war. The fate of the world's only republic, Clay implied, might depend on the fact: "God grant us a happy result to this new & untried experiment to which the only free government upon earth is about to be subjected! That such will be the issue of the contest I entertain no doubt if the people possess the fortitude and firmness which I believe they do."

It is therefore understandable that men should have viewed the War of 1812, its beginning and outcome, as demonstrating that the American Republic could function effectively in international life. Reviewing the recent contest in a speech delivered in 1816, Henry Clay could thus avow:

> Have we gained nothing by the war? Let any man look at the degraded condition of this country before the war; the scorn of the universe, the contempt of ourselves; and tell me if we have gained nothing by the war? What is our present situation? Respectability and character abroad—security and confidence at home. If we have not obtained in the opinion of some the full measure of retribution, our character and Constitution are placed on a solid basis, never to be shaken.

The second war with Great Britain had proved, if it accomplished nothing else, that the Republic was not utopian.

5

THE MONROE DOCTRINE: DECEMBER 2, 1823

At the proposal of the Russian Imperial Government, made through the minister of the Emperor residing here, a full power and instructions have been transmitted to the minister of the United States at St. Petersburg to arrange by amicable negotiation the respective rights and interests of the two nations on the northwest coast of this continent. A similar proposal has been made by his Imperial Majesty to the Government of Great Britain, which has likewise been acceded to. The Government of the United States has been desirous by this friendly proceeding of manifesting the great value which they have invariably attached to the friendship of the Emperor and their solicitude to cultivate the best understanding with his Government. In the discussions to which this interest has given rise and in the arrangements by which they may terminate the occasion has been judged proper for asserting, as a principle in which the rights and interests of the United States are involved, that the American continents, by the free and independent condition which they have assumed and maintain, are henceforth not to be considered as subjects for future colonization by any European powers. . . .

It was stated at the commencement of the last session that a great effort was then making in Spain and Portugal to improve the condition of the people of those countries, and that it appeared to be conducted with extraordinary moderation. It need scarcely be remarked that the

From J. D. Richardson (Ed.), *A Compilation of the Messages and Papers of the Presidents*, 1789–1897 Vol. II, pp. 209 ff. Washington, D.C.: U.S. Government Printing Office, 1899.

result has been so far very different from what was then anticipated. Of events in that quarter of the globe, with which we have so much intercourse and from which we derive our origin, we have always been anxious and interested spectators. The citizens of the United States cherish sentiments the most friendly in favor of the liberty and happiness of their fellow-men on that side of the Atlantic. In the wars of the European powers in matters relating to themselves we have never taken any part, nor does it comport with our policy so to do. It is only when our rights are invaded or seriously menaced that we resent injuries or make preparation for our defense. With the movements in this hemisphere we are of necessity more immediately connected, and by causes which must be obvious to all enlightened and impartial observers. The political system of the allied powers is essentially different in this respect from that of America. This difference proceeds from that which exists in their respective Governments; and to the defense of our own, which has been achieved by the loss of so much blood and treasure, and matured by the wisdom of their most enlightened citizens, and under which we have enjoyed unexampled felicity, this whole nation is devoted. We owe it, therefore, to candor and to the amicable relations existing between the United States and those powers to declare that we should consider any attempt on their part to extend their system to any portion of this hemisphere as dangerous to our peace and safety. With the existing colonies or dependencies of any European power we have not interfered and shall not interfere. But with the Governments who have declared their independence and maintained it, and whose independence we have, on great consideration and on just principles, acknowledged, we could not view any interposition for the purpose of oppressing them, or controlling in any other manner their destiny, by any European power in any other light than as the manifestation of an unfriendly disposition toward the United States. In the war between those new Governments and Spain we declared our neutrality at the time of their recognition, and to this we have adhered, and shall continue to adhere, provided no change shall occur which, in the judgment of the competent authorities of this Government, shall make a corresponding change on the part of the United States indispensable to their security.

The late events in Spain and Portugal shew that Europe is still unsettled. Of this important fact no stronger proof can be adduced than that the allied powers should have thought it proper, on any principle satisfactory to themselves, to have interposed by force in the internal concerns of Spain. To what extent such interposition may be carried, on the same principle is a question in which all independent powers whose governments differ from theirs are interested, even those most remote, and surely none more so than the United States. Our policy in regard to Europe, which was adopted at an early stage of the wars which have so long agitated that quarter of the globe, nevertheless remains the same, which is, not to interfere in the internal concerns of any of its powers; to consider the government *de facto* as the legitimate government for us; to cultivate friendly relations with it, and to preserve those relations by a frank, firm and manly policy, meeting in all instances the just claims of every power, submitting to injuries from none. But in regard to those continents circumstances are eminently and conspicuously different. It is impossible that the allied powers should extend their political system to any portion of either continent without endangering our peace and happiness; nor can anyone believe that our southern brethren, if left to themselves, would adopt it of their own accord. It is equally impossible, therefore, that we should behold such interposition in any form with indifference. If we look to the comparative strength and resources of Spain and those new Governments, and their distance from each other, it must be obvious that she can never subdue them. It is still the true policy of the United States to leave the parties to themselves, in the hope that other powers will pursue the same course. . . .

PART 4
THE AGE OF
MANIFEST
DESTINY

INTRODUCTION

The 1840's was one of the most energetic decades in the history of American foreign policy. Buoyed by an extravagant sense of nationalism and a popular conviction that the republic was destined to be the vehicle for the spread of democracy throughout the hemisphere, the nation made its final surge to the Pacific. Within five years, Texas was annexed, a settlement to the long-standing dispute with England over Oregon was arranged, and an empire was wrested from Mexico.

The passionate rhetoric of this period may leave the impression that expansion was a new idea to Americans. In reality, however, it antedated the republic. Long before independence, colonial leaders had looked anxiously toward Canada and the day when the whole of North America would be part of the British Empire. During the revolution the United States had made a military assault on Quebec, and after the war Canada remained an object of incessant interest to American diplomatists. In 1803 Jefferson doubled the land area of the United States by purchasing Louisiana and sought persistently to acquire the Floridas, an ambition ultimately achieved during the Monroe administration when John Quincy Adams negotiated the Transcontinental Treaty of 1819 with Spain.

There was, however, something unique about the expansionism of the 1840's. Earlier American territorial growth, at least before the acquisition of the Floridas from Spain, had been motivated in large measure by a concern for national security. The early republic, sharing borders on the north and south with hostile monarchies and menaced on its frontiers by unfriendly Indians, sought to eliminate threats to its security through expansion. By the 1840's, if not before, the republic was too powerful to fear any longer its foreign neighbors. Spain had been eliminated altogether; the Indians had been subdued; and the English had long since given up any aggressive designs against the United States.

If security was not a significant factor in the unfolding drama of national expansion, ideology was. The extravagant rhetoric of the age relied heavily on the idea of Manifest Destiny to explain and justify American behavior. Indeed, some historians believe that in that national passion is the principal explanation for the drive of American foreign policy in the 1840's. According to this view an ebullient democracy, riding a wave of nationalism and committed to the belief that the territorial expansion of the United States was equivalent to expanding the area of freedom and democracy, rushed headlong to the Pacific. The vigorous young republic tumbled Englishmen, Indians, and Mexicans alike onto the scrapheap of history and emerged powerful and unscathed. All this came about, it has been suggested, because Americans were persuaded that their divinely inspired destiny was to spread liberty across the continent. During the decade there was more than enough rhetoric to make a case for the argument (selection 1).

However, the suggestion that a national passion for Manifest Destiny explains American foreign policy in the 1840's suffers from serious weaknesses. The first is an assumption built into the argument that the power of the ideology was sweeping and that there was no significant opposition to it. On the contrary, large areas of the body politic in all parts of the nation and in both major political parties were opposed to expansion. The key issue in the presidential election of 1844 was expansion. Certainly, had this been a broadly popular idea among Americans, that astute politician Henry Clay, the Whig candidate, would never have committed himself so early in the campaign to oppose the annexation of Texas. Moreover, though it is true that Clay lost a close contest to the expansionist Democrat James K. Polk, Polk's margin of victory in the electoral college was razor thin. Indeed, it is generally agreed that his victory came as a result of the fact that in New York popular votes were siphoned away from Clay by the Abolitionist Party candidate, James G. Birney, himself an opponent of expansion. Between Clay and Birney, the two anti-expansionist candidates actually marshaled a popular majority in the election of 1844. If Birney had not entered the race, it is at least likely that Clay would have won New York and an electoral majority.

Another weakness in the argument for Manifest Destiny as the prime motivating factor behind American foreign policy is the assumption that America's policy makers simply reflected popular opinion, that their decisions were made in consequence of the pressure of public sentiment. Unhappily, the translation of popular feeling into an effective foreign policy is never easily proven. There remains the distinct possibility that public support for expansion was used by diplomatists to defend policies decided upon for other reasons.

In selection 2, from Charles G. Sellers' definitive biography of Polk relating to events immediately preceding and following the declaration of war against Mexico in 1846, a great deal is revealed about the man and his diplomacy. Polk was evidently a ruthless and supremely confident politician, unwilling to allow any obstacles, foreign or domestic, to interfere with his carefully defined purposes. Polk did indeed have a continental vision. The annexation of Texas, the settlement of the Oregon dispute with Britain establishing a Canadian-American boundary to the Pacific along the forty-ninth degree of north latitude, the acquisition of California, and the land between California and the established United States boundary were all part of a well-conceived program. It does not follow from this, however, that Polk viewed himself as an instrument of God chosen to fulfill some ill-defined destiny for America. Expanding the area of freedom does not seem to have been a particular concern of his.

If a commitment to Manifest Destiny is not an acceptable explanation for Polk's expansionist policies, how are they to be explained? Why did he press England almost to the point of war before settling the Oregon question? Why was he so anxious to acquire California? Norman A. Graebner offers a commercial explanation for Polk's aggressive diplomacy, suggesting that the President's major purpose was to acquire deep-water ports on the Pacific that might be used to fulfill an age-old dream, the penetration of the markets of Asia and the Pacific (selection 3). In a strange way, Polk was realizing the Columbian dream of a "passage to the Indies."

1

PUBLIC DINNER TO COMMODORE STOCKTON
NILES NATIONAL REGISTER

The entertainment was of the most splendid character. The Musical Fund hall was thronged on the occasion. Among the guests were Senator Downs, of La., Hon. D. D. Thurston of Rhode Island, R. J. Thomas of Tennessee, Morris and Gibson, of La., Judges Burnside and Bell, V. S. Macauley, L. C. Levin, M. Hampton, L. B. Chase, &c., &c.

The Hon. John Swift presided, assisted by vice presidents, H. D. Gilpin, Josiah Randall, J. M. Read, H. L. Benner, Mayor Belstering and W. G. Alexander.

Sumptuous eating was succeeded by toasts as usual. The U.S. President—the vice president—the governor of Pennsylvania, were successively toasted without appendage. The fourth toast was,

"Our country—may she ever be right—but right or wrong, our country."

After drinking this toast, the chairman rose, and addressed the assembly in reference to the distinguished officer who was the guest of the occasion, his high commendation of whom was repeatedly interrupted by loud applause. He concluded by giving the following toast—

Com. R. F. Stockton—As distinguished for his civil acquirements as he is for his military reknown—equally at home, whether on land or sea, when called upon to meet the enemies of his country—the soldier and the sailor. A man who never turned his back on friend or foe .

The toast was received with indescribable enthusiasm. After the

From *Niles National Register*, Jan. 22, 1848, "Manifest Destiny Doctrines."

cheering subsided, Com. Stockton rose to respond. He was again loudly cheered.

We have not space for the whole of his remarks. His acknowledgments for the honor conferred were happily expressed. Omitting them, we proceed to his remarks respecting California.

"Attributing, as I will, your congratulations today, on the general result of things in California, without reference to the causes or agents by which it was produced, and applying to myself but a small portion of your approbation, I may be permitted to mingle, without stint, my congratulations with yours, that California is now under the protection of the United States. [Great cheering.] Her agricultural, her horticultural, her mineral resources are abundant. She has beautiful skies and verdant fields. Her population consists of a fine looking race of men and women; they are kind, hospitable and valiant.

"Annexation, nay acquisition, is not a necessary consequence of conquest—and, therefore, it is not on that account that I would offer my congratulations here today—oh, no!

"I care not for the beautiful fields and healthful skies of California. I care not for her leagues of land and her mines of silver. The glory of the achievements there—if any glory there be, is in the establishment of the first free press, in California—[Great applause]—in having built the first school house in California—in having established religious toleration as well as civil liberty in California. [Tremendous applause.] May the torch grow brighter and brighter, until from Cape Mendocino to Cape St. Lucas, it illumines the dark path of the victim of religious intolerance and political despotism. [Thunders of applause.]

"The inhabitants of California, number, I believe about 12 or 15,000. A large portion of them, if not all of them, prefer the institutions of the U.S.; and it is much to be hoped, may I not say, fervently, devoutly to be prayed for, that they shall in some way or other be secured in the permanent enjoyment of civil and religious liberty—[great applause]—and that our friends there may not pay the dreadful penalty the Mexican always demands—his life for his fidelity to us! [Great applause.] Well, however this may turn out, if it should be otherwise—if these pleasing anticipations should not be realized—other hands must tear down the school houses—other hands must put out the light of liberty! [Great cheers.] For me and mine, before God, we'll take no part in such a business! [Enthusiastic applause.]

"California has within herself the elements of wealth and power; and when art, and science, and religion—when all the genial influences of civilization, which in our day is advancing with such marvellous rapidity, are brought to bear upon her, may we not reasonably assert that the years will be but few, before we behold her standing erect in the attitude of a free and independent nation." [Great applause.]

Excusing himself on account of the investigation going on at Washington on the military operations in California, he left to faithful history to vindicate what related to his own conduct there, under embarrassing circumstances—far from home and from resources, and out of the reach of instructions. "In the midst of these embarrassments we thought as sailors, we had done very well." [Loud laughter.]

Having closed what he had to say in reference to California, the commodore proceeded to a consideration of, What Has Been Done, and What Is to Be Done with Mexico?

"No thoughtful observer of the progress of the U. States, can fail to be impressed with the conviction that we enjoy a degree of happiness and prosperity never heretofore vouchsafed to the nations of mankind. With an unexampled measure of political liberty; unbroken social order; extraordinary growth of the arts and sciences—philanthropic and benevolent institutions, the fair offspring of the Christian faith, extending their blessed agency, in all directions—unbounded religious toleration, heaven's best gift; for which our fathers risked and suffered most—with all these rich endowments, do we not indeed present an example of the beneficent care of Providence for which we can find no parallel in the history of man? And now when engaged in war, we find ourselves, followed by the same blessed influences. Wherever our soldiers have carried our arms, victory has awaited them. We see them rushing against walls, bristling with bayonets and artillery, and lined with legions of armed men; we see our youthful heroes precipitating themselves from parapet to parapet, and charging from bastion to bastion; we hear the crash of grape and canister; and amid the smoke and thunder of the battle, we behold the flag of our counrty, waiving—[The remainder of the sentence was lost in the tremendous cheering which here burst forth from the assemblage.] We behold the flag of civil and religious freedom waiving over what had been regarded as impregnable fortresses and the remains of armies fleeing to the mountains.

"Gentlemen, how has all this been accomplished? Whence those achievements? I speak to intellectual men. All in the hearing of my voice entertain, I doubt not, a just and abiding sense of their deep responsibility not only on this earth, but in time hereafter. I ask you, then, how has all this happened? Is it to be attributed exclusively to the wisdom of our cabinet and the powers of our armies? These are all well—admirably well. But our successes have overlapped the bounds of all human calculation and the most sanguine hope. Therefore we must look beyond all this for the secret of our successes and the source of our remarkable prosperity. It is because the spirit of our pilgrim fathers is with us. It its because the God of armies and the Lord of hosts is with us. [Tremendous applause.] And how is it with poor, unfortunate, wretched Mexico? Ever since the day of the last of the Montezumas, intestine broils have disturbed her peace. Her whole territory has been drenched with the blood of her own children. Within the last quarter of a century, revolution has succeeded revolution. Now in the encounter with us she has been beaten in every field. She has been driven from fortress to fortress—from town to town, until the scattered remnants of her broken armies are fleeing to the mountains and calling upon the rocks to hide them. [Applause.] Is it not, therefore, in this disposition of public affairs, proper to rise superior to the consideration of party influences, and in true philosophical spirit and patriotic fidelity, take an honest view of our condition, in the sight of God and beneath the scrutiny of the Christian and civilized world?

"What you may think of it, I know not; and you must permit me to add, I care not; but for myself I speak not to you as a party man. Remember, gentlemen, that I go for my country. I cannot be bound, I cannot be kept within the restraints of party discipline when my country calls me forth. [Tremendous cheering, which lasted several minutes.] I go for my country—my whole country and nothing but my country. I desire to address you now in the spirit of the father of a large family, desirous to transmit to his latest posterity the blessings of civil and religious liberty. I speak to you as a Christian man—as a son, perhaps an unworthy son of this great republic, but one whose heart burns with an ardent desire to transmit, not only to his own immediate descendants, the blessings of which I speak, but to extend them to our neighbors on this continent. [Great applause.]

"But do not mistake me. Do not misunderstand me. I am no propagandist in the common reception of the term. In my judgment, principles depend much upon relations and circumstances, and that which in the abstract may be well enough, often wastes itself in fanaticism. All things must bide their time.

"I have no respect for the man or set of men who will recklessly disturb the social order of any community and produce civil war for the purpose of hastening such a result, no matter how beneficial in the abstract it may seem to be. [Cheers.] And I am bound to say farther, that I have quite as little respect for the man or set of men, who have in the Providence of God been placed in stations, when the great questions of civil and religious liberty are to be determined, who will shrink from the responsibilities of that station. [Cheers.] In the application of these principles to the future policy of this country, let it not be supposed for a moment that I would presume to censure the great men of this nation. Nor would I attempt to instruct the most humble of my countrymen. I present these views merely for the purpose of rendering more distinct and clear the remarks which I have offered, and which I may not have stated with sufficient explicitness.

"I suppose the war with Mexico was caused by the repeated insults which time after time had been heaped upon this nation. [Great applause.] I regard this much talked of indemnity as merely collateral or incidental, arising out of the circumstances of the war. In my opinion, that question will be set aside, if not wholly lost sight of in the pressure of the great considerations which are to grow out of the high responsibilities and delicate duties crowding upon us, and the unexampled victories which have attended our arms. [Cheers.] In pursuing a legitimate object of war—in the providence of God we are placed, or are likely so to be placed, in a position where by a fair and legitimate construction of the law of nations, the fate of Mexico and the peace of this continent, to a greater or less extent, will devolve upon the virtue, the wisdom, and the humanity of our rulers. [Applause.] In these rulers I have the greatest confidence, and for them I entertain the most profound respect. [Applause.]

"I tell you again gentlemen, this matter of indemnity, in money or anything else, will be secondary, altogether secondary, in comparison with the considerations which I have no doubt will be presented to this nation in the farther prosecution of this war. The insults have been resented—nobly resented—they have been wiped out—they have been washed out with blood. [Enthusiastic applause.] If, then, indemnity, means money, any financier will tell you that if that is what you seek as the only object of the war, you had better withdraw your troops as soon as possible, and you will save money. [A laugh.]

"But indemnity is not the object of the war. No man here or elsewhere will consent to weigh blood against money. [Great applause.] I do not care who presents the proposition—when it is presented; or to whom it is presented, whig or democrat. No man will weigh blood for money. [Loud applause.] But this is not, I repeat, our condition. Higher and nobler objects present themselves, for the attainment of which you must increase your armies in Mexico, cost what it may. [Great applause.] Fifty thousand men must go to Mexico. [Renewed applause.] Let me then state the objects for the attainment of which, in my judgment, this augmentation of our force in Mexico, is required.

"Mexico is poor and wretched. Why? Misgovernment—insatiable avarice—unintermitted wrong unsparing cruelty and unbending insolence—these have inflicted their curse on the unhappy country, and made her what she is. But as the darkest hour is that which just precedes the advent of the morning sun, so let us hope that a better and happier day is now about to dawn upon unfortunate Mexico. Be it ours, now to forgive her all her trespasses, and returning good for evil, make her free and happy! [Enthusiastic applause which lasted several minutes.]

"If I were now the sovereign authority, as I was once the viceroy— [laughter]—I would prosecute this war for the express purpose of redeeming Mexico from misrule and civil strife. If, however, such a treaty were offered me as that offered to the government of the United States, before God, I would consider it my bounden duty to reject it. [Loud applause.] I would say to them, we can pay the indemnity ourselves. But we have a duty before God which we cannot—we must not evade. The priceless boon of civil and religious liberty has been confided to us as trustees—[cheers]—I would insist, if the war were to be prolonged for fifty years, and cost money enough to demand from us each year the half of all that we possess, I would still insist that the inestimable blessings of civil and religious liberty should be guaranteed to Mexico. We must not shrink from the solemn duty. We dare not shrink from it. We cannot lose sight of the great truth that nations are accountable as well as individuals, and that they too must meet the stern responsibilities of their moral character—they too must encounter the penalty of violated law in the more extended sphere adapted to their physical condition.

"Let the solemn question come home to the bosom and business of every citizen of this great republic: "What have I done—what has this generation done for the advancement of civil and religious liberty! [Applause.]

"It is in view of this responsibility—of our obligations to the infinite source of all our peace, prosperity and happiness—of our duty to fulfill the great mission of liberty committed to our hands, that I would insist, cost what it may, on the establishment of a permanent, independent republic in Mexico. [Cheers.] I would insist that the great principle of religious toleration should be secured to all—that the Protestant in Mexico should be guaranteed enjoyment of all the immunities and privileges enjoyed by Mexicans in the United States. [Loud cheers.] These great and benevolent objects I would accomplish by sending into Mexico a force adequate to maintain all the posts which we now occupy, to defend them against any assaults that might be made against them, and to keep open our communications. I would seize upon Paredes, Arista, and other military chieftans, and send them to St. Helena, if you please. [Laughter and applause.] I would declare an armistice; and the executive should be called upon to issue a proclamation, and send six or more commissioners to meet Mexico in a liberal and generous spirit.

"We have vanquished Mexico. She is prostrate at our feet—we can afford to be magnanimous. Let us act so that we need not fear the strictest scrutiny of the Christian and civilized world. I would with a magnanimous and kindly hand gather these wretched people within the fold of republicanism. [Loud applause.] This I would accomplish at any cost.—'Oh!' but it is said, 'this will bring us to direct taxation.' Well, let it come. We must not shrink from our responsibility. We have ample means. Throwing aside long financial reports which nobody understands [Laughter], let us in a manly, upright and philanthropic spirit meet every emergency which we may be called upon to counter in the discharge of duty. [Applause.]

"But I have already detained you too long. Let me conclude, and again returning my heartfelt thanks for your kindness, offer you the following sentiment:

"Philadelphia—Renowned for her encouragement of the fine arts; with one moiety of the public patronage bestowed elsewhere, she would stand as unrivalled in the mechanic arts, as the state of Pennsylvania now does to her agricultural and mineral resources."

This toast was received with great enthusiasm, and the distinguished guest resumed his seat amid long continued cheering.

2

HARD WAR AVERTED—
EASY WAR GAINED
CHARLES G. SELLERS

By a remarkable combination of nerve, judgment, and disingenuous manipulation of men, Polk had completed the first two phases of his continentalist program, Texas and Oregon, and begun the third. American sovereignty had been carried to the banks of the Rio Grande and the northern shores of the Pacific, while already American armies were on the march to round out the continental domain at the expense of Mexico. To accomplish this last objective Polk was prepared to expend much in both blood and money, but how much he did not yet faintly imagine.

. . . .

ONE

The idea of a war with Mexico had from the beginning encountered strong opposition in Congress and the country. But in hectic conferences on Sunday, May 10, the administration had worked out a strategy for compelling reluctant congressmen to endorse it almost unanimously. Consulting with Polk and Marcy, the House Committee on Military Affairs had drafted a war bill appropriating ten million dollars and authorizing the president to call out fifty thousand volunteers. This measure was submitted to the House along with the war message at noon the next day. The disciplined Democratic majority allowed

From Charles G. Sellers, *James K. Polk, Continentalist*, 1843–1846, Vol. 2 (copyright © 1968 by Princeton University Press), pp. 415–426. Omission of Footnotes. Reprinted by permission of Princeton University Press.

only two hours for debate, three fourths of it consumed by the reading of documents accompanying the message. Only in the last moments of the debate did the Democratic leadership propose a preamble to the bill declaring that "by the act of the Republic of Mexico, a state of war exists between that government and the United States." The preamble thus suddenly sprung on the House was to serve in lieu of a declaration of war. Members would be compelled either to endorse the administration's interpretation of events on the Rio Grande or to vote against money and troops for rescuing Taylor's imperilled army.

The Whigs and a handful of Calhounites struggled desperately against the war juggernaut. Since the first news of hostilities on Saturday night, Calhoun had been feverishly trying to organize a new peace coalition. Now the South Carolinians Holmes and Rhett tried in vain to separate the preamble from the bill. They would gladly vote military supplies, they said, but the question of war should be referred to the Committee on Foreign Relations for deliberate consideration. Just as vainly various Whigs proposed amendments that would authorize military measures while refusing to sanction the march to the Rio Grande or barring offensive operations west of the Nueces. But the administration spokesmen insisted that Taylor's perilous situation demanded immediate, unquestioning action; and by a vote of 123 to 67 they grafted the preamble onto the bill. Seventeen Whigs (from the South and Pennsylvania) felt compelled to go along with the administration's interpretation of the war, while fourteen Calhounish Democrats from the South opposed it.

As ruthless use of the previous question pressed the amended measure toward a vote, the boldest of the antiwar men bitterly watched most of the Whigs "desert us and go over to the support of the outrageous war waged by the Executive, upon an unoffending people who merely oppose the robbery which we [are] attempting to perpetrate on them." Just before the final vote, and by the parliamentary device of asking to be excused from voting, the Whig congressman from Henry Clay's district got the floor to "protest solemnly against defiling this measure with the unfounded statement that Mexico began this war." "The river Nueces is the true western boundary of Texas," said Garrett Davis. " . . . It is our own President who began this war." But even Davis finally felt compelled to vote for the bill, and it passed 174 to 14. Over twenty members refused to vote at all, and ex-President Adams headed the fourteen northern Whigs who dared to vote Nay.

Adams told a colleague that he hoped Taylor's officers would resign and his soldiers desert rather than fight such a war, and another of the fourteen observed with grim satisfaction that the Whigs who had felt compelled to vote for the bill were "as sick a set of fellows as you ever saw." "While we must all stand by our country," confided one of these to a friend, "it is grievous to know that when we pray 'God defend the right' our prayers are not for our own country."

While the Whigs in the House grieved over the hard choice that had been inexorably forced on them, their colleagues in the Senate saw in Calhoun's activities some hope of slowing if not stopping the war juggernaut. Calhoun had been arguing that Congress should confine itself to military measures for rescuing Taylor's army and maintaining the status quo along the border. "I distinguish between hostilities and war," he declared after the war message was read in the Senate on Monday afternoon. Only Congress could constitutionally declare war, he said, and peace might still be preserved if the Senate refused to be stampeded and gave "high, full, and dispassionate consideration" to the question of formally declaring war.

At first it seemed that Calhoun's view was supported not only by the Whigs but by Benton as well, and would prevail in the Senate. When Polk had called in Benton Monday morning for an advance view of the war message, the Missouri senator had criticized the march to the Rio Grande and expressed his opposition to an "aggressive war on Mexico." He had told the president that he was willing to vote men and money for the defense of United States territory, but he clearly did not think that United States territory extended beyond the Nueces. It was on Benton's motion that afternoon that the Senate refused to act immediately and disposed of the war message in accordance with Calhoun's views. That part dealing with military preparations was referred to Benton's Military Affairs Committee and that part dealing with the question of war to the Foreign Relations Committee, still headed by Allen. Then the Senate turned routinely to other matters. These maneuvers in the Senate on Monday afternoon convinced the president that Calhoun, Benton, and the Whigs were joining forces to defeat his war policy. The only thing that could save it, he concluded, "is the fear of the people by the few Democratic Senators who wish it defeated."

That night the administration threw all its energies into arousing Benton's "fear of the people." Polk, Buchanan, and Marcy remonstrated with him, and his friends of the Van Buren group were enlisted to warn him of the political consequences of siding with Calhoun, the Whigs, and Mexico. When these entreaties failed to move the stubborn Missourian, Senator Dix "in distress" summoned Frank Blair from his suburban home. Blair hastened to town early Tuesday morning, played adroitly on Benton's suspicions of Calhoun, and concluded by telling his old friend bluntly "that he was bound to stick to the War party or he was a ruined man." Finally Benton said, "I see *you are right.*" Hastily he assembled the Military Affairs Committee, while Allen was convening the Foreign Relations Committee; and at a Senate Democratic caucus later that morning Benton and Allen announced that their committees would support the House war bill and press it to a vote before adjournment that day.

Thus when the Senate convened at noon, an impatient and implacable Democratic majority confronted the startled peace men, who had not expected the committees to report for several days. Desperately the peace men sought some means of voting for military measures without voting for the odious declaration that war existed by the act of Mexico. "It was just as impossible for him to vote for that preamble as it was for him to plunge a dagger into his own heart, and more so . . . ," said Calhoun. "As to . . . all that was called popularity, he did not care the snap of his finger. . . . He could not agree to make war on Mexico by making war on the Constitution. . . . It was monstrous." But the peace amendments were voted down by an unvarying count of 20 to 26, Calhoun and McDuffie siding with the Whig minority. The Whigs, as Dallas described the scene, "after struggling hard for hours, almost got upon their knees to beg to be spared from voting on the preamble; but the democrats were resolved that they should speak out." On the final vote only John Davis of Massachusetts and Thomas Clayton of Delaware dared to vote Nay; two more Whigs answered "Aye, except the preamble"; and two Whigs and Calhoun refused to vote. All of Calhoun's southern allies, even McDuffie, deserted him to vote Aye; and the measure passed at 6:30 p.m. by a vote of 40 to 2. The House was reconvened an hour later to concur in several technical amendments inserted by the Senate, and the president had his war bill.

The passage of the war bill was a striking demonstration of a determined president's ability to compel a reluctant Congress to support a jingoistic foreign policy. Even many of the Democrats resented bitterly the action the president had forced upon them. "I am too sick of the miserable concern here to write or say anything about it . . . ," confessed Senator Dix. "I should not be surprised if the next accounts should show that there is no Mexican invasion of our soil." Dix's coadjutor in persuading Benton to support the war bill, Frank Blair, concluded after reading the documents concerning the Slidell mission that Polk "has got to lying in public as well as private." Blair was convinced that speculators in the American private claims against Mexico had provided much of the pressure for war, and that Secretary Walker was "knee deep in those claims." Senators Benton, Allen, and Dix shared Blair's views; but nevertheless, said Dix, "we are all determined . . . to support the President in his measures."

These men were compelled to support the president because they knew he had calculated accurately the public's reaction to the situation he had produced on the Rio Grande. "Nobody talks of Oregon now," reported a Georgian on the day the Senate passed the war bill. "It is Mexico and War. I never saw the people more excited. A volunteer company could be raised in every county in Georgia. Our government has permitted itself to be insulted long enough. The blood of her citizens has been spilt on her own soil. It appeals to us for vengeance." In Ohio's Whiggish, antislavery Western Reserve, geographically and ideologically at the other extremity of the country, one of Giddings' supporters ruefully reported that "we are sadly inclined to Huzza for the Mexican war." And farther west a shrewd but still obscure Whig candidate for Congress, Abraham Lincoln, exhorted the country's "citizen soldiery, to sustain her national character" by volunteering for the war. The war found defenders even in the ranks of organized idealism. When an antiwar resolution was proposed to the American Union of Associationists, one of its officers, Parke Godwin, protested hotly: "The questions of war and slavery are only incidental ones, which can easily be put aside, but the question of extending *constitutional republican institutions* over this whole continent is one of the broadest, noblest and most important that was ever presented to any nation."

Calhoun's friends agreed that his opposition to the war bill had been "perfectly suicidal," and one of them apologized to the administration for having helped persuade him to return to the Senate. His most devoted political supporter and manager Franklin Elmore told Polk that he "found Mr. Calhoun more irritable than he [Elmore] had ever known him," and promised to try to persuade him to support the administration. A Democratic congressman from Virginia who had followed Calhoun's lead in refusing to vote on the war bill promptly received warnings of "opposition to you among the democrats of your district." Such portents of political retribution were not lost on other politicians.

The country's mood of patriotic jingoism set in sharp relief the political courage of the handful of Whigs who not only voted against the war bill, but sought the first opportunity of expressing publicly their sense of moral outrage at "this illegal, unrighteous, and damnable war." "We had seen an American President, without provocation, and without right, planting the standard of the United States on a foreign soil, and using the military forces of the United States to violate every principle of international law and of moral justice," said Giddings of Ohio. "The war has not been commenced by Mexico, but by the President of the United States, without the authority of Congress," said Severance of Maine. Polk had sent Taylor into the Mexican department of Tamaulipas, "and it is there on Mexican soil that blood has been shed." If the Mexicans "have made a manly resistance to General Taylor," he concluded, "they are to be honored and applauded for doing so." Culver of New York charged that "The war had been planned and declared" against Mexico, because "We wanted to get her territory." Calling Polk "a President who has sprung up in a night," Culver asked: "Where was his right to enter into a country which did not belong to us, and point his cannon at a Mexican town to which we could have no pretensions?" And yet this "mushroom President" had dared to send "a bill into this House, commencing with a falsehood, and couched under a shameful whereas." Polk should no longer be called Young Hickory. "He did not dare to recommend to Congress to declare war, but came to the House with a 'whereas' and a 'whereas.' "

TWO

Having got his war, Polk lost no time in making clear to his associates just what he expected to gain by it. At a special Cabinet meeting on the day the war bill was signed, Buchanan, with an obtuseness extraordinary even for him, proposed informing other governments that "in going to war we did not do so with a view to acquire either California or New Mexico or any other portion of the Mexican territory." With the Oregon settlement still trembling in the balance, Buchanan seems to have feared that Great Britain, and probably France also, would declare war to prevent the United States from acquiring California. Polk instantly retorted that he would "stand and fight until the last man among us fell in the conflict" before he would pledge that "we would not if we could fairly and honorably acquire California or any other part of the Mexican Territory which we desired." The rest of the Cabinet backed the president, Walker vehemently so; and after a discussion of more than two hours, "one of the most earnest and interesting which has ever occurred in my Cabinet," Polk peremptorily directed Buchanan to eliminate the proposed pledge from the circular he had drafted to United States ministers abroad. Instead the world was told that "We go to war with Mexico solely for the purpose of conquering an honorable and permanent peace."

Polk's preoccupation with the territorial objectives of the war was most evident in the administration's early strategic planning. As soon as passage of the war bill was assured, on Tuesday, May 12, the president's first thought was of faraway California and the United States naval squadron on its coast. To reassure himself he had Bancroft bring and read to the Cabinet the repeated orders to Commodores Sloat and Stockton, dating back to the administration's third month in office, to seize the California ports in the event of war with Mexico. The next day, after signing the war bill, Polk conferred with Secretary Marcy and Commanding General Winfield Scott. As a result of these deliberations a special messenger was dispatched that night to Missouri with orders for Colonel Stephen Kearny's regiment of regular dragoons to start for New Mexico. The same messenger carried a requisition on the governor of Missouri for a thousand volunteers to follow Kearny as quickly as they could be organized. In a further conference with Marcy and Scott on Thursday evening, Polk laid down the principle that "the first movement should be to march a competent force into the Northern Provinces and seize and hold them until peace was made."

In these early deliberations on strategy Polk showed scant interest in the main army on the lower Rio Grande, though he did decide that General Scott should be sent to supersede Taylor as its commander. When the Cabinet met on Saturday of the first week of the war, the president outlined to them "the plan of the campaign against Mexico

. . . & particularly against the Northern Provinces. . . . My plan was to march an army of 2000 men on Santa Fé & near 4000 men on Chihuahua and at once conquer the Northern Provinces, leaving Gen'l Scott to occupy the country on the lower Del Norte and in the interior." During the following weeks General John E. Wool was selected to command the Chihuahua expedition and ordered to assemble his invading force at San Antonio, Texas.

But Polk's major preoccupation continued to be the almost undefended California, which he feared the naval forces might not be able to control without assistance. "If the war should be protracted for any considerable time, it would in my judgment be very important that the U.S. should hold military possession of California at the time peace was made," he told his Cabinet on Saturday, May 30. ". . . I declared my purpose to be to acquire for the U.S. California, New Mexico, and perhaps some others of the Northern Provinces of Mexico, whenever a peace was made. In Mr. Slidell's Secret instructions last autumn those objects were included. Now that we were at War the prospect of acquiring them was much better, and to secure that object military possession should with as little delay as possible be taken of all these Provinces." The president had devoted most of that week to planning a special military expedition to the Pacific, but it was doubtful whether a force could be organized to march from the Missouri frontier in time to cross the Sierra Nevada before the winter snows set in. The plan finally adopted was to have Colonel Kearny proceed on to California after occupying lightly defended New Mexico.

Bancroft calculated that Sloat could have heard the war news by May 17, and by the middle of June he was hoping that "California is now in our possession, never to be given up." To his Boston friend, the California trader Samuel Hooper, he wrote, "We were driven reluctantly to war; we must make a solid peace, that shall open the far west to religious freedom, political rights, schools, commerce and industry." Hooper replied with a plea for seizing the California coast south to the thirty-second parallel, so as to take in the entire populated area and all the good harbors down to San Diego. Below 32°, he explained, hundred of miles of desert separated California from the settled parts of Mexico.

Up to this time the administration had been preoccupied primarily with obtaining San Francisco and had been thinking of a 35° boundary. But Hooper's letter had an immediate effect. "If Mexico makes peace this month the Rio [Grande] del Norte and the parallel of 35 may do as a boundary," wrote Bancroft on June 22; "after that 32 which will include San Diego." Hooper expounded further on the benefits of a 32° boundary, and on July 12 orders went out to Commodore Sloat to seize San Diego as soon as San Francisco and Monterey were securely in hand. "The object of the United States has reference to ultimate peace with Mexico," Sloat was told; "and if, at that peace, the basis of *uti possidetis* shall be established, the government expects, through your forces, to be found in actual possession of Upper California."

Meanwhile, on June 30, the Cabinet had taken up the question of the administration's exact territorial objectives. By now Buchanan was willing to fight for a Rio Grande boundary up to El Paso and thence west along the thirty-second parallel to the Pacific, so as to include New Mexico and Upper California; but he strongly opposed annexing any Mexican territory south of 32°. Doubtless with an eye to his presidential prospects, he argued that the North would be unwilling to "acquire so large a Country that would probably become a slave-holding country if attached to the U.S." Again Walker took fire, arguing for a boundary due west from the mouth of the Rio Grande along the twenty-sixth parallel to the Pacific. This time, and in a similar discussion a week later, Polk declared that he preferred Walker's 26° boundary if it could be obtained by paying a few more millions for it; but if not, he was willing to take 32°. "In any event," he said, "we must obtain Upper California and New Mexico in any Treaty of Peace we would make." Privately he was shocked to find Buchanan "entertaining opinions so contracted and sectional."

Meanwhile, leaving nothing to chance, Polk was supervising personally every detail of the further arrangements for the possession of California. An additional thousand volunteers from Missouri were ordered after Kearny. A regular artillery battery and a large store of munitions and supplies were dispatched from New York around Cape Horn. The president himself drafted the part of Kearny's orders that emphasized the importance of conciliating the Californians; and the naval commanders were similarly instructed to hold California, "if possible, with the consent of the inhabitants." So intent was the administration on this golden prize that in June still another regiment of volunteers was ordered to proceed from New York to California by sea.

The New York regiment had one curious feature: volunteers for it had to agree to accept discharge in California. The government's anxiety to recruit a large body of permanent settlers arose from fears of a massive migration of Mormons to California. Driven from one home after another in the settled parts of the United States by vigilante harassment, these unpopular people had now been forced to abandon their thriving center at Nauvoo, Illinois, and strike out across the Great Plains in search of a haven beyond the reach of American persecution. Their destination was said to be California; and while the main body of many thousands started on the overland trek, a smaller party of over two hundred had embarked at New York in February for San Francisco.

The Mormons had helped carry Illinois for Polk in the presidential election, and he had refused the demands of Illinois politicians that he block their plan to settle on the Pacific coast. "The right of emigration or expatriation was one which any citizen possessed," he had told an Illinois senator. ". . . I would not interfere with them on the ground of their religious faith, however absurd it might be considered to be; . . . if I could interfere with the Mormons, I could with the Baptists, or any other religious sect; . . . by the constitution any citizen had a right to adopt his own religious faith." Nevertheless Brigham Young's mighty host would overwhelm the small United States–born population in California, and might well cooperate with the British or the Mexican residents to prevent the flag of their persecutors from following them across the continent. Polk was anxious to "conciliate them, attach them to our country, & prevent them from taking part against us," while at the same time building up the non-Mormon population of California. Therefore in addition to recruiting the New York regiment of potential settlers, he authorized Colonel Kearny to accept up to five hundred Mormon volunteers for his California expedition. The impoverished exiles, anxious for the government's favor and military pay, hastened to supply them.

The public got its first unequivocal indication of the administration's designs on California from the requirement that the New York volunteers accept discharge there, and considerable criticism followed. This was the occasion for one of the most incredible statements Polk ever made. Just at this time he made another overture to New York's disgruntled Van Burenites by inviting Senator Dix to replace the exhausted McLane as minister to England. "The President desired me to say to you, if I should write," reported the straightforward and trusting senator to Governor Wright, "that he had no schemes of conquest in view in respect to Mexico, no intention to take possession of any portion of her territory, with a view to hold it, and that his only object was to push military operations so vigorously that she should be made willing to adjust the matters in dispute between her and us on fair terms. As to the regiment designed for California, the intention was to have it discharged there, and it was, therefore, deemed wise to have it composed of persons who would be willing to remain and become citizens of our own territory on the Pacific, *i.e.*, Oregon."

3

EMPIRE ON THE PACIFIC
NORMAN A. GRAEBNER

ONE

Manifest destiny persists as a popular term in American historical literature to explain the expansion of the United States to continent-wide dimensions in the 1840's. Like most broad generalizations, it does not bear close scrutiny. Undoubtedly, the vigor of the American people in that decade, their restless and sometimes uncontrollable energy, their idealism and faith in their democratic institutions convinced them of a peculiar American mission. Perhaps for many expansionists the American purpose remained that of spreading democracy over the land from ocean to ocean.

Public sentiment in 1844 seemed to favor the extension of the United States into Oregon. But lands along the Pacific were not for the taking, and public opinion is never simply defined or casually conveyed into specific proposals by a national administration. This was especially true in the forties when political leaders at no time were in agreement on precise objectives on the Pacific. There was, in fact, sufficient disagreement over expansionist purpose that the territorial gains of the Polk administration were achieved amid vigorous political opposition. Nor did these acquisitions prevent the American people from voting from power the party that gave them their immense foothold on the distant sea. Diverse are the elements which shape the course of history.

From Norman A. Graebner, *Empire on the Pacific—A Study in American Continental Expansion*. Copyright 1955, pp. 217–228. The Ronald Press Company, New York.

The concept of manifest destiny, as a democratic expression, represented an expanding, not a confining or limiting, force. As an ideal, it was not easily defined in terms of precise territorial limits. In 1844, when the claims of the ideal had fully taken hold, American expansionism looked far beyond Texas and Oregon. Indeed, it had no visible limit. The New York *Herald* prophesied that the American Republic would in due course embrace all the land from the Isthmus of Panama to the polar regions and from the Atlantic to the Pacific. One Texas correspondent wrote that "the fact must be no longer disguised, that we, the people of the United States must hold, and govern, under free and harmonious institutions, the continent we inhabit."

Some suggested that American laws be extended to include the downtrodden peons of South America. "And who does not wish to have them finally reach Cape Horn if their democratic character can be preserved?" demanded one expansionist. "Certainly no friend of the largest liberty of oppressed humanity." In their enthusiasm to extend the "area of freedom," many even looked beyond the continental limits to Cuba, the Sandwich Islands, the far-flung regions of the Pacific, and even to the Old World itself. This was a magnificent vision for a democratic purpose, but it hardly explains the sweep of the United States across the continent.

For American expansion to the Pacific was always a precise and calculated movement. It was ever limited in its objectives. American diplomatic and military policy that secured the acquisition of both Oregon and California was in the possession of men who never defined their expansionist purposes in terms of a democratic ideal. The vistas of all from Jackson to Polk were maritime and they were always anchored to specific waterways along the Pacific Coast. Land was necessary to them merely as a right of way to ocean ports—a barrier to be spanned by improved avenues of commerce. Any interpretation of westward extension beyond Texas is meaningless unless defined in terms of commerce and harbors.

TWO

Travelers during the decade before 1845 had created a precise vision of the western coasts of North America. It was a vision born of the sea. With the exception of Fremont, every noted voyager who recorded his impressions of Oregon and California had approached these regions via the Pacific. Some traders had sailed these coasts directly from Boston; others had first traversed the broad Pacific world as captains of merchant vessels or as explorers. But whatever their mission on the great ocean, they were without exception struck by the excellent quality of the Strait of Juan de Fuca, San Francisco Bay, and the harbor of San Diego, as well as the possible role of these ports in the development of Pacific commerce.

Charles Wilkes, as the commander of the United States exploring expedition to the Pacific, studied minutely not only the islands and sea lanes of the entire area, but also the important harbors and bays along the North American coast from Fuca Strait to San Francisco. Wilkes was not certain that these coastal regions, separated as they were in the early forties by almost two thousand miles of wilderness from the settled portions of the Midwest, would become other than a prosperous and independent maritime republic. Eminently qualified, however, to speculate on these Western harbors as stations in a Pacific commerce, he predicted a sizable stream of traffic emanating from them:

> This future state is admirably situated to become a powerful maritime nation, with two of the finest ports in the world,—that within the straits of Juan de Fuca, and San Francisco. These two regions have, in fact, within themselves every thing to make them increase, and keep up an intercourse with the whole of Polynesia, as well as the countries of South America on the one side, and China, the Philippines, New Holland, and New Zealand, on the other. Among the latter, before many years, may be included Japan. Such various climates will furnish the materials for a beneficial exchange of products, and an intercourse that must, in time, become immense; while this western coast, enjoying a climate in many respects superior to any other in the Pacific, possessed as it must be by the Anglo-Norman race, and having none to enter into rivalry with it but the indolent inhabitants of warm climates, is evidently destined to fill a large space in the world's future history.

American officials and expansionists refused to accept his prediction of a separate commercial nation across the mountains. The threat of European encroachment convinced them that the grandeur of the

Pacific Coast must accrue to the wealth, prosperity, and commercial eminence of the United States. By 1845 the American press accepted the dreams of Webster and Calhoun who had anticipated an American Boston or New York situated on some distant harbor. For those who perpetuated the expansionist program after Polk's inaugural, ports of call in Oregon and California were as vital as had been land empires in Texas during the preceding year. Except for what remained of the whole-of-Oregon fever, American expansionism had lost its broad nationalism and had become anchored to the mercantile interests of the United States.

After California entered the American consciousness, the expansionist purpose increasingly embraced both Oregon and California as two halves of a single ambition. Thereafter the complete vision of empire on the Pacific included the harbors from Puget Sound to San Diego. It called for a peaceful settlement of the Oregon controversy at 49° and the acquisition of Upper California. Writing to President Polk in July, 1845, Charles Fletcher pictured an American Union stretching from the Atlantic to the Pacific and from the thirtieth to the forty-ninth degree of north latitude. The St. Louis *Missourian* demanded both the Strait of Fuca and San Francisco harbor to fulfill the maritime destiny of the United States. Quite typically William Field, a Texan, advised the President to accept the parallel of 49° and then purchase California for as much as fifty million if necessary. He wrote, "I will only remark that if you can settle the Oregon difficulty without war and obtain California of Mexico, to the Gulf of California and the river Gila for a boundary, you will have achieved enough to enroll your name *highest* among those of the benefactors of the American people."

By 1846 this unitary but limited view of the Pacific Coast had penetrated the halls of Congress, where Meredith P. Gentry, of Tennessee, observed: "Oregon up to the 49th parallel of latitude, and the province of Upper California, when it can be fairly acquired, is the utmost limit to which this nation ought to go in the acquisition of territory."

With the Oregon treaty of 1846 the United States had reached the Pacific. Its frontage along the sea from 42° to Fuca Strait and Puget Sound fulfilled half the expansionist dream. On those shores the onward progress of the American pioneer would stop, but commercial expansionists looked beyond to the impetus that the possession of Oregon would give to American trade in the Pacific. "Commercially," predicted Benton, "the advantages of Oregon will be great—far greater than any equal portion of the Atlantic States." This Missourian believed that Oriental markets and export items would better complement the mercantile requirements of the United States than would those of Europe.

Through Fuca Strait, moreover, lay the new passage to the East which would bring to America the wealth and splendor which had always gone to those who commanded the trade of the Orient. The editor of the Baltimore *American* declared that

> The commerce of the world is to be ours, and both oceans are to be subject to us. The splendors of Eastern cities which grew into greatness by the trade between the Valley of the Nile and the Valley of the Ganges, will shine but dimly, even in the enhanced illumination of fancy and tradition, when compared with the stately magnificence and colossal structure of the cities which are to concentrate the rich elements of the Valley of the Mississippi. The ruins of Thebes and Memphis, of Palmyra and Balbec remain still to attest a wonderful degree of former greatness; but they grew up by means of a caravan trade on camels, or by a commerce of galleys on the Red Sea and the Persian Gulf. From such a traffic let the eye turn to the rivers, canals, and railroads of this continent of our, to the mighty agency of steam, propelling innumerable vessels and cars, and the immense expanse of alluvial soil, fertile in products under the culture of a people who for enterprise, energy and invention have no superiors—we may say no equals.

For decades after 1846 British travelers in the Far Northwest recognized the magnitude of this American diplomatic achievement. With a Columbia River boundary, complained one British observer in 1872, Canadian shipping in the north Pacific might have competed with that of the United States. Upon viewing the waters of Puget Sound, another English traveler acknowledged dejectedly the significance of the American triumph in Oregon: "It is not easy to conceive what reasons for claiming the country north of the Columbia could be urged by the United States Government. But they knew the prospective value of the magnificent inland waters of Puget Sound, and acted upon that knowledge. With the possession of that grand inlet British Columbia could easily compete with California and Oregon; without it, it becomes a difficult matter to do so." British observers in western Canada agreed that the American negotiators knew the value of the waterways they sought, whereas the British did not.

Following the outbreak of the Mexican War in May, 1846, metropolitan editorialists soon regarded that conflict as the agency whereby the United States might consummate her westward movement and annex the harbors of California. To them the Oregon settlement had been made particularly acceptable by the anticipation of adding certain Mexican ports to the American Union. In May the New York *Herald* urged the Polk administration to seize San Francisco Bay so that men would forget the whole of Oregon. One California correspondent predicted the result of the speedy occupation of the Pacific ports by the American naval squadron: "We shall have then a country, bounded at the North latitude by 49 degrees, to the Pacific—and the South on the same ocean by 32 degrees—and the western and eastern boundaries, being what Nature intended them, the Pacific, with China in the outline, and the Atlantic with Europe in the background."

Such prospects pleased the editor of the New York *Herald*. He noted that the proposed boundaries gave the United States 1,300 miles of coast on the Pacific, several magnificent harbors, and "squared off our South-Western possessions." One writer for the New York *Journal of Commerce* in December, 1846, rejoiced that with the acquisition of New Mexico and California the territory of the United States would "spread out in one broad square belt from one ocean to the other, giving us nearly as much coast on the Pacific as we possess on the Atlantic." The imaginary line of 42° meant little to these commercial expansionists of a century ago.

This vision was not lost on the Midwest. The Mississippi Valley responded eagerly to the call to arms, stimulated perhaps by the prospect of conquering Mexican soil. Such enthusiasm was not misplaced, for future trade routes through the great valley lay in the direction of California as well as Oregon. During the Oregon debates Andrew Kennedy and John McClernand had revealed the significance of the Strait of Fuca to the grain regions of the Midwest. Now this agrarian concept of commercial empire in the Pacific encompassed also the harbors of California. It was the editor of the Baltimore *American* who analyzed cogently in September, 1847, the possible mercantile relationships between this Mexican province and the broad prairies of the Mississippi Valley:

The Mississippi River . . . stretches out its arms east and west to lay hold of both oceans. That vast alluvial region, the garden of the civilized world . . . is to be, and that before many generations shall have passed, the centre of the world's commerce and its most prolific source. It must have access to the sea coast on both shores, and along the whole extent, communicating freely with the Atlantic sea board, which we already possess, entire, and with the Pacific which we must possess, entire. . . . Besides, it is clear that California must have its connections with the Mississippi Valley. . . . Without these connections California would be insulated. Confined to her own resources . . . her fine harbors without the materials of commerce would not avail her much. But once drawn into the embrace of the great valley and suffused with the rich currents of its ample products, California, from her position alone, becomes important, and her commercial greatness stands revealed.

American expansion over contiguous territory was complete with the Treaty of Guadalupe Hidalgo. Thereafter United States frontage on the Pacific remained unchanged. In 1848, it is true, some did not believe that American continental expansion had run its course. Tom Corwin anticipated demands for even greater annexations in the future. He wrote to William Greene in March, 1848, that the treaty gave to the United States a third of Mexico immediately "with the implied understanding that the balance is to be swallowed when our anglo-saxon gastric juices shall clamor for another Cannibal breakfast." The New York *Herald* recognized the same feeling but with considerably more pleasure: "We will take a large portion now, and the balance at a more convenient season." Both were wrong, for American expansion was a deliberate movement, and the United States had achieved what two decades of observers had thought essential for this nation's future development.

THREE

Polk alone could fulfill the expansionist goals of the forties. Although he was an advocate of agrarian democracy, his expansionist outlook as President was as narrowly mercantile as that of Webster or Winthrop. He accepted the wisdom of compromise in Oregon for the precise reasons that the Whigs and the metropolitan press called for a settlement along the forty-ninth parallel. His wartime expansionist policy was aimed primarily at San Francisco and San Diego, and as the war neared completion Polk acknowledged no other objectives to Congress. In his message of December, 1847, he declared that the bay of San Francisco and other harbors on the California coast "would afford shelter for our navy, for our numerous whale ships, and other merchant vessels employed in the Pacific ocean, [and] would in a short period become the marts of an extensive and profitable commerce with China, and other countries of the East."

With the ratification of the Treaty of Guadalupe Hidalgo, the weary President could at last contemplate the success of his arduous foreign policy. In July he delivered to Congress a personal appraisal of his success in expanding the boundaries of the United States. Again his eyes were focused solely on the ports of San Diego, Monterey, and San Francisco. These, he declared, "will enable the United States to command the already valuable and rapidly increasing commerce of the Pacific." Under the American flag they would "afford security and repose to our commercial marine; and American mechanics will soon furnish ready means of ship-building and repair, which are now so much wanted in that distant sea." The President prophesied the growth of great commercial cities on these capacious harbors which would secure "the rich commerce of the East, and shall thus obtain for our products new and increased markets, and greatly enlarge our coasting and foreign trade, as well as augment our tonnage and revenue."

Democratic spokesmen in 1848 likewise measured the diplomatic settlements of the Polk administration in terms of harbors and trade. Lucien Chase of Tennessee limited the important acquisitions of the United States to Puget Sound, Monterey, San Diego, and San Francisco. His particularism focused his attention even more narrowly. "In the Bay of San Francisco," he wrote, "will converge the commerce of Asia and the model Republic. It possesses advantages over every other harbor upon the western coast of North or South America. . . . The vast and increasing commerce of Asia, and the islands of the East, is now open to our adventurous seamen. . . ."

Similarly a Democratic electioneering pamphlet singled out the California ports as the key acquisition of recent United States expansionist policy which had placed the American nation firmly on the distant coast. "From our cities on the Pacific," it predicted, "a speedy communication will be opened with China, and a profitable trade enjoyed, which must soon pour the wealth of that nation into our laps." For Whigs who had flayed Polk's Mexican policy, San Francisco Bay possibly made somewhat more palatable the huge swallow of territory acquired by the war.

During the succeeding years observers at San Francisco continued to appraise the acquisition of California in commercial terms. The French consul at this port viewed the region as the controlling element in the development of Pacific trade. He concluded in 1852 that "all the archipelagoes of the Pacific Ocean, the entire American continent from Sitka to the Straits of Magellan, China, Japan, are destined to submit to the influence of this state [and] to be attracted into the sphere of its commercial activity." One Californian in the fifties revealed the importance of that region's waterways to the total commercial growth of the United States in the following words:

> The commerce of the Pacific is in the hands of New York, Boston, New Bedford, Bangor, Cape Cod, and all-along-shore to New Orleans, and whatever benefits commerce derives hereby, is felt throughout the whole country. Neither are other portions of the sunny south, or the rich valleys of the west unrepresented there. Though the ships may be of Eastern construction, and commanded by the indomitable and enterprising Yankee skipper, yet he and his hardy crew are but the carriers for the products of the East and South.

FOUR

Historians have tended to exaggerate the natural urge of the American people to expand in the forties. For that reason they have attributed an unrealistic importance to the impact of pioneers, public sentiment, and war on American continental expansion. None of these had any direct bearing on the determination of United States boundaries along the Pacific. American frontiersmen never repeated the role they played in the annexation of Texas. In time they might have secured possession of California, but in 1845 hardly a thousand had reached that province. More numerous in Oregon, American pioneers were still limited to regions south of the Columbia. If they prompted the British to retreat from that line, they hardly explain why the United States insisted on that British retreat.

What mattered far more in the definition of American purpose were the travelers who toured the Pacific coasts and recorded the location and significance of waterways. These men, not pioneers, formulated the objectives of American officials from Adams to Polk. For two decades the official analysis of United States needs on the Pacific changed imperceptibly. Pioneers undoubtedly strengthened the American urge to expand westward, but they had little effect on the extent to which the nation would expand.

Public opinion as reflected in the spirit of manifest destiny played no greater role in the determination of United States ocean frontage than did the pressure of pioneers. Politicians had aroused sufficient interests in Oregon by 1844 to turn it into a popular issue. But to the extent that the Oregon settlement was a mandate, the American people voted for 54° 40', a boundary which they never acquired.

California was never a campaign issue at all. Its annexation was never the result of popular demand. After the metropolitan press turned its attention to that region in 1845, the Mexican province undoubtedly became a coveted objective for thousands of Americans. Yet for the mass of citizens it remained a remote, unknown region. California persisted probably as an area of vital concern for those relatively few merchants, politicians, travelers, and officials who appreciated its commercial significance. Whig success in attacking Democratic expansionist policy during 1848 reveals an extensive lack of interest in Polk's diplomatic achievement. The Washington *National Intelligencer* interpreted the Whig victory as proof that the American people had rejected the seductive visions of manifest destiny.

American triumphs in Mexico were essential to the success of the expansionist program, but they had no bearing on administration goals. These had been defined by Polk and his cabinet before the war was hardly under way. Manifest destiny revealed itself in the Mexican War only when it clamored for the whole of Mexico, but even that final burst of agrarian nationalism was effectively killed by the Treaty of Guadalupe Hidalgo. Polk's objectives, clear and precise, were ever limited to two ocean ports. Victories along the road to Mexico City were important only in that they eventually brought to the President the opportunity to secure what he had once hoped to achieve by diplomacy alone.

Nor can Nicholas P. Trist be overlooked in the fulfillment of United States territorial growth, for in the final analysis it was he, lonely and unobserved, who secured the southern boundary of California. If the nation achieved all this through the dictates of manifest destiny, that destiny revealed itself through some exceedingly devious patterns.

Particularism had its way in both the Oregon and Mexican treaties. Administration goals, therefore, had to be achieved through private diplomacy, England assuming the leadership in the former negotiations. This was essential, for only thus could the President defy that public opinion and avoid those pressures of American politics that sought to prevent both the peaceful settlement of the Oregon question and the acquisition of California.

Indeed, manifest destiny is an inadequate description of American expansionism in the forties. The mere urge to expand or even the acceptance of a destiny to occupy new areas on the continent does not create specific geographical objectives. Nor do these factors take into account the role of chance or the careful formulation and execution of policy. It was not by accident that the United States spread as a broad belt across the continent in the forties. It was rather through clearly conceived policies relentlessly pursued that the United States achieved its empire on the Pacific.

PART 5
THE AMERICAN
CIVIL WAR AND
BRITISH NEUTRALITY

INTRODUCTION

The American Civil War, which began in April 1861, cast the United States in a new and unusual role in international affairs. From the beginning the republic had based its foreign policy on the assumption that it would remain at peace, a neutral in the conflicts that continually plagued Europe. Indeed, during the wars of the French Revolution and Empire, the United States had been the staunch defender of the rights of neutrals against belligerent incursions and had done much to establish the respectability of liberal maritime principles. The Civil War, however, created a new situation. The United States was now the belligerent in a major war, and Europe remained at peace.

In sharp contrast to foreign policy in the age of Manifest Destiny, American diplomacy during the war focused on a negative task, keeping two great European powers, England and France, from intervening in behalf of the Confederacy. The Palmerston government in London was the key to the situation, for although Louis Napoleon of France was extremely sympathetic to the south, his policy was to do nothing without British cooperation.

Keeping England neutral was no simple task. In the first place influential segments of the British public and press opinion were anxious for a Southern victory and the collapse of the American republic. Demands for political reform in England had grown strident since the first major reform act of 1832, and the British aristocracy was feeling a good deal of pressure. John Bright and other English democrats had continually relied on the American example in their arguments for greater democracy in England. Only naturally then, the Civil War, which marked the disruption of America's political institutions, was greeted with delight by many in England who took the side of the aristocracy in the struggle against greater democratization. It seemed convincing evidence of the superiority of English political institutions (selection 1).

Both Lord Palmerston, the Prime Minister, and his Foreign Secretary, Lord John Russell, realized that many advantages were to be gained by the dissolution of the United States. The balance of power in the Western Hemisphere would be significantly altered, and Canada would enjoy greater security than she had known since the American Revolution. Moreover, England would be afforded a superb opportunity to restore her prestige in the Caribbean and throughout Latin America, tarnished in recent years as a result of several losing confrontations with the United States. Finally, at a time when the government in Washington was moving rapidly in the direction of a protectionist economic policy, a Confederate victory would guarantee Britain access to a free market in the South and a continuing supply of raw cotton at reasonable prices.

There is some evidence that during the early part of the war the British government went beyond sympathy for the South, taking a pro-Confederate position in its handling of some important questions relating to the war. For example, as soon as President Lincoln declared a blockade of the southern coastline, the Palmerston ministry responded by declaring its neutrality, thus recognizing the belligerency of the Confederacy and conferring upon the new government of Jefferson Davis a legal status and international legitimacy it would otherwise have been denied. During the first two years of the war the British government demonstrated in at least one other significant way a bias in favor of the Confederacy. It adopted a narrowly legalistic attitude about questions raised by the construction of Confederate commerce destroyers in British shipyards. Perhaps as many as 250 American merchant vessels fell victim to Confederate raiders built in Britain. Although the United States government protested vigorously, London maintained that under its neutrality law, the Foreign Enlistment Act of 1819, it had no power to stop the construction of raiders so long as they did not actually arm before leaving British jurisdiction. Had the Palmerston government been unsympathetic to the Confederacy, it would have found it a simple task to exert the requisite pressure on shipbuilders to halt the construction of Confederate war vessels in British shipyards.

Adding to the difficulties created by British predispositions in favor of the Confederacy were frequent incidents at sea between war vessels of the United States and British merchant ships. The most dramatic issue of this sort was the *Trent* affair, which took place on November 8, 1861. On that day the U.S.S. *San Jacinto*, commanded by Captain Charles Wilkes, overhauled the British mail steamer *Trent* in the Caribbean. After a show of force Wilkes took prisoner two Confederate diplomatic agents, James M. Mason and John Slidell, then on their way to Europe to seek recognition and aid from France and England. In the United States Captain Wilkes was treated as a national hero. In Britain, however, he was considered a pirate. His imprudence in seizing from under the protection of the Union Jack the two Confederate diplomats was considered even by Sir George Cornewall Lewis, a friend of the Union in the Palmerston ministry, reason for war. Passions on both sides of the Atlantic were at white heat.

In the weeks following the *Trent* affair, the Lincoln administration faced an unpleasant dilemma. The British position seemed clear. If the prisoners were not released, it would mean war. On the other hand, to repudiate Wilkes would be to arouse the ire of an American public grown sullen as a result of continuing military defeats at the hands of the Confederacy. Ultimately Lincoln and his Secretary of State, William H. Seward, took the only logical course, releasing the prisoners and taking their chances with public opinion. Seward put the best face on this American surrender, averring that by releasing the two diplomats he was living up to a long-established American principle against impressment and expressing his pleasure that Britain had at long last accepted the American view first laid down during the Jefferson administration.

Although no other maritime confrontations were as serious as the *Trent* affair, incidents did continue as a result of American enforcement of its naval blockade of the Confederacy. The blockading of more than thirty-five hundred miles of southern coast was an impossible task even for the rapidly expanding American Navy. In an effort to make the blockade more effective the United States resorted to practices that earlier, while a neutral during the wars of the French Revolution and Empire, she had denounced. Stuart L. Bernath, in his account of the hotly contested *Peterhoff* incident, reveals that the United States could and would reject its earlier principles when the requirements of belligerency so dictated (selection 2).

Southern diplomats were doing everything possible to force Britain to intervene on behalf of the South. During the years preceding the outbreak of the war, there had been a good deal of talk about the likelihood of secession by the Southern states and the possibility of a war that would halt the flow of cotton abroad. Southern leaders had become convinced, partially as a result of speculation in foreign capitals and partially as a result of their own rhetoric, that cotton was "king" and that England and France, because of their economic dependence on a continued supply of cotton for their factories, could not allow the North to prosecute a disruptive war against the South. Writing in January 1861, one Southern publicist predicted that secession would be accomplished peacefully, for Britain would not allow a war to interfere with her access to the South's cotton.

> The first demonstration of blockade of the Southern ports would be swept away by the English fleet of observation hovering on the Southern coast to protect English commerce and especially the free flow of Cotton to English and French factories. The flow of cotton must not cease; because the enormous sum of £150,000,000 is annually due to the elaboration of raw cotton and because 5,000,000 people derive their daily and immediate support therefrom in England alone and every interest throughout the kingdom is connected therewith. The stoppage of the raw material from the cotton states of the South, either by failure of crop or civil war and its consequences, would produce the most disastrous political results—if not a revolution in England.

Convinced that cotton was "king," the Confederate leaders decided to halt the sale of cotton abroad in an effort to coerce England and France into recognition and possibly intervention.

England did not intervene in the war, despite an initial partiality for the Confederacy among certain elements in and out of the ministry, the violation of British neutral rights by war vessels of the United States, and the pressure of "king cotton diplomacy." The failure of the cotton embargo was significant, and many scholars have tried to explain why it did not work. When all the arguments have been reduced to their first principles, however, it seems clear that the South made a catastrophic error, misjudging the adaptability of Britain's industrial system. There is something striking about the degree to which the South deceived itself about this. The belief that the world's foremost power would crumble in despair and revolution as a result of an economic boycott cannot be described in any other terms. It was at once the sheerest nonsense and a characteristically American response to a difficult diplomatic situation. Economic sanctions had repeatedly been used in the service of certain foreign policy goals, sometimes with success. Jefferson's experience with the embargo, however, should have forewarned the Confederates that there was room for failure too. Seldom have Americans placed more unjustified reliance on economic sanctions of this sort than the South did in the Civil War.

The failure of the cotton embargo helps to explain Britain's reluctance to intervene. However, other more compelling reasons deserve consideration. A negative factor of indeterminate consequence was that at least until the end of 1862, Englishmen, almost to a man, were convinced that in any event the Confederacy was going to win independence; this was true even among those who hoped the Union might be preserved. Thus, until 1863, by which time the tide of battle had turned in favor of the North, few saw any reason to urge intervention.

Even if pro-Southern leaders in Britain had pressed for recognition and aid for the South, there is considerable doubt that they could have managed it. That England, a leading nation in the struggle to abolish slavery, could have allied herself with the world's foremost slave power is extremely questionable, especially after Lincoln's Emancipation Proclamation turned the war into a struggle against this evil.

Finally, British intervention made neither economic nor military sense. England was enjoying a vast war trade with both sides in America as well as a virtual monopoly on the world's commerce. Intervention would have meant war with the United States and great economic loss. Moreover, Canada, ill prepared to defend herself, was a hostage to Northern arms. Had Britain intervened, she would have had to finance a major land war in North America in defense of this vulnerable province.

Recent scholarship has made it clear that aside from a brief moment in 1862, few in the British government gave any serious thought to active intervention in the war. Nor was any effective effort made to bolster Canada's defenses, certainly a prerequisite to involvement. Norman A. Graebner suggests that British policy was fundamentally consistent throughout the war and that it was in keeping with the traditional practice of neutrals toward belligerents and of established powers toward revolutions (selection 3). There were of course aberrations. However, if the ministry did act hastily in recognizing Southern belligerency, it also acquiesced in the North's violation of its neutral rights and never considered extending full diplomatic recognition to the Confederacy until such time as she had established her sovereignty on the battlefield. After 1862 there was scarcely a chance of that.

1

THE CONFEDERATE STRUGGLE AND RECOGNITION

LONDON QUARTERLY REVIEW

Among many strange things in the conduct of the Federals during the course of this terrible war, one of the strangest has been the value they have attached to English expressions of opinion. It is certainly not in repayment of any similar compliment from us. During the Russian war and the Indian mutiny, American comments upon England's conduct were not restrained or weakened by any false tenderness for our susceptibilities. The sympathy of our kinsmen for any one, whether Czar or Sepoy, whose conduct was embarrassing to England, was expressed with the most demonstrative cordiality, and spiced with all the verbal condiments with which they know how to flavour the insipidity of political discussion. Yet we cannot remember that their noisy criticism provoked any feeling, good, bad, or indifferent, in London. Nobody knew what the Americans were saying, or cared to ask. The opinion of New York upon the subject was of no more practical importance than the opinion of Rio Janeiro. And as a question of sentiment, it was a matter of profound indifference to us whether our neighbours praised or blamed us. The magnitude of the perils we had to meet, and the arduous exertions we were called upon to make, were subjects of anxiety too engrossing to leave us much leisure to ask what others thought of us. The solicitude, therefore, with which the Americans scan our newspapers, watch the speeches of our public men, and scrutinize every vehicle of English opinion, in order to discover some phrase or sentiment distasteful to themselves, is absolutely inex-

From "The Confederate Struggle and Recognition," *London Quarterly Review* (London, July and October, 1862), Vol. 112, pp. 535–545; 549–553.

plicable to us. One would have thought that a bloody civil war, a broken empire, and ruined liberties, would have left little room in their minds for susceptibility to the criticisms of foreigners.

If they are resolved to overhear the discussions we carry on among ourselves upon the events which cause us so much domestic misery, we do not deny that they are likely to suffer a listener's proverbial fate. There are many points in the strictures which the mass of Englishmen make upon this war which must be very distasteful to the Federals. English opinion has wavered a good deal; but it is in the main unfavourable to them now. When the war broke out the general bias was slightly Northern. The recent reception of the Prince of Wales had made a favourable impression; and it was not till the affair of the 'Trent' that that impression was wholly effaced. Then the real issues of the war were a good deal misapprehended just at first. The *prima facie* interpretation of the Secession movement was, that the slaveowners desired to subject more territory to slavery; and that they had rebelled because the North had been inspired, by a holy horror of slavery, to resist this unhallowed project. This view of the facts was unquestionably true to a certain extent; and at first it was believed in England to be the whole truth. So long as this impression was entertained, it could not be doubtful which way the sympathies of Englishmen would incline. The anti-slavery movement was no longer in its first vigour; but it still retained power enough to pledge England to look with aversion upon a revolution commenced for the purpose of perpetuating slavery. But as time went on, and the issues of the war came out more clearly, this spring of Northern sympathies began to fail. It soon became apparent that the grievance of the South went very far beyond the mere refusal to allow slaves to be held in the territories of the United States; and it became still more clear that whatever the North were fighting for, it was not for the emancipation of the negro. It was impossible to continue to believe that the North were crusading for abolition, in the face of the President's reiterated denials, and of the inhuman treatment which negroes were constantly receiving at Northern hands. If anything was wanting to confirm their scepticism, it has been supplied by the President's recent proclamation. That he should have reserved Emancipation to be the military resource of his extreme necessity, shows how little he cared for it as a philanthropist. He values it, not for the freedom it may confer, but for the carnage he hopes that it may cause. It must be confessed that the absolute quiescence of the negroes under circumstances which in Jamaica or Hayti would have excited a bloody revolt, is a cogent answer to the sensation descriptions of the 'Uncle Tom' school which have worked so powerfully on this side of the Atlantic.

But the practical argument against the North is the one that has weighed the most heavily here. War of any kind is only excusable when it is waged with a tolerable likelihood of success. A war for a reconstruction of the Union bore failure upon its face. The conquest of the South was a difficult undertaking, but it was not necessarily impossible. It might have been done, if the North could have found a Napoleon, and would have placed themselves unreservedly under his command. Even without a Napoleon, but with generals of average ability, they might have carried devastation far and wide through the South. But to compel the Southerners to return as willing citizens and take their part as of old in the political mechanism of the Republic, was an undertaking beyond the power of the highest genius and the mightiest armies. It was impossible for Englishmen to sympathize in a war which could have no end but desolation. And it was impossible for the keenest friend of the Federals not to mark how the war grew in horror as it progressed, and developed more and more the character of a mere war of revenge. The objectless devastation perpetrated by Pope and Blenker—men dragged from their homes and shot in the presence of their wives and children, without a pretence of trial, as in Missouri—young girls deliberately given over to a brutal soldiery by Federal commanders, as at Athens—women adjudged by public proclamation to suffer the vilest outrage for speaking, or even looking as though they loved the cause for which their brothers and husbands were dying, as at New Orleans—all these things fell lightly on the ears of the Federals themselves, but they have sunk deep into the hearts of Englishmen. We must have bidden farewell to every feeling both of humanity and honour before we can sympathize with a war of this kind, or with the men who wage it.

But there is no doubt that American proceedings would have been discussed less eagerly in England, and possibly criticised with less freedom, if they had not been made the turning point of a political controversy of our own. For a great number of years a certain party among us, great admirers of America, who even in this last extremity still worship faithfully at the old shrine, have chosen to fight their English battles upon American soil. That their antagonists should follow them there is one of the inevitable exigencies of war. Those who originally chose the battle-field must be responsible for the choice—not those who perforce accepted it. If Englishmen have taken almost a domestic interest in American institutions—if they have watched this, their first ordeal, with peculiar solicitude, and have passed their comments on it with outspoken freedom,—the Federals must impute it entirely to the indiscreet fervour of their own particular friends.

The impression produced upon the majority of spectators in England has undoubtedly been that democratic institutions have failed. Probably this feeling would not have been so general or so decided if the peculiar virtue of democratic institutions had not been so strenuously vaunted. Their advocates now tell us that the American civil war is not the first civil war on record, and that the evil passions of which it is the fruit, and the evil deeds of which it has been the parent, have many a precedent in monarchical and aristocratical states. To a certain extent this is true. But this is not the tone in which they were wont to speak before the war broke out. If Mr. Bright or his friends had been formerly content to claim for their pet democracy nothing more than that it was no worse than some of the old European monarchies, few people would have cared to question their modest panegyric. But it is the background of their extravagant adulation which throws forward into so strong a relief the calamities under which the Americans are suffering. They never ceased to assure us that democracy was a cure for war, for revolution, for extravagance, for corruption, for nepotism, for class legislation, and, in short, for all the evils with which the states of Europe are familiar. It is too late for them, now that America is a prey to all these old-world maladies at once, to turn round and tell us that the model Republic is no worse than an average despotism, or no worse than England was four hundred years ago. For years they have been proclaiming to us that it is infinitely better. For years America's small debt and scanty estimates have been the text upon which homilies to corrupt, extravagant old England have been preached. For years these have furnished the triumphant proof that political equality was the parent of pacific and thrifty government. A twelvemonth of stern experience has covered with confusion the foolish boasting of twenty years. A man would be laughed at now who should claim for democracy any special thrift, or purity, or love of peace. Its keenest admirers will hardly venture to invest it with those particular virtues just at present. But yet, if the admirers of America had had their way two or three years back, we should have altered our well-tried institutions for the sake of curing that lavishness of expenditure and that pugnacious policy which we were told was the special disease of an aristocratic system, and from which democracy had made America so gloriously free.

Something of the same effect upon English opinion has been produced by the eulogies of American freedom with which our ears have been incessantly regaled. Long before the days of Mr. Bright they formed the favourite commonplace of democratic orators on both sides of the Atlantic. We have placed at the head of this article the names of two books, published during the present year, which contain a curious record of the vaunting prophecies in regard to America in which the Liberal party of old and those connected with them delighted to indulge. It is instructive to compare the America of reality with the America of partisan prediction. Our first extract is from the reflections penned by Mr. Bewick, in 1822:—

> George III. and his advisers never contemplated the mighty events they were thus bringing about—rearing and establishing the wisest and greatest of republics and nations the world ever saw. When its enormous territory is filled with an enlightened population, and its government, like a rock, founded on the rights and liberties of man, it is beyond human comprehension to foresee the strides the nation will make towards perfection. It is likely they will cast a compassionate eye on the rest of the world grovelling under arbitrary power, banish it from the face of the earth, and level despots with the ground.

They will have to commence this compassionate operation with their own territory, and their own President, if they are to fulfil the prophecy. Our next extract shall be from a speech of Mr. Washington Irving's, delivered at New York thirty years ago:—

> It has been asked, Can I be content to live in this country? Whoever asks that questions must have an inadequate idea of its blessings and delights. What sacrifice of enjoyments have I to reconcile myself to? I come from countries cowering *with doubt and danger, where the rich man trembles and the poor man frowns—where all repine at the present and dread the future.* I come from these to a country where all is life and animation—where I hear on every side the sound of exultation—where every one speaks of the past with triumph, the present with delight, the future with growing and confident anticipation.

Mr. Irving has not lived to see the insults he cast upon England—doubly bitter as coming from one who had been cherished among us for years till his own countrymen, equally with ourselves, regarded him as almost an Englishman—retorted by Fate upon the people for the sake of whose applause he uttered them. The same tradition has been carried on by the prophets of a later day. It would be endless to quote the panegyrics and predictions of Mr. Bright. So late as May last, he could venture to congratulate the Northern States as being the freest country on the face of the earth. He, and the other admirers of America, have always been peculiarly severe upon the measures of repression which in times of public danger English governments have thought it necessary to adopt: and they have been loud in their admiration of the liberty, overstepping the bounds of licence, with which Americans have till recently disputed, almost at will, the decisions of their Government. They have always warmly denounced the hesitating measures of coercion which have been practised in Ireland during critical emergencies. It is not unnatural, therefore, that we should view with considerable surprise, and no little amusement, America, their model state, resorting to measures compared with which our severest have been mild and partial. There is no doubt that in times of public danger all states have felt the necessity of sharpening their laws against treasonable writing and speaking, though they have rarely dispensed so entirely with legal checks in the employment of this extreme remedy, or displayed so little judgment or moderation in applying it. But whether their course is abstractedly defensible or not, it cannot fail to strike observers in this country as contrasting oddly with the principles which have been so loudly proclaimed by Americanizing zealots here. And the comparison between past boasts and present facts does not lose in interest, when we find the liberty-loving eulogists of the past coolly persisting in their eulogy now that the very pretence of liberty has been thrown aside.

There is no doubt that the decision with which English opinion has pronounced itself upon the failure of democracy in America is due, in a considerable degree, to the extravagant adulation with which in former years that democracy was besmeared. But this is not the whole of the motive cause, or even the most powerful ingredient. It would be grievously understating the case to say that the American system has only fallen short of the extreme expectations which had been formed by a knot of fanatics here: or that it teaches us no more important lesson than that of disbelieving the extravagances of Mr. Bright. The civil war has a terrible interest of its own, both on account of the horrors it involves, and of the misery it is bringing upon a portion of our own countrymen. But it is fraught with instruction as well as interest. Every step that it takes teaches us something with respect to the working of the political system which has been tried in America for the first time on a large scale, and which England has been so frequently called upon to imitate. And the more the civil war progresses, the more important its teaching becomes. At first it may be said to have conveyed lessons that were comparatively elementary. The essential weakness of a Federal form of governmnt was a moral that lay on the surface of Secession. But as we have nothing Federal in the form of our Government, and are never likely to have, the moral had no peculiar interest for us. The injurious effects of a temporary and elective sovereignty were also a very obvious inference from the conduct of President Buchanan. For the last four momentous months of his Presidency he was obviously dominated by no other desire than that of putting off the evil day of bloodshed till his successor's time. He was a traitor, if not by his action, at least by his passive acquiescence: and if he acquiesced in that which it would have been wearisome and arduous to resist, it was because he had no motive for action. His recklessness to all that might happen, when once his tenure of office should have closed, was a striking illustration of the value of an hereditary throne. Sovereignty by birth, and sovereignty by election, do not appear to differ very widely in the average intellectual merit of the sovereigns they produce. Kings and Presidents alike have only in very exceptional cases any special fitness for the posts they occupy. But the enormous and paramount advantage of the hereditary principle is this—that the Sovereign whose son is to succeed to the throne he leaves is bound over by the strongest of human motives to be faithful to his trust. He cannot, like the elective President, view with indifference the turmoil or the danger that may await his successor.

But this truth was not of much practical interest to us. We have never had any taste for elective sovereigns in England. The advantages of a hereditary crown have never been seriously impugned. Mr. Bright has occasionally let slip the sentiment that a president is a much cheaper official than a monarch; but he has never ventured to enlarge upon this unpopular topic. In truth, even if there were any inclination among us to agitate such a question, and if the present wearer of the

Crown were less popular than she is, no one could feel that the question was a very practical one. The powers of the Crown, though legally they are very large, are so much held in reserve under a constitutional system that we are scarcely conscious of their existence. They make so little show that they present no mark for an agitator's aim. The truth is that the Crown is not a combatant in the real political struggle of our age. In this country, at least, republicanism and monarchy have ceased to be pitted against each other. It is agreed on all hands that— through the Crown—the nation is to rule. But what class is to preponderate within the nation? How is the nation's voice to be expressed? The struggle for power in our day lies not between Crown and people, or between a caste of nobles and a bourgeoisie, but between the classes who have property and the classes who have none. If property, and the intellectual advantages and moral securities which property as a rule implies, are to be taken into account, the propertied classes will be supreme, as they are now in England. If property is to be of no account, and absolute political equality is to prevail, the mere multitude will rule, as it does now in the Federal States. For many years past the advocates of the multitude have claimed that the merits of democracy shall be judged by its working in the Northern States. And unless we renounce the guidance of experience altogether, and mould our polity to suit a mere theory, it is evident that this claim must be admitted. The Northern States are the only communities who have tried the rule of the multitude on any considerable scale, and therefore we must abide by the results of their experiment, if we mean to defer to any experiment at all.

Let us, then, eliminate from the problem all disturbing and collateral causes. The mere event of Secession was, in a considerable degree, due to the defects of the Federal system; and the Federal system has no necessary connexion with Democracy. Let us, then, pass by the question of Secession, and confine our attention to more recent events. Since the Secession, at all events, the Federal principle has not interfered. The government of the United States for fifteen months has been in practice as centralized as that of France. Those fifteen months will form a fair test of the working of government by the multitude. We have seen how that form of government works when the political sky is perfectly unclouded. With boundless lands, high wages of labour, low taxation, cheap food, and no foreign enemy to fear, the system of government in the United States has succeeded passably well. It has not been favourable to moral progress; for their commercial morality has been the lowest in the world. They have not upheld the national credit with very great good fortune; for the States' governments have repudiated in several instances; and the late Secretary for War, Mr. Stanton, had already begun to speak of the future repudiation of its whole debt by the Federal government as a very possible hypothesis. It has not been successful in executing justice between man and man; for the elective judges, holding their offices for brief periods, have been in most places the creatures of the people; and the mob has always set the law at defiance, in eastern or western States alike, whenever it thought fit. With these reservations, the democratic government has answered fairly enough under the conditions of absolute sunshine which it has enjoyed. But under such conditions most governments would succeed. The most vicious despot could hardly prevent the mass of his people from being contented under such circumstances; and until discontent arises, the government cannot well help succeeding. War, the curse of nations, and the crucial test of governments, would not come near their borders. They did their best to invite him, by invading their neighbours and insulting their rivals; but for a time they invited him in vain. That boundless natural resources, and peace which they could not contrive to terminate, should have given them material prosperity, may reflect credit on the energy of the people, but is of little use in proving the excellence of their form of government. It is in stormier weather that forms of government are tested. They are, in their nature, precautions against disturbance; and it is only by their behaviour when disturbance comes that their true merits can be ascertained. The anchor that only holds ground in perfectly smooth water might almost as well be left at home. Englishmen, therefore, have watched this year of civil war with no little interest, to see how the government of the multitude would bear the strain. While the experiment was yet in progress, and its issue doubtful, political disputants on both sides have appealed to it in confirmation of their own views. Opinions may have been divided so long as the upshot was in suspense; but now that the great experiment is verging to its close, it is only a few choice spirits, whose iron-sided fanaticism no facts can penetrate, that will maintain that the democracy has worked well. Most men are now agreed that it has failed; and that, not in any subordinate detail, but in the two great opposite functions which are the final cause, the *raison d'être*, of all political institutions. It has failed to repress rebellion; it has failed to uphold liberty: it has failed as a machine of government; and it has failed as a guarantee for freedom.

These failures scarcely need a formal proof. They lie on the surface of a history too fresh to be forgotten, and too plain to be misread. The condition in which they find themselves is the best proof that the rulers of the United States have utterly failed as administrators. Fifteen months back they started upon the war with every condition in their favour. That they would succeed in so subjugating the Southerners as to restore them to the Republic as loyal fellow-citizens, was never possible: but that they would have all the success which military victories could give, ought to have been a certainty. Their population exceeded that of their opponents in the proportion of more than two to one. Their preponderance in wealth was still more overwhelming. They had the absolute command of the sea, and of the navigable rivers which give such enormous facilities for the invasion of the Confederate territory. The workshops of all Europe were open to them; while to their enemies Europe was almost absolutely cut off. The Confederates have had to supply themselves at a few months' notice, from their own internal resources, with arms, ammunition, clothing, and food, for all of which, up to the time of the Secession, they had been dependent on importations. Nothing but the most conspicuous incompetence could have prevented the Federals from winning in a race with a competitor so fearfully weighted; and it has been incompetence such as the world has rarely seen equalled or approached. If it had been the incompetence of one single official, there might have been no cause for surprise. Such accidents will happen in the best-constructed governments. But it has been all-embracing, all-pervading. It has infected all departments of the Government; it has been as marked in the legislature as in the executive, in the civilian as in the commander, in the subordinate as in the chief. With the exception of the naval operations of Commodore Farragut before New Orleans, there has been no operation of the Federal Government that has not been paralyzed by incompetence at every step. It has dogged with equal pertinacity the operations in the field to which America is comparatively strange, and the operations of legislation and finance with which her statesmen are as conversant as our own. It has produced a military campaign opened with unparalleled vauntings, and issuing in unparalleled disaster; a policy which has neither given heart and ardour to the

North, nor conciliated the South; a finance, caricaturing in its absurdest lineaments the worst blunders of our own, and better fitted than any that was ever devised to burden the industry of the future, while it stifles commerce for the present; and a recklessness in tampering with the currency, which we must recur to mediaeval history to parallel. The servants of the United States Government have failed as commanders—witness M'Clellan, and M'Dowell, and Pope: they have failed as administrators—witness Cameron and Stanton: they have failed as financiers, as in the case of Chase: and they have failed as independent governors, as in the instances of Butler and Wool. There is no species of administration, no section of a Government's operations, in which those who have been intrusted by the multitude at a time of trial to manage its affairs have not disgracefully and ignominiously failed.

.   .   .

If it be an object that the multitude should directly govern, democracy does not seem to have approached nearer to that object than any other form of government. The people still follow their leaders in America as elsewhere. The only difference is that the lead has passed from the hands of the independent and highly-cultivated classes into the hands of wire-pullers and caucus-mongers. The evils of such a state of things may be tolerable during a period of profound tranquillity. While a nation's political sky is bright, the vanity of its pettier minds may be soothed by the idea that the people can do without great men. But, whatever the advantage of the nation may be, the fair weather cannot last for ever. The day of trial will come, when institutions are tried in the fire of civic dissension; and then such a collapse as that upon which the eyes of all Christendom are riveted at the present moment will throw abundant light upon the wisdom of governing by little men.

But it may be said, as it has been often said, that the upper classes in the Federal States are excluded from power, not by the constitution, but by their own act. They have voluntarily withdrawn from politics, and refuse to mingle in them. It is their own doing that the 'political blacklegs' have been left without competitors. The people have not deposed their natural leaders, but the leaders have abdicated their trust.

The fact is unquestionably so; but it is not the less a direct result of Democratic institutions. Whether the better classes of North America are or are not to blame for their withdrawal from the political arena, is not very material to the question. It is possible that if they had been men of superhuman virtue, they would have braved every discouragement, accepted every degradation, and served their country in her own despite. But though individuals may be actuated by super-human virtue, classes never are; they will always act according to the average morality of their time. And the reproach of Democratic insti-tutions is, that there is that in them which, according to the average working of human motives, will always drive the refined and educated classes to abandon politics, and to seek fame or occupation upon other fields. The reason is not far to seek. They will not stoop to the acts by which alone it is possible to rise. Every one who is familiar with election work in England, knows how much humiliation a popular candidature involves. It is only in such places as our metropolitan con-stituencies that the evil assumes its most revolting type; and we know how rarely it is that a man of position or repute can be induced to submit himself to the ordeal of a metropolitan election. In America the degradation of a metropolitan election multiplies itself tenfold. The dependence which is exacted is more absolute; the pledges re-quired are larger, and must be swallowed more completely; the repre-sentative is more of a delegate, and less of a free agent. Moreover, the odious necessity is still more imperative upon the candidate of making himself pleasant to persons whom in his heart he utterly despises; and the necessity lasts longer, and recurs oftener. Sometimes able men may be found who are not fastidious, and they will not feel the hardship of professing what they do not believe, or exhibiting an enforced geniality towards men from whom they would naturally recoil. But the best men of a community will not do this. A man who has to swallow a string of pledges dictated to him by an unreasoning and passionate herd of ignorant men must have first seared out from his mind, by the strong caustic of self-interest, all feelings of self-repect. The man who forces himself to a familiarity, which under any other circumstances he would disdain, with the coarsest, and often the vilest, of mankind, in order to procure his election, cannot look back to the operation with complacency, or feel that he has raised himself in his own esteem. Under a system where these initiatory sacrifices are required, only those will take part in politics who are too thickskinned to wince at the humiliations through which they must pass, or whose wants are sufficiently pressing to have numbed their usual sensibilities. In England, now that the generation which was trained before the Reform Bill is worn out, it has become increasingly difficult to supply the best class of candidates for the more important seats; and yet among us it is only a mitigated type of the evil that prevails. In America it early became impossible. It has been attested by numberless travellers—it has been sufficiently proved by the utter helplessness of the men who have been tossing hither and thither upon the waves of the present storm—that the best, the calmest, the acutest, the noblest spirits of the community have preferred to turn away from politics altogether, rather than bend to the yoke of degradation which a popular candidature in a Democratic State implies.

Of course this deterioration of political life reacts upon and intensifies itself. Its humiliating conditions expel the best men, and their place is filled up by adventurers; and then, over and above the previous repulsiveness of a political career, is added the necessity of working with the rascals who are making the commonwealth a prey. Thus the evil becomes worse and worse, accelerating its own progress at each downward stage. Even in America the degeneracy has been gradual. At the time of the Revolution, the profession of politics involved risks and sacrifices which made it the noblest of all pursuits. The men of the Revolution were a splendid race, who had risen to their eminence by daring and ability alone. Political life, illustrated by their career, drew to it the best blood of the nation. Science, literature, commerce, did not, perhaps, flourish as they have done of recent years, but the Republic was better governed and better served. But the poison introduced by Jefferson was already at work, and was not slow to manifest its effects. The great men of the Republic became fewer and fewer, and, with Webster, they have absolutely disappeared. The standard of admiration is reversed now; politics has fallen from the highest to the lowest grade of honourable occupations, or rather it has fallen out of the category altogther. Matters have come to that pass that, as Mr. Trollope puts it, 'If A calls B a politician, A intends to vilify B by so calling him.'

But it is not only by driving from the field of politics its natural leaders that the American Democracy has brought its present disasters upon itself. It is far more directly responsible. The incompetence of the President is the most conspicuous cause of the present calamities;

and the incompetence of the President is the direct result of the mode in which he is chosen. The framers of the Republic placed an unlimited confidence in their favourite nostrum of popular election. In England we trust, for the choice of our chief magistrate, to a principle confessedly fortuitous, and therefore uncertain in its results. But then we provide guides to inform his mind, and constitutional checks to arrest his errors; so that his action is, in practice, reduced to those matters upon which the public opinion of his subjects is either agreed with him, or is not strongly opposed to him. But in America, the chosen of the people draws his title from too lofty an origin to be hampered by any such suspicious precautions. In England the King reigns, but does not govern. In America the President does not pretend to reign, but there is no doubt about his governing. His ministers are so, only in the etymological sense of the term. Every act of his government is actually, as well as constitutionally, his own. He draws out the campaign, he appoints the generals, he settles the foreign policy, he decides whether emancipation is to be proclaimed or not. Whether legally or not, he has now claimed and seized the additional power of imprisoning every citizen at pleasure; overriding the decisions of the law-courts; instituting a passport system and a conscription by his mere fiat; and declaring martial law wherever he thinks fit. And all these prerogatives he puts in force by the summary action of the Provost Marshal. No need of a Mutiny Act stays his arm. His ministers are liable to no interpellations, and are responsible to no majority in Congress. No dread of a ministerial crisis arrests his action; and his fears for the future, if he chances to be a lukewarm patriot, are limited to a vista of four years. Invested with such powers, and clogged by so few checks, the whole responsibility of disaster must rest on him. With a man of Mr. Lincoln's incapacity and obstinacy, intrusted with the enormous prerogatives of an American President, the ablest public servant would have been powerless to save his country. No doubt he has been very inefficiently served. But if M'Clellan had been a Wellington, he would have done nothing under a superior who had laid it down, as the plan of his campaign, to disperse, instead of concentrating his forces; and who put an empty braggart like Pope over his head, because he had 'known him in the West.' If Mr. Chase had been a Turgot, he could have done nothing with a master who had made up his mind not to levy a farthing of direct taxation till the elections for Congress were over. It is difficult to blame these subordinates, incapable as they are, as long as the system under which they act allows them, without reproof, to be the agents of a policy they disapprove. Wise counsels may be offered to the President, but he need not take them; powerful talents may be tendered to him, but he need not use them. For the space of four years he is master without appeal; and if his talents or his morality happen to be insufficient for his duties, he is at full liberty to do all that in four years can be done towards the ruin of his country. And the example of Buchanan living in Pennsylvania, absolutely forgotten, shows that, even if he have misused his powers for the furtherance of actual treason, he may yet securely count upon retiring into safe obscurity when his term is over.

The strange peculiarity of the American Constitution, as it now works, is that it stakes everything upon a single throw. The whole destiny of the country is hazarded, without possibility of recall, upon the result of the Presidential election. Our rulers in England are chosen in many different ways, and owe their position to a variety of converging causes. Parliamentary distinction, official experience, social popularity, distinguished birth, all go for something in the selection of the statesmen by whom our empire is governed. But yet we do not absolutely trust any of these things, nor all of them combined. We never so resign ourselves into the hands even of the most honoured ruler that we cannot recall the trust in case of need. If he deceives our expectations, and his incompetence is proved by some striking failure, the ousting vote is always ready, and the rival is always at hand to take his place. But the Americans bind themselves over, by indentures that cannot be broken, to serve their master absolutely during the space that has been fixed. It is a grievous error to say that the Americans are governed by mob-law. We could almost find it in our hearts to wish they were. They are governed by that which is much worse—the irremovable ruler of a mob's choice. At least, if the mob had any voice in the government, they would not feel themselves bound to persevere in a ruinous policy as a matter of personal consistency or to fulfil election pledges. The American President is the corner-stone of the democracy which for years past we have been so often called upon to admire and to copy, and he appears to combine in himself all the evils which it is possible for a ruler to unite. He has not a king's interest to preserve the country with which his own and his dynasty's interests are bound up; he has not a constitutional minister's constant responsibility; and he extends his tenure of office over a term of years which is amply sufficient to enable him to conduct his country to destruction. If he were chosen by angels, he might succeed. If even the results of popular election had been those which the founders of the Republic fondly counted on, something better might have come of it. We need not describe what the Presidential elections have really been. The jealousy of merit by which democracies have been haunted in all times has worked with fatal effect. It has become a standing maxim of policy with the conventions by whom the candidate of each party is chosen, that he must be obscure enough to have excited no enmity by his previous public career; for, though a distinguished candidate might better serve the country, it is the obscure candidate who is most likely to appease all jealousies and to secure a party victory. As Mr. Trollope puts it, 'But one requisite is essential for a President: he must be a man whom none as yet have delighted to honour.'

These several causes are abundantly sufficient to explain the fact that the chief magistrate is incapable, and that he can find nothing but incapacity to serve him. Everything has been staked on the ability of the President, and of the subordinates whom he selects; and every precaution has been taken to place the office in imbecile hands. All the best men have been effectually driven from the arena of politics; and of those who remain, the obscurest is selected to wield a power nearly as large, and quite as uncontrolled, as the power of the Emperor of the French. No other explanation is needed to account for the 'swaggering imbecility' of the Washington statesmen, or the piteous plight in which their country lies.

2

SQUALL ACROSS THE ATLANTIC: THE PETERHOFF EPISODE

STUART L. BERNATH

Late in November 1862 the American consul at London, Freeman H. Morse, acquired a copy of a letter privately circulated by the shipping concern of James J. Bennett and Wake of London. This communication announced plans for dispatching a vessel to the Rio Grande. A purchasing agent for the Confederate government would handle the exchange of the ship's cargo for cotton at Matamoros, Mexico, across the Rio Grande from Brownsville, Texas. Shippers were assured of large profits. It did not take long for Morse to identify the vessel selected for the mission as the *Peterhoff*, a screw-propeller steamer which had recently run the Union blackade of the Confederacy at Charleston, South Carolina, and had returned to England with a valuable cargo of cotton. He informed Secretary of State William H. Seward of the situation, and the steamer was soon placed on the Union black list of vessels suspected of intending to carry goods into the Southern states.

The *Peterhoff* sailed late in January 1863. Her manifest, shipping list, clearance, bills of lading, and other papers indicated that her destination was Matamoros. She would anchor off the Rio Grande since she was too heavy to cross the bar at the mouth of the river, and her cargo would be transferred to lighters which would carry it up the Rio Grande to Matamoros. Her freight, valued at $650,000, included 36 cases of artillery harness, 14,450 pairs of army boots, 5,580 pairs of

From Stuart L. Bernath, "Squall Across the Atlantic: The *Peterhoff* Episode," *Journal of Southern History*, XXXIV (August 1968), pp. 382–401. Copyright 1968 by the Southern Historical Association. Reprinted by permission of the Managing Editor.

"government regulation gray blankets," 95 casks of large horseshoes, 52,000 horseshoe nails, iron, steel, shovels, large amounts of morphine, chloroform, and quinine. The cargo was consigned to the ship's captain, Stephen Jarman, and to three passengers.

After a brief stop at St. Thomas in the Danish West Indies, the *Peterhoff* was captured on February 25 by the Union ship-of-war *Vanderbilt* on suspicion of intent to run the blockade and of having aboard contraband—warlike goods, such as arms and ammunition, which a neutral is prohibited by the laws of war from transporting to either belligerent. The *Peterhoff*'s seizure was made on order of Acting Rear Admiral Charles Wilkes, notorious in England for having removed two Confederate commissioners from the British mail packet *Trent* in November 1861. Repercussions from this act had brought England and America close to war.

When it became apparent that his vessel would be seized, Captain Jarman ordered papers burned and a package thrown overboard. He later testified before a prize court that the papers destroyed were letters from his family and that the package thrown overboard was, to the best of his knowledge, white powder and nothing more, as its owner Frederick Mohl claimed. Unknown to the captors and to the Union courts was a letter from Mohl to Confederate Secretary of State Judah P. Benjamin indicating that the package dropped overboard contained dispatches from Confederate commissioners in England and France and that the *Peterhoff* mails also contained dispatches. Had this been known in England, that nation would have had no grounds for protest, for the seizure and condemnation of a vessel carrying enemy dispatches was standard practice according to contemporary interpretations of international law.

The officer of the *Vanderbilt* who boarded the ship asked her captain to bring the *Peterhoff*'s papers to his vessel. Jarman refused, contending that it was impossible since he was in charge of Her Majesty's mail. He agreed to an examination of the papers on board the *Peterhoff*, however. The Union officer scrutinized the papers, considered them suspicious, and seized the vessel. A prize crew took the *Peterhoff* to Key West, Florida, but finding the prize court there closed for an indefinite period, took her north for adjudication.

During the Civil War maritime cases similar to this one were not uncommon. Complications frequently resulted from the differing views of England and the United States with respect to the legality of captures and the treatment of personnel, vessels, cargoes, and mails by American captors. The *Peterhoff* case, following a number of such incidents, precipitated others and had a pernicious influence upon Anglo-American relations. The Supreme Court ruling on this case and on similar ones had a significant impact upon international law. In addition, the *Peterhoff* incident provides considerable insight into the interrelations of the State and Navy departments and the American courts. In spite of certain differences in approach to the resolution of problems which arose in this case, the ultimate aim of the agencies of the American government involved was less to preserve the sanctity of the law than to serve the national interests of the United States.

Prior to the Civil War American interpretations of international law held that if a neutral port was the destination of a neutral ship in wartime, neither vessel nor cargo could be captured, nor could they be condemned in a belligerent prize court. A belligerent could make no inquiry into the ultimate destination of the cargo once it was landed at the neutral port. On the other hand, if contraband goods were shipped directly from a neutral port to a belligerent, the vessel and cargo were subject to capture and condemnation since transport of contraband to a belligerent or breaking a blockade was illegal.

To enforce the blockade imposed on the South and to frustrate devious traders, Union naval officers broke with American tradition and seized neutral vessels traveling between neutral ports. Northern courts, likewise deviating from the traditional American position, condemned the ships on the basis of the British "doctrine of continuous voyage." Fundamental to this legal concept was the idea that a person cannot do indirectly what he is forbidden to do directly. Thus, as applied during the Civil War, if a ship carrying contraband to a belligerent merely touched at an intermediate port, that act did not break the continuity of a voyage or remove the stigma of illegality. A vessel like the *Peterhoff*, ostensibly bound for a neutral port but with an ulterior destination for her cargo in enemy territory, could be seized and sent to a Union prize court for adjudication. If it could be proved that the cargo was directly or indirectly destined for the enemy, vessel and cargo could be condemned. The *Peterhoff* case itself extended the doctrine, which in the cases of the *Bermuda, Stephen Hart,* and *Springbok* was only applied to goods supposedly intended to be conveyed to the Confederate States by sea, either directly or by means of a transshipment at a neutral port. In the *Peterhoff* case goods which were designated as contraband by the American courts were ultimately to have reached their destination overland.

The doctrine of continuous voyage had arisen originally as a consequence of efforts to evade the British rule of war of 1756, under which neutrals were not allowed in time of war to engage in a trade from which they were excluded in time of peace. The American Treaty Plan of 1776 and most subsequent American commercial treaties included what were thought to be safeguards against the effects of this rule by providing that in case of war the trade of neutrals in noncontraband would be free between belligerent ports and between those ports and the ports of neutrals. Hence, the ultimate destination of a cargo would have no bearing on a case if the freight was carried in a neutral vessel. England would not accept this position.

During the Napoleonic Wars Secretary of State James Madison made frequent protests against the rule of 1756, and American shippers landed cargoes from the French West Indies in ports of the neutral United States, hoping thereby to break the illegal voyage to France and to render it legal. Sir William Grant ruled, however, in 1805, that the landing of goods and payment of duties in a neutral port did not interrupt the continuity of the illicit carriage of the cargo unless there was an honest intention to dispose of it in the neutral nation. This ruling firmly established the doctrine of continuous voyage in the British interpretation of international maritime law.

After the Napoleonic Wars American secretaries of state concluded numerous treaties with various countries containing provisions for neutral trade from port to port of a belligerent. When Britain in 1854 was considering rules to be applied during the Crimean War, Secretary of State William L. Marcy warned that if the British tried to apply the doctrine of continuous voyage, such act might disturb friendly relations with the United States. Several American treaties signed between 1854 and 1861 provided for freedom of neutral trade between belligerent ports. As noted earlier, during the Civil War the American courts reversed their traditional position and decreed the legality of the doctrine of continuous voyage.

Popular opinion in England rejected the American legal stand on seizures based on the doctrine of continuous voyage. Captures on this basis had not taken place for half a century; to blow the dust off a doctrine which had become conveniently obsolete in the minds of many Englishmen could only be "illegal"—especially since its employment was now detrimental to British commerce. The British government, however, perceiving a possible future use for American recognition of the legality of the doctrine, acquiesced in its utilization by American courts during the Civil War. Half a century later, during World War I, England employed the doctrine against American shipping.

When news of the *Peterhoff*'s seizure arrived in England, the press reacted with vehemence. The excitement reached a height second only to that which resulted from the *Trent* affair. Fear of a possible war with the United States caused falling stock prices, and the exchanges closed. Marine insurance rates rose conspicuously, and shipping interests unsuccessfully urged the government to increase the number of warships in the British squadron in the West Indies in order to give greater protection to their legitimate trade with neutral nations.

The *Saturday Review* of London suggested that the North was trying to provoke hostilities in order to escape the humiliation of having to acknowledge openly the military superiority of the South. The London *Observer* typified the view of many in its feeling that the American policy of taking English ships sailing between neutral ports "must inevitably lead to a rupture." The London *Times,* conveniently overlooking England's introduction and extensive usage of the doctrine of continuous voyage against American commerce during the Napoleonic Wars, attacked its revival and application by the United States as a new doctrine; America was now advancing "extraordinary pretensions." In addition, the journal suspected that the *Peterhoff,* like other vessels seized, had been taken without consideration of destination or cargo, but upon suspicions derived from the inclusion of the ship's name in the black list. The *Times* ominously cautioned the United States: "There are limits to the forbearance which even a great nation can exercise towards a struggling but still petulant and presuming Government. In the case of the Peterhoff these limits have been passed . . . ."

Seymour Fitzgerald of Horsham brought the *Peterhoff* case before the House of Commons, criticizing the English government for failing to protect neutral rights. John A. Roebuck of Sheffield commented that "the conduct of the North American dis-United States has been . . . humiliating to the people of England." Bernal Osborne of Liskeard did not wish to provoke America and proposed a halt to offensive language under the existing combustible circumstances.

The British Foreign Office, however, could hardly ignore the situation. On March 26 the *Peterhoff*'s owner wrote to Secretary of State for Foreign Affairs Lord John Russell, pointing to the illegality of the capture and the necessity for government action to prevent the recurrence of such incidents. Lord Russell replied through Edmund Hammond of the Foreign Office that the American government had no right to seize vessels bona fide bound from England to neutral ports "unless such vessels attempt to touch at, or have an intermediate or contingent destination to some blockaded port or place, or are carriers of contraband of war destined for the Confederate States . . . ." But the British could not claim any exemption from the right of visit by belligerent cruisers. Vessels suspected of transgressions of international law were clearly subject to capture, and more than a few Englishmen had been found guilty of such violations by American courts during the current conflict. The British government could not "deny the belligerents in this war the exercise of those rights which, in all wars in which Great Britain had been concerned, she has claimed herself to exercise." On the basis of the documents seen, however, the *Peterhoff* appeared to be guiltless, and representations would be made by the British minister in Washington. But if legal grounds for capture were brought to his attention, the case would go through the usual channels—the prize courts.

The London *Shipping and Mercantile Gazette* observed that this opinion favored the rights of belligerents over those of neutrals. Her Majesty's government was reluctant to press neutral rights to a point which might later hinder the exercise of English sea power. The favoring of Northern belligerent practices could mean advantage to British belligerency in a future conflict.

Russell instructed the English minister in Washington, Lord Richard B. P. Lyons, to urge the release of the *Peterhoff* and her cargo and to obtain compensation for detention of the ship and her passengers. Lyons acted even before receiving the Foreign Secretary's message because of advice from British Vice-Admiral Sir Alexander Milne. This officer had warned from the West Indies that the seizure of the *Peterhoff* had aroused great indignation in the fleet. American seizures of British vessels passing between neutral ports on the basis of mere suspicion was becoming intolerable. Lord Lyons received no satisfaction, however. Secretary of State Seward advised him that the American government did not choose to restore the vessel. The case would go through the prize court at New York, where the *Peterhoff* had been taken, though with as little delay as was necessary. He made no mention of claims.

The British minister was far from pleased with Seward's answer. He informed the Secretary of State that Her Majesty's government could not accept his proposition of turning the matter over to a prize court. Lyons demanded compensation for the shippers, who had been damaged to the extent of several thousand pounds by the unjustifiable seizure of the *Peterhoff* and the detention of their agents. He added gratuitously that there was an impression in England that the American government had decided to stop legitimate trade with Matamoros by means of capture without cause, by delays in adjudication, and by "wanton imprisonment" of masters and crews of ships seized. To pretend that goods carried to Matamoros might be afterwards transported to Texas could not alter the legal character of the trade, for the direct destination of the cargo was Matamoros.

Seward replied that the executive department of the government would consider the question of claims only if it was not within the jurisdiction of the prize court—and he thought it was. Any negative impression in England of American behavior was groundless. The suddenly enlarged Matamoros trade, which had grown "as palaces, cities, states, and empires rise in the tales of the Arabian Nights under the waving of a wand," had occurred simultaneously with a suspiciously rapid construction of roads across Texas. Southern cotton was passing through Matamoros in exchange for articles needed by the Confederacy. The *Peterhoff* was the first vessel discovered in this illicit trade and would, with certainty, be handled in the prize court. Nevertheless, renewed instructions had been given to naval officers to be cautious and to conform strictly to the principles of maritime law in conducting searches and seizures. In addition, Seward and Secretary of the Navy Gideon Welles decided to transfer Wilkes from the West Indies in order to avoid friction with England. This was especially helpful in mollifying British public opinion, which had renewed its outcries against Wilkes when the *Peterhoff* was seized.

The question of mail on board the *Peterhoff* became almost as explosive as the issue of ship and cargo. On April 9 Lord Lyons protested that the vessel's mails had been dealt with in a manner incompatible with the directions given in Seward's letter to Secretary of the Navy Welles dated October 31, 1862. This communication had suggested that neutral mails found on captured ships should not be searched or opened but should be sent on to their destination. Prize Commissioner Henry H. Elliott had opened the *Peterhoff* mailbag in the presence of a United States district attorney and against the protest of a British consul. The sealed packages of letters within the bag were not touched. With little delay, Seward telegraphed the American district attorney who was prosecuting the case to "Let the mail of the *Peterhoff* remain inviolate until further directions from me."

The Secretary of State next urged Welles to release the mails on the bases of his letter of October 31, of international law, of the necessity of avoiding war with England, and of the future requirements of America as a neutral. Welles had never bothered to effect the suggestions in the letter, writing in his diary that its "tone and manner . . . were supercilious and offensive, the concession disreputable and unwarrantable, the surrender of our indisputable rights disgraceful, and the whole thing unstatesmanslike and illegal, unjust to the Navy and the country, and discourteous to the Secretary of the Navy . . . ." Welles refused to approve releasing the mails and argued that they might contain evidence useful in condemning the *Peterhoff*—which would mean prize money for captors and Navy Department. The Secretary of the Navy was certain that neither Lincoln nor Seward had any right to interfere; the matter must be left to the courts.

Disgusted, Seward turned to the President. Lincoln requested both secretaries to prepare their arguments and present them to him. This was done, and the President took Seward's side, horrified at the prospect of war resulting from the inspection of English mail. The Secretary of State shortly afterwards informed Lyons that he had directed the *Peterhoff* mails to be released. A month later Lincoln instructed Welles to order naval commanders to forward captured neutral mails to their destinations.

American newspapers responded to the decision on the *Peterhoff* mails with surprise, regret, displeasure, indignation, and mortification. Except for the most bellicose of Englishmen, British opinion was pacified when the mails were released—and this was the important thing. The London *Globe* lauded Lincoln's moderation and fairness, praising the President and his secretary of state for staving off "great troubles." Wells, however, was so furious at the outcome of the dispute that a decade later he devoted 38 pages of a 215-page book to reviewing the incident, justifying himself, and castigating Seward.

The seizure of the *Peterhoff*, in addition to all the other difficulties it caused, eventually rendered voyages between England and Matamoros too hazardous for British insurance companies to provide protection —at least until the prize court made its decision on the case. As a result two Americans went for assistance to the United States minister in London, Charles Francis Adams. They had supplies and munitions which they hoped to send to the Mexicans to help them in their struggle against France. They requested a letter which they hoped would satisfy the underwriters at Lloyd's that their trade was of neutral character and could therefore be safely insured. The evidence they presented convinced Adams that their freight was not intended for the Confederacy, and he drew up a letter to Admiral Samuel F. Du Pont of the South Atlantic Blockading Squadron indicating this fact. The note was thus intended to satisfy Lloyd's and to induce Du Pont to let the traders go on their way if members of his squadron should stop them at sea. Not expecting his note to be published, Adams added some unwelcome remarks on "the multitude of fraudulent and dishonest enterprises" emanating from England. He was pleased to distinguish this one as having "a different and creditable purpose."

One of the American merchants took the letter to Lloyd's and presented it. The note infuriated the firm and a copy was sent to the *Times*, which immediately published it. The attack was merciless. Ignoring the citizenship of the traders, the newspaper accused Adams of constituting "himself as a kind of 'Prize Court,' sitting in London, passing judgment on cargoes" before their being dispatched from port. English merchants had no intention of going as supplicants to the representative of a foreign nation for "licences" to transact legitimate business. "For the assumption of power in a written instrument by a foreign Minister there has been nothing to equal it since the Legates of the Pope published Bulls, dated from the Vatican, overriding the laws of England." Adams' note, the *Times* continued, seemed to imply that vessels without such a certificate should be captured. The whole proceeding was monstrous. Other journals recorded similar sentiments, the *Morning Herald's* editorial, for example, being entitled "BRITISH SUBMISSION TO YANKEE INSULTS." If British ire was not aroused sufficiently already, the New York *Times* did its part to keep things moving: "Certifying to the good faith and honor of British traders, in these days of blockade-runners and privateers, is extrahazardous. . . . The London *Times* which in this, as in most other matters, embodies the national wrath and swagger, would do well to turn its indignation upon the real offender. The fact that British shippers apply to Mr. Adams for certificates of character, may be a very good reason why *they* should be hung, drawn and quartered,—or blown from the cannon of the London *Times*."

Members of Parliament launched a heavy verbal assault on the United States. The Marquess of Clanricarde, before Charles Wilkes had been removed from his command, said that if British merchants were obliged to American ministers to protect English trade, then "Commodore Wilkes might set a broom at his mast head . . . and proclaim that he had swept British ships and British trade away from that coast." Lord Russell, under pressure from Lloyd's and the shipping interests, found Adams' actions "very extraordinary" and "most unwarrantable"; it was inconceivable for a diplomat to issue such a permit.

Both England and France formally protested. Lord Lyons observed that Adams' note was an interference with England's legitimate trade since it rendered vessels without certificates suspect and liable to unjustifiable detention and capture. French Secretary of State for Foreign Affairs Édouard Drouyn de Lhuys complained bitterly that Adams had taken pleasure in describing the shippers as having an honorable intent when their vessel was bound to Mexico with arms intended for the killing of Frenchmen. Seward was compelled to disavow the American minister's letter and to apologize for its issuance; only then were England and France pacified.

Adams felt that Seward's apologies were a national disgrace, measures he personally would never have taken. Nevertheless, Adams had made a serious mistake. He certainly should have considered the possibility that his note might have been published, and he should have limited his message to the essential information he wished to convey. Instead, he used language which could not fail to antagonize powerful private interests and two national governments. One of his own secretaries in London considered the proceeding "indefensible," worthy of "the severest censure." Adams' most recent biographer considers the incident "as the single significant example of imprudence in a mission remarkable for restraint and tact."

The *Peterhoff* case opened on July 10, 1863, in the United States District Court, Southern District of New York. Two weeks later, after the arguments for the government and claimants had been ably presented, Judge Samuel R. Betts ruled that the ship was laden in whole or in part with contraband. Her papers were simulated and false with regard to her real destination. The *Peterhoff*, he continued, was not truly destined for Matamoros, but rather for a terminal point in Confederate territory. Betts therefore condemned both ship and cargo and promised that a more extensive opinion would soon follow.

By the time Judge Betts made his decision, British contentiousness on the subject of American seizures had abated somewhat. Lord Russell had suggested recently that bellicose members of Parliament wait for the decisions in the cases of the *Peterhoff* and the other vessels pending in the United States courts before criticizing the verdicts. He believed that American jurists would act fairly and without intent to interfere unnecessarily with British commerce. The *Saturday Review* confirmed the Foreign Secretary's position, and even the easily excitable *Times* observed calmly that the principles being recognized and extended by the Union prize courts might "well be very precious to England in some future crisis."

When news of the decision reached Britain, the *Times* saw no need for wrath or indignation and published the refutations of the judgment by the owner of the *Peterhoff* and the brokers for the cargo without a derogatory comment. Only the London commercial interests' *Shipping and Mercantile Gazette* was convinced that American rulings were not sustained by the evidence. It contended that Judge Betts's "innovation" of basing his judgment on the doctrine of continuous voyage had been done solely to gratify the animosity of the federal government toward England. American journals, not unexpectedly, felt that the decision was entirely sound.

After the law officers of the crown examined copies of the prize court transcripts, Lord Russell wrote Lyons in Washington that the evidence would not change Her Majesty's government's position on the inexpediency of any official interference in the *Peterhoff* case. The facts appeared to sustain the verdict. Without positively confirming the judgment, the English government could only suggest that the aggrieved claimants appeal to the United States Supreme Court.

Judge Betts's 104-page opinion became available in March 1864. Betts noted that while Captain Jarman had admitted to ordering the destruction of papers and a package, once a member of his crew revealed the incident, the descriptions of the items involved differed considerably. Betts was convinced that Jarman had ordered papers destroyed when capture became imminent because they would have revealed that vessel and cargo were liable to seizure and condemnation —that the *Peterhoff* was carrying contraband to the enemy. Although destruction of papers was not sufficient grounds for condemnation, it did provide good reason for suspicion when combined with the captain's prevarications.

The nature of the cargo was simple to determine. Most of it was especially adapted to army use without further processing. If its destination was the Confederacy, the freight must be described as contraband. When articles of such character were destined for enemy use, all other articles found on the same ship must, despite their innocence, share the fate of the contraband.

What then was the destination of the cargo? Aside from the title page of the logbook, there was nothing substantial to show where the *Peterhoff* was bound. The only testimony as to the freight's destination was made by the sailors who heard a passenger say that it was to be Texas by way of Matamoros. The character and quantity of the articles composing the cargo were such as to be quite useful to the Confederacy, but were ill adapted to the Mexican market or the little port of Matamoros. The cargo included, for example, "negro brogans." Such items would be useful in Texas where a Negro population existed, but not in Mexico, where Betts was certain there were no Negroes. Finally, the captain's behavior, erasure of the listing of a contraband item in the manifest, and the failure of manifest and bills of lading to indicate the nature of the cargo and its destination, taken together, proved that ship and freight were destined for the Confederate States.

To exempt vessel and cargo from condemnation because the latter was to pass through a neutral port on its way to Texas would open a wide door to the practice of fraud upon the belligerent rights of the United States. The ultimate destination of the cargo determined the character of the trade, no matter how circuitous the route by which it reached that destination. If contraband was to be transported from a neutral to an enemy country by enemy means of conveyance, the trade was illicit. Under the circumstances, Judge Betts concluded, the voyage of the *Peterhoff* was illegal at its inception. English rulings provided ample precedent for condemnation of steamer and cargo.

Russell wrote Lyons after the law officers of the crown had reviewed Betts's detailed opinion that Her Majesty's government could see no justification for intervention on behalf of the claimants. In fact, the verdict rendered and the reasons given for it appeared to be in harmony with English prize court judgments.

Lord Lyons did, however, ask for a postponement of the sale of the *Peterhoff* and her cargo until an appeal could be submitted by the claimants to the Supreme Court and a decision made on it. Seward referred it to the Navy Department and then notified the British through Assistant Secretary of State Frederick W. Seward that the question must be handled by the prize courts. Shortly thereafter the court sold the cargo at public auction for $273,628.99. The Navy Department purchased the steamer for $80,000 from the prize tribunal and used her until March 6, 1864, when she sank off the coast of North Carolina as a consequence of a collision.

3

NORTHERN DIPLOMACY AND EUROPEAN NEUTRALITY

NORMAN A. GRAEBNER

Europe's diplomatic tradition cautioned against any recognition of the Confederacy until the South had demonstrated the power required to establish and maintain its independence. Without the assurance of ultimate Southern success, European involvement would assume the risk of either an eventual ignominious retreat from a declared diplomatic objective or an unlimited military commitment to guarantee the achievement of Southern independence. Confronted with Europe's traditional realism, the Southern diplomatic cause in London and Paris could be no more successful than the Southern military cause in Virginia and Pennsylvania. Diplomacy reflects the status of power, and Southern power never appeared greater than during the summer and autumn months of 1862.

News of General George B. McClellan's retirement from before Richmond in the early summer of 1862 merely confirmed a general European conviction that the American Union was doomed. To European military experts, diplomats, and statesmen, Northern power seemed incapable of overcoming the defensive nature of the Southern military commitment. The North, Europe understood, enjoyed an immense industrial superiority, but the advantages of strategy, terrain, and leadership appeared to lie with the South. Confederate armies had no obligation to conquer the North, but only to beat off the Union forces. This they appeared capable of doing. In June, 1862, the London *Times* broached the issue of European intervention, convinced that

From David Donald ed., *Why the North Won the Civil War*, Louisiana State University Press, copyright 1960, pp. 61–75. Used by permission of the publisher.

Southern independence was inevitable. "It is plain," said the *Times*, "that the time is approaching when Europe will have to think seriously of its relations to the two belligerents in the American war. . . . That North and South must now choose between separation and ruin, material and political, is the opinion of nearly every one who, looking impartially and from a distance on the conflict, sees what is hidden from the frenzied eyes of the Northern politicians." Recognition of a successful cause could be both legitimate and effective.

For many British editors and politicians, McClellan's retreat from the peninsula during the summer of 1862 was like redemption. So dominant was the pro-Southern trend in British opinion that Henry Adams wrote from London, "There is no doubt that the idea here is as strong as ever that we must ultimately fail, and unless a very few weeks show some great military result we shall have our hands full in this quarter." Only a decisive Northern victory, he observed, could prevent European intervention. Public hostility, Charles Francis Adams wrote on July 10 to his son in America, was "rising every hour and running harder against us than at any time since the Trent affair." There was nothing to do but retreat. "I shut myself up," he lamented, "went to no parties and avoided contact with everyone except friends." Reports in the British press of the capture of McClellan's entire army, Adams believed, had been fabricated "to carry the House of Commons off their feet" as it commenced its crucial debate on William Shaw Lindsay's resolution calling for a more vigorous pro-Confederate British policy.

In defense of his resolution, Lindsay pointed to the inevitability of final separation between North and South. He declared that the Southern cause was just and that the North would now accept mediation. Lancashire was in distress. Lindsay quoted from a letter written by a mill hand, "We think it high time to give the Southern States the recognition they so richly deserve." Friends of the North were assured that the British Ministry would not be influenced by the parliamentary debate and therefore chose the strategy of permitting the pro-Confederates to wear themselves out against a stone wall of silence. After two days of verbal effort Lindsay asked for a postponement of his motion to "wait for king cotton to turn the screws still further." Somehow the debate created a strong impression in England that public opinion favored intervention.

That critical summer found the European diplomats confused and divided. Napoleon pondered the Southern victories, convinced that the moment for intervention had arrived. He informed the British Ministry that France would recognize Southern independence if the London government would follow. Edouard Antoine Thouvenel, the French Minister in Paris, did not share the Emperor's enthusiasm for intervention. He doubted that the French public had any interest in such involvement or that the Confederacy would win. He warned that French intervention, unless supported by both Britain and Russia, would result in an overcommitment of French power. Russia, he surmised, would reject every proposal for joint action. He was correct. Prince Gortchakov made it clear that his government would regard the dissolution of the Union as a catastrophe. In an interview with Bayard Taylor of the American Embassy in October, 1862, he said: "You know that the government of the United States has few friends among the Powers. England rejoices over what is happening to you; she longs and prays for your overthrow. France is less actively hostile; her interests would be less affected by the result; but she is not unwilling to see it. She is not your friend. . . . Russia, alone, has stood by you from the first, and will continue to stand by you. We are very, *very* anxious that some means should be adopted—that *any* course should be pursued—which will prevent the division which now seems inevitable."

In Washington Mercier, still counseling mediation, stood alone. Lyons had no interest in confronting Seward with that issue again. To Stoeckl he observed, "We ought not to venture on mediation unless we are ready to go to war." Lyons did not share the European hostility toward the American Union. During his visit to England in the summer of 1862 he wrote to the British chargé d'affaires in Washington, with reference to McClellan's defeat, "I'm afraid no one but me is sorry for it." He believed that the debate on British policy in Parliament was ill-timed. "I do not think we know here sufficiently the extent of the disaster [to McClellan] to be able to come to any conclusion as to what the European Powers should do," ran his warning. Stoeckl concluded that the ravages of war would prompt the North eventually to beg for mediation, but not yet. He doubted, moreover, that British or French recognition of the South would achieve anything. "It will not end the war and what is more," he predicted, "it will not procure cotton for them, and the distress of the manufacturing districts will not be lessened. It can be accomplished only by forcing open the Southern ports, thus leading to a clear rupture with the North."

In London Mason, misled by the public evidence of British interventionism and unmindful of the distrubing doubts in the Foreign Office, moved to drive home his apparent advantage. He dispatched a brief note to Lord Russell requesting an interview. This Russell refused, assuring Mason that no advantage would result from it. In a second dispatch the Confederate Commissioner phrased his position in great detail, but again Russell replied that the moment for recognition had not arrived. For Mason the official British position had suddenly become clear. The Ministry would not alter its policies until the South revealed its ability to gain and maintain its independence, and reports from America indicated that the South was faltering at New Orleans, Memphis, and Shiloh. From Vienna John Lothrop Motley observed with accuracy that diplomacy would continue to reflect the course of war in America.

In Paris Slidell met with equal opposition. Thouvenel convinced him that it would be unwise even to ask for recognition. France, he said, was involved in Italy, but Slidell understood clearly the cause for French hesitancy. To the Confederate government he wrote on August 24: "You will find by my official correspondence that we are still hard and fast aground here. Nothing will float us off but a strong and continued current of important successes in the field." England, he warned, would avoid intervention until the North and South had become entirely exhausted. "Nothing," he lamented, "can exceed the selfishness of English statesmen except their wretched hypocrisy. They are continually casting about their disinterested magnanimity and objection of all other considerations than those dictated by a high-toned morality, while their entire policy is marked by egotism and duplicity."

Despite the lack of conviction in Europe's judgment of Confederate prospects, Southern victories were prompting the British Ministry to consider intervention. Russell admitted that nothing less than further Confederate successes would force mediation on the North. "I think," he wrote to the Embassy in Washington, "we must allow the President to spend his second batch of 600,000 men before we can hope that he and his democracy will listen to reason." Russell was convinced privately that October, 1862, will be the anticipated time for action. Stonewall Jackson's victories in Virginia prompted him to inform Lord Palmerston, the Prime Minister, that "it really looks as if he might end the war." Palmerston agreed, writing on September 14: "The Federals . . . got a very complete smashing . . . even Washington or Baltimore may fall into the hands of the Confederates. If this should happen, would it not be time for us to consider whether in such a state of things England and France might not address the contending parties and recommend an arrangement upon the basis of separation." The British Cabinet awaited word from France.

Before Napoleon could commit France to intervention, the British government passed the moment of decision. The wise and respected British politician, Earl Granville, warned Russell that involvement would mean war. "I doubt," he cautioned, "if the war continues long after our recognition of the South, whether it will be possible for us to avoid drifting into it." If Granville's words lacked conviction, Northern arms did not. Before the end of September news reached London of McClellan's success at Antietam and Lee's retreat down the Shenandoah Valley. Russell, who had been the ministry's most vigorous spokesman for involvement, now admitted, "This American question must be well sifted." Palmerston's support of Russell's position had been conditioned on the Southern invasion of Maryland. Now on October 2 in a letter to Russell he also acknowledged the wisdom of Granville's argument. Since mediation would favor the Southern position, its acceptance in the North hinged on Southern triumphs. Ten days earlier the necessary conditions seemed impending; now Palmerston counseled delay. He had no interest in exposing Canada and British commerce to a war against the United States. Nor would he venture into a quarrel without the support of France and Russia. "The whole matter is full of difficulty," he concluded, "and can only be cleared up by some more decided events between the contending armies."

William E. Gladstone, Britain's liberal cabinet leader, continued to urge British involvement in the American conflict as a moral obligation. At Newcastle on October 7 he declared: "Jefferson Davis and the other leaders have made an army, they are making, it appears, a navy, and they have made what is more than either, they have made a nation." Gladstone denied that British mediation would be met by insult or war, for, he predicted in a memorandum to the Prime Minister, "America would feel the influence and weight of a general opinion on the part of civilized Europe that this horrible war ought to cease." Whatever the immediate Northern reaction, the British proposal would produce a powerful effect on opinion and alter affairs in America in favor of peace. But perhaps Gladstone was motivated by more than a moral revulsion to war. He had recently toured the North of England and was fearful that the unemployment in the cotton districts would produce a violent upheaval. By serving the cause of peace the great liberal might also serve the cause of the British cotton textile industry.

Palmerston, under pressure from the Cabinet, sought the advice of the Earl of Derby, leader of the opposition. Derby vigorously opposed both mediation and recognition. He reiterated the fundamental conviction of European conservatives that either action would merely irritate the North without advancing the cause of the South or procuring a single bale of cotton. Mediation, he added, would gain its apparent objective only if England were prepared to sweep away the blockade and invite a declaration of war from the Lincoln administration. Intervention was hopeless because there was no way in which England could influence events in America short of military involvement. Palmerston's decision reflected this fundamental reality. Britain, he informed Lord Russell, "could take no step nor make any communication of a distinct proposition with any advantage." The North, he pointed out, demanded no less than restoration of the Union and the South no less than independence. To offer mediation would merely pledge each party in the conflict more firmly to its uncompromising objective. Russell added his conviction that no British action would be effective unless it were supported by Russia, Prussia, Austria, and France. For nations of such diverse interests agreement on interventionist policy was impossible.

During the crucial months of October and November, 1862, Napoleon never disguised his sympathy for the Confederate cause. But sentiment and policy are not synonymous, and the French Emperor balked at involvement in the American conflict. He complained to Slidell of troubles in Italy and Greece and acknowledged his fear that if he acted alone England would desert him and would attempt to embroil him in a war with the United States. Slidell assured him that recognition would not be regarded by the North as a *casus belli* and that with his powerful navy he could defend French interests on the seas without difficulty. To Slidell joint mediation was worthless, for he had no faith in England or Russia. Napoleon answered with a proposal acceptable to the Southern Commissioner. France and Britain might seek a six-month armistice in the American Civil War in the interest of humanity. Napoleon's final program for joint action was dispatched to both London and St. Petersburg.

In London the tripartite proposal threw the Cabinet into confusion. Palmerston was displeased, for he no longer had any interest in European intervention. Lord Russell favored action provided European leaders could discover terms upon which the warring sections in America would agree. In lieu of this elusive formula he favored a Cabinet discussion of the French dispatch. At the Cabinet meetings of November 11 and 12 Russell conceded the issue to Palmerston. Reported Gladstone to his wife: "The United States affair has ended and not well. Lord Russell rather turned tail. He gave way without resolutely fighting out his battle." In its reply to the French government, the British Ministry declared that mediation in any form was useless since Lincoln would not accept it.

At issue in the final Cabinet decision was the attitude of Russia. As early as November 8, St. Petersburg had informed the Foreign Office that the Russian government had rejected Napoleon's proposal. Prince Gortchakov advised the French that it was "essential to avoid the appearance of any pressure of a nature to offend American public opinion, and to excite susceptibilities very easily roused at the bare idea of intervention." Russell yielded on this key question to Palmerston when he wrote, "We ought not to move at present without Russia." Russia's inflexibility created the basis for a harmonious decision within the British Cabinet, and even Gladstone could write, "As to the state of matters generally in the Cabinet, I have never seen it smoother."

Throughout the months of decision in Europe, Seward exerted relentless pressure on the British and French governments. When Mercier transmitted a French offer of mediation to him in July, 1862, the Secretary warned that "the Emperor can commit no graver error than to mix himself in our affairs. At the rumor alone of intervention all the factions will reunite themselves against you and even in the border states you will meet resistance unanimous and desperate." It was not in the French interest, he continued, to compromise the kindly feeling which the United States held for France. Mercier thereupon advised caution in Paris, adding that intervention could easily result in war. When Mercier apprised Seward of Europe's reaction to McClellan's withdrawal from Richmond, the Secretary again stormed back: "I have noticed it but as for us it would be a great misfortune if the powers should wish to intervene in our affairs. There is no possible compromise . . . and at any price, we will not admit the division of the Union."

Seward acknowledged the kindly sentiments of Europe but replied that the best testimony of those sentiments would be Old World abstention from American affairs. When Mercier suggested that restoration of the Union was impossible, Seward told him: "Do not believe for a moment that either the Federal Congress, myself or any person connected with this government will in any case entertain any proposition or suggestion of arrangement or accommodation or adjustment from within or without upon the basis of a surrender of the Federal Union."

Above all Seward sought to disabuse European leaders of their conviction that a Northern victory was impossible. Nothing had occurred, he once wrote to Dayton in Paris, to shake the confidence of the Federal government in the ultimate success of its purpose. To those Europeans who insisted that the United States was too large for one nation, Seward retorted that it was too small for two. When Europe gave evidence of interventionist tendencies in August, 1862, Seward wrote to Adams: "The nation has a right and it is its duty, to live. Those who favor and give aid to the insurrection, upon whatever pretext, assail the nation in an hour of danger, and therefore they cannot be held or regarded as its friends. In taking this ground, the United States claim only what they concede to all other nations. No state can be really independent in any other position."

In denying Europe the right to intervene, Seward insisted that he was defending the principle of civil government itself, for at stake was nothing less than the existence of the United States. "Any other principle than this," he said, "would be to resolve government everywhere into a thing of accident and caprice, and ultimately all human society into a state of perpetual war." American policy was dictated by the law of self-preservation, and no nation, he added, "animated by loyal sentiments and inspired by a generous ambition can ever suffer itself to debate with parties within or without a policy of self-preservation."

Seward, therefore, instructed Adams not to debate, hear, or receive any communication from the British government which sought to advise the United States in its relations with the Confederacy. This nation was fighting for empire, he admitted in October, 1862, but it was an empire lawfully acquired and lawfully held. "Studying to confine this unhappy struggle within our own borders," he wrote to Dayton, "we have not only invoked no foreign aid or sympathy, but we have warned foreign nations frankly and have besought them not to interfere. We have practised justice towards them in every way, and conciliation to an unusual degree. But we are none the less determined for all that to be sovereign and to be free."

Seward's reaction to the British Cabinet debate of November revealed both confidence and dismay. It was not pleasant for a loyal American, he admitted to Adams, to observe an English cabinet discuss the future of the American Republic. But the United States, he added, enjoyed the right and possessed the power to determine its own destiny; never before was it better prepared to meet danger from abroad. The wheel of political fortune continued to turn. England had once desired American friendship; she would do so again. "Neither politicians nor statesmen control events," the Secretary concluded. "They can moderate them and accommodate their ambitions to them, but they can do no more."

After November, 1862, all wartime diplomacy receded into insignificance. Whatever Southern hopes of European intervention still remained were shattered by the Confederate disasters at Gettysburg and Vicksburg in July, 1863. In September Mason informed Russell by note that his mission had been terminated. The British Secretary replied coldly: "I have on other occasions explained to you the reasons which have inclined her Majesty's Government to decline the overtures you alluded to. . . . These reasons are still in force, and it is not necessary to repeat them." Europe's final refusal to involve itself in the American struggle was nothing less than a total vindication of Seward's diplomacy. Whatever the North's diplomatic advantages, he had understood them and exploited them with astonishing effectiveness. He made it clear that any European nation which committed itself to the destruction of the American Union would pay dearly if it sought to fulfill that commitment.

In one sense there was nothing unique in the diplomatic issues raised by the American Civil War. Many nations in the past had undergone internal revolutions in which elements seeking power had sought either to overthrow the established government or to establish the independence of some portion of its territory. Such uprisings had succeeded and failed, but when major power was involved they had demonstrated invariably that other nations, whatever their moral and material interests, really could not intervene diplomatically without running the risk of military involvement.

Unfortunately Union diplomacy after 1861 placed this nation in the unprecedented and embarrassing position of appearing to defy its own democratic principle of self-determination. Americans in the past, Europe recalled, had not only made declarations in favor of the Greek and Hungarian revolutions and applauded such revolutionary leaders as Louis Kossuth, but they had furnished them money for the declared purpose of assuring new disorders. Now Americans were compelled to recognize what they had often denied Europe—that governments cannot exist without authority and that to maintain their authority, they must resort to force. Cassius Clay, to explain American purpose, once declared that the United States was fighting for nationality and liberty. To this the London *Times* recalled sarcastically that it was difficult to understand how "a people fighting . . . to force their fellow citizens to remain in a confederacy which they repudiated, can be called the champions of liberty and nationalism." The Confederates were fighting for their independence, observed the *Times*, adding, "But with the Northerners all is different. They are not content with their own. They are fighting to coerce others."

Europe might have recalled that idealism had never established the official diplomatic tradition of the United States toward revolution and oppression. Whatever the concern of individual Americans toward events abroad, the nation's dictum since Washington's presidency had been one of abstention. John Quincy Adams had given it classical form in his Marcellus letters of 1794: "It is our duty to remain, the peaceful and silent, though sorrowful spectators of the European scene." Again in July, 1821, Adams declared that "America is the well-wisher to the freedom and independence of all. She is the vindicator only of her own." All national leaders prior to the Civil War, when holding positions of responsibility, agreed that any foreign intervention in behalf of liberal causes might well commit the United States beyond its national interest. President James Munroe recognized this when he refused to render aid to the revolting states of Latin America. They would receive recognition, he informed them, when they had demonstrated sufficient strength to establish their own independence. Palmerston was merely reflecting this diplomatic tradition when he admitted in October, 1862, that Britain "must continue merely to be lookers-on till the war shall have taken a more decided turn."

Tangible British and French interests were involved in the Southern struggle for independence, and to that extent neither nation could ignore events across the Atlantic. But until the South could demonstrate, as did the Latin American republics, that it could overcome the power and purpose of the North, European recognition would have defied one of the most significant and thoroughly established traditions of modern diplomacy. Except for one fleeting period in 1862, neither Britain nor France revealed any serious intention of breaking from their own past and assuming commitments which would endanger their territorial and commercial interests in the New World. Had Europe given expression to its moral sentiment by supporting the cause of the seemingly oppressed, it would merely have magnified the horror and confusion. Of this Seward left no doubt. He warned Europe in May, 1862, that its involvement in the affairs of the United States would not serve the interests of humanity. "If Europe will still sympathize with the revolution," he wrote, "it must now look forward to the end; an end in which the war ceases with anarchy substituted for the social system that existed when the war began. What will then have become of the interests which carried Europe to the side which was at once the wrong side and the losing one? Only a perfect withdrawal of all favor from the insurrection can now save those interests in any degree. The insurrectionary states, left hopeless of foreign intervention, will be content to stop in their career of self-destruction, and to avail themselves of the moderating power of the Federal government. If the nations of Europe shall refuse to see this, and the war must therefore go on to the conclusion I have indicated, the responsibility for that conclusion will not rest with the government of the United States."

Seward here touched the central issue of Europe's relationship to the conflict in America. If after the summer of 1862 it was still within the power of the Old World to bring injury to the North, it was beyond its power to bring salvation to the South. There were no inexpensive means available to Europe to achieve the liberation of the South against the North's determination to hold it. Those Europeans who sought to cast from the South the yoke of alien rule might have been moved by the moral sentiment of Gladstone, but they had no influence on Palmerston. And since the realities of power are always the determining factors in international affairs, a Gladstone in office, whatever his sentimentalism and faith in moral pressure, could have influenced the internal affairs of the United States, wrapped in civil war, with no more success than the masters of *Realpolitik* who rejected such purpose as a matter of principle.

PART 6
POST-CIVIL WAR
EXPANSIONISM

INTRODUCTION

Sentiment favoring further American expansion did not expire with the Mexican War. However, the sectional controversy of the 1850's and the Civil War offered insurmountable obstacles to its effective continuation. Moreover, in the period immediately following the Civil War, problems of political reconstruction, the growth of a new industrial order, and the fact that after the Franco-Prussian War of 1870 Europe began another long period of relative quiescence, all tended to distract the national consciousness from questions of foreign policy. Nevertheless, a careful scrutiny of the period after the Civil War indicates that the spirit of expansionism remained very much alive in America and that industrialism, surely the most significant aspect of postwar American life, was perhaps in the process of changing its nature.

Secretary of State William H. Seward, who served from 1861 to 1869, distinguished himself not only as an able diplomat during the war but as the foremost prophet of American expansion in the years immediately following. A fit successor to his mentor and friend John Quincy Adams, he stands as a transitional figure in the history of American expansion, partially committed to the old idea of a continental empire reaching from Alaska to Mexico but thinking too of a broader economic empire in which domination of the markets of Asia was the ultimate goal (selection 1).

By the 1880's the phenomenal growth of industry in the United States dramatized the significance of Seward's vision. For many it made the expansion of foreign trade seem not simply economically important but socially imperative as well. The Panic of 1873 and the long depression that followed, these observers believed, were the results of overproduction and the accumulation of vast surpluses of manufactured goods in the United States. According to this view, the national market having been surfeited, there followed a reduction in demand, a falling off in productivity, and the concomitant growth of massive unemployment. This disastrous economic situation gave rise to radicalism and labor violence among the working classes and ultimately threatened revolution. The solution, so it seemed to some, was to eliminate the surplus by penetrating new foreign markets.

Many stumbling blocks were in the way of the fulfillment of this vision, not the least of which was traditional isolationism. Even among those who thought primarily in economic terms and were not impressed by isolationist ideas, there was little unity on the subject. A powerful sector of the business community was wedded to the principle of a high tariff designed to protect the American market against foreign competition. This policy invited retaliation and of course denied America easy access to many foreign markets.

During the administration of Chester A. Arthur, in the early 1880's, Secretary of State Frederick Frelinghuysen sought, without much success, to find a middle road between the demands for protection from foreign competition at home and the warning that America would have to adopt a free trade policy in order to compete for world trade. The policy of reciprocity, in itself no solution to the problems created by the expanding productive capacities of the American industrial machine, nevertheless does stand as solid evidence that by the early 1880's America's policy makers had identified the industrial surplus as a matter of fundamental social and economic importance and were attempting to deal with it. By the end of the decade, as America's productivity soared, the problem became more acute and many voices were raised urging a reconsideration of earlier economic foreign policy. Among the most important spokesmen was Captain Alfred Thayer Mahan. He argued that America's future literally depended on her ability to compete in the international struggle for control of foreign markets (selection 2).

At the end of the century, and as a direct result of the Spanish-American War, Seward's vision of a Pacific empire with access to the markets of Asia was brought to fruition. America became the major power in the Caribbean and extended a chain of naval bases all the way to the Philippines. The causes of the war and the reasons behind the McKinley administration's decision to acquire the Philippines are not easily explained, for although one may perceive in the history of American foreign policy after the Civil War a growing interest in trade expansion, it is not always easily demonstrated that this feeling was effectively translated into military and political action. Moreover, an economic interpretation of the war and of American imperialism must either ignore or find some way to incorporate intellectual, psychological, and political factors that have little to do with economics but do help to explain the events.

Historians have had broad differences of opinion about the causes of war and imperialism. Some have suggested that a key to understanding why America went to war against Spain is to be found in the fact that the 1890's was a decade of deep frustration in the United States. The Panic of 1893 and the depression that followed created doubt about the viability of the American economic system. The persistence of labor violence, the rise of the Populist Party, and the increasing popularity of alien economic and political philosophies emphasizing class struggle, all seemed to be warnings of the deterioration of the system. Too, the end of the frontier denied to the nation for the first time in its history the optimism born of the knowledge that virgin lands offered fresh opportunity. The safety valve had seemingly closed. The United States, it appeared, had run out of time and space simultaneously. In their frustration Americans looked outward, seeking to vent their hostilities or perhaps to prove their worth as a people in some militant way. Thus the decade was filled with international crises. The first was with Chile in 1892. This was followed by a dispute with Great Britain over the boundary between British Guiana and Venezuela. Finally American attentions fixed on Spain and her attempt to crush the latest in a long series of insurrections in Cuba. The agony of Cuba quickly became a major issue in the United States, and the McKinley administration, despite struggles to avoid a war to free Cuba, was driven to war by the power of public opinion (selection 3).

Other scholars cannot accept this view. They believe that the war with Spain and its result—the creation of American naval bases and coaling stations reaching all the way to the Philippines, as well as political and naval dominance in the sensitive Caribbean area—cannot have been chance happenings. According to some historians, the war and its fruits were products of a long-term program of economic imperialism. Thomas McCormick, for example, does not debate the question of whether the war was a part of the administration's grand scheme (selection 4). He does, however, take issue with the argument that imperialism was the result of psychological or intellectual factors, or even the pressure of public opinion. He suggests that the decision to take Hawaii, Guam, and particularly the Philippines was "part of an effort to construct a system of coaling, cable, and naval stations into an integrated trade route which could facilitate realization of America's one overriding ambition in the Pacific—the penetration and, ultimately, the domination of the fabled China market."

1

YEARS OF PREPARATION
WALTER LAFEBER

In the unfolding drama of the new empire William Henry Seward appears as the prince of players. Grant, Hamilton Fish, William M. Evarts, James G. Blaine, Frederick T. Frelinghuysen, and Thomas F. Bayard assume secondary roles. Although Seward left the stage in the first act of the drama, only a few of the other players could improve on his techniques, and none could approach his vision of American empire.

Henry Adams described Seward near the end of his career as "a slouching, slender figure; a head like a wise macaw; a beaked nose; shaggy eyebrows; unorderly hair and clothes; hoarse voice; offhand manner; free talk, and perpetual cigar." Seward nevertheless attracted an urbane, educated person like young Adams, for the Secretary of State, like Adams, was an intellectual in nearly every sense of the word. He won Phi Beta Kappa honors at Union College while still in his teens and for a short time taught school. His son later noted that Seward regularly read Chaucer, Spenser, Ben Jonson, Ariosto, Macaulay, Carlyle, Burke, Lieber, and Prescott's histories "as fast as they came out." He also knew the Latin classics but his favorite, appropriately enough, was the theorist of the British Empire, Francis Bacon. Seward also learned from John Quincy Adams. It was not coincidental that Seward's ideas of American empire so resembled those of Adams; after Adams' death, Seward eulogized, "I have lost a patron, a guide,

Reprinted from Walter LaFeber: *The New Empire: An Interpretation of American Expansion, 1860–1898*, pp. 25–32. © 1963 by the American Historical Association. Used by permission of Cornell University Press.

a counsellor, and a friend—one whom I loved scarcely less than the dearest relations, and venerated above all that was mortal among men."

He also understood more mundane things—such as the value of political parties for his own advancement. When once asked how to fight slavery he answered: "Organization! Organization! Nothing but organization." This served as the motto for most of his political operations. He was tabbed by many political observers as the Republican nominee for the White House in 1860. But paradoxically, he was cut off from the strongest segments of the Republican party during the 1865–1869 period, the years when he most actively worked for the advancement of the new empire.

Seward deserves to be remembered as the greatest Secretary of State in American history after his beloved Adams. This is so partially because of his astute diplomacy, which kept European powers out of the Civil War, but also because his vision of empire dominated American policy for the next century. He based this vision, as would be expected of an intellectual, on "a political law—and when I say political law, I mean a higher law, a law of Providence—that empire has, for the last three thousand years . . . made its way constantly westward, and that it must continue to move on westward until the tides of the renewed and of the decaying civilization of the world meet on the shores of the Pacific Ocean." In the same speech he noted, "Empire moves far more rapidly in modern than it did in ancient times." In this single pronouncement, noting the historic movement of empire westward across America and into the Pacific and Asia, Seward anticipated many (especially Brooks Adams) who would ring the changes on this theme in the 1890's; he emphasized that this imperial movement traveled at a much faster speed during an industrial age than it did in ancient times; and he reiterated the theme of imperial manifest destiny ordained by Providence for the American people.

Seward spent much of his life attempting to prepare the United States for its proper role in this westward flight of empire. It was his misfortune that he tried to unify and strengthen the nation for this role at the very time slavery made his task impossible. After the Civil War he renewed his quest. He always envisioned an empire which would not be acquired haphazardly, but would develop along carefully worked out lines. The best word to describe his concept of empire, perhaps, is integrated. The empire would begin with a strong, consolidated base of power on the American continent and move into the way stations of the Pacific as it approached the final goal of Asia. Each area would have its own functions to perform and become an integrated part of the whole empire.

Seward prophesied that the battle for world power would occur in Asia, since "commerce has brought the ancient continents near to us." But the victor in this battle would be the nation operating from the strongest economic and power base. Therefore he advised in 1853:

> Open up a highway through your country from New York to San Francisco. Put your domain under cultivation, and your ten thousand wheels of manufacture in motion. Multiply your ships, and send them forth to the East. The nation that draws most materials and provisions from the earth, and fabricates the most, and sells the most of productions and fabrics to foreign nations, must be, and will be the great power of the earth.

Seward offered concrete suggestions to realize this base of power. First, he advised the passing of a high tariff to protect small industries and attract foreign laborers. Once Europe was drained of her cheap labor, the ocean could be "reduced to a ferry" for American products. High tariffs would also allow effective planning and allocation of resources by the federal government and give the government money for internal improvements (an idea from John Quincy Adams' repertoire). Second, Seward wanted to offer the public lands quickly and at low prices. This would not only attract cheap labor, but would also provide adequate agricultural products; "commercial supremacy demands just such an agricultural basis" as American lands, when inhabited, could supply. Third, he hoped to obtain cheap labor, especially by enticing Asian workers. He accomplished this with the 1868 treaty between the United States and China, which gave Chinese laborers almost unrestricted entry into the country. Finally, he would tie the continent together with canals and one or more transcontinental railroads. Money was no object: "It is necessary; and since it is necessary, there is the end of the argument." Seward summed up these views with a favorite story of the barbarian looking at King Croesus' great hoard of gold and then remarking: "It is all very well; but whoever comes upon you with better iron than you have, will be master of all this gold." Seward would add: "We shall find it so in the end."

Latin America and Canada would inevitably become a part of this continental base. Seward declared that he wanted no American colonies in Latin America, but this did not mean he found no interest in the area. He feared that establishing colonies would result in either a standing army in the United States or anarchy in the colonies. Instead, he wanted to hold islands in the Caribbean which would serve as strategic bases to protect an Isthmian route to the Pacific and also prevent European powers from dabbling in the area of the North American coastline. But Central America would come into the Union eventually when "the ever-increasing expansion of the American people westward and southward" began. Soon Mexico would "be opening herself as cheerfully to American immigration as Montana and Idaho are now." Then Mexico would not be a colony, but a state, fulfilling Seward's prophecy that Mexico City was an excellent site for the future capital of the American empire. Canada would also eventually be a part of the continental base. In an 1860 speech Seward noted that "an ingenious, enterprising, and ambitious people" are building Canada, "and I am able to say, 'It is very well, you are building excellent states to be hereafter admitted into the American Union.' "

In the same speech he made a similar comment about Alaska. Seward realized this particular dream when he negotiated its purchase in 1867. The United States bought "Seward's Icebox" for several good reasons, including traditional American friendship for Russia, the hope that the deal would sandwich British Columbia between American territory and make inevitable its annexation, and the belief that Alaskan resources would more than pay the $7,200,000 price tag. But given Seward's view of empire, perhaps his son, a distinguished diplomat in his own right, later offered the best reason: "To the United States, it would give a foothold for commercial and naval operations accessible from the Pacific States." Nathaniel P. Banks, Chairman of the House Foreign Affairs Committee in 1867 and a strong supporter of Seward's imperial ideas, called the Aleutians the "drawbridge between America and Asia."

Seward approached the Asian market cautiously and methodically. Alaska protected one flank. An American-controlled canal would provide a southern corridor. In the center would be California and Hawaii. California, Seward exulted:

> California that comes from the clime where the west dies away into the rising east; California, that bounds at once the empire and the continent; California, the youthful queen of the Pacific. . . . The world

contains no seat of empire so magnificent as this. . . . The nation thus situated . . . must command the empire of the seas, which alone is real empire.

Hawaii offered the next step west. Here Seward promoted the American representative to Minister Resident in 1863 and four years later tried to prepare the islands for the hug of annexation by pulling Hawaii into a reciprocity treaty. The Senate was too busy with Reconstruction to deal with Seward's proposal, but he nevertheless told the American Minister in September, 1867, that annexation was still "deemed desirable by this government." He was immediately successful in placing the Stars and Stripes above the Midway islands in 1867. These islands, 1,200 miles west of Hawaii, became an important outpost for America's Pacific interests.

And beyond lay the bottomless markets of Asia, "the prize" for which Europe and the United States contended, "the chief theatre of events in the world's great hereafter." Here lay the crucial area if the United States hoped to control "the commerce of the world, which is the empire of the world." Here too the United States moving westward would meet another great nation moving eastward. "Russia and the United States," the new Secretary of State wrote to the American Minister to Russia in May, 1861, "may remain good friends until, each having made a circuit of half the globe in opposite directions, they shall meet and greet each other in the region where civilization first began." Seward had few illusions about the implications of his expansionist policy.

America's success in Asia depended upon the success of its open-door policy, which advocated equal commercial rights for all nations and no territorial aggrandizement by any. Seward cooperated with European powers in order to protect this American policy. The open-door concept was nothing new, dating back to the most-favored-nation clauses in the first American-Chinese treaty in 1844. What was new was Seward's vigorous moves to protect the policy. He could deal gently with China; the Burlingame Treaty of 1868 provided for the preservation of American rights of travel and residence in China as well as freer entry into the United States for Chinese laborers. But the Secretary of State was tough with Japan. When that nation proved reluctant to correct what Seward considered to be infringements upon American rights, he ordered naval units to participate in a show of strength that climaxed with the powers dictating to Japan from a British gunboat. He was equally vigorous in Korea. At one point he proposed to the French that they cooperate with the United States to force open the Hermit Kingdom to outside interests. When the French refused this offer, Seward sent his nephew, George F. Seward, to sign a trade treaty with Korea, but this attempt also failed. Fifteen years later, however, Korea grudgingly opened its doors to American traders and missionaries.

Henry Adams summed it up: "The policy of Mr. Seward was based upon this fixed idea [of expansion], which, under his active direction, assumed a development, that even went somewhat too far and too fast for the public." Seward's Caribbean plans, especially the purchase of the Danish West Indies and Santo Domingo, came to nothing. Nor did he bring Hawaii into the American orbit when he wanted. But he did outline in some detail his ideas of an integrated empire with a great continental base which would produce vast quantities of goods for hundreds of millions of consumers in Asia. He did see the completion of the transcontinental railroad, industries supported by tariffs and internal improvements, and the acquisition of Alaska and Midway as way stations to the Asian market. He accomplished much of his work, moreover, despite the Civil War and a strong antiexpansionist feeling in the late 1860's.

The antiexpansionists effectively used several arguments to thwart Seward's ambitions. . . . They claimed that the United States suffered from a land glut already; no more land could properly be developed. If the Union acquired more territory, it might be Latin-American, and this would aggravate the race problem. Others argued that the United States should avoid a colonial policy, especially at a time when England was trying to dispose of her own unprofitable outlying areas. Finally, some antiexpansionists urged financial retrenchment in order to start American industries and farms booming again rather than paying fancy price tags for noncontiguous territory. The most notable characteristic of these arguments is not that they were effective in the late 1860's, but that they melted away in large measure after the 1870's, as the frontier closed, an open-door commercial policy eliminated colonial problems, and American factories and farms boomed so successfully that the resulting glut of goods threatened to inundate the economy. With these changes, Seward's successors were able to complete much of what he had been unable to finish.

2

THE UNITED STATES
LOOKING OUTWARD
ALFRED THAYER MAHAN

Indications are not wanting of an approaching change in the thoughts and policy of Americans as to their relations with the world outside their own borders. For the past quarter of a century, the predominant idea, which has successfully asserted itself at the polls and shaped the course of the government, has been to preserve the home market for the home industries. The employer and the workman have alike been taught to look at the various economical measures proposed from this point of view, to regard with hostility any step favoring the intrusion of the foreign producer upon their own domain, and rather to demand increasingly rigorous measures of exclusion than to acquiesce in any loosening of the chain that binds the consumer to them. The inevitable consequence has followed, as in all cases when the mind or the eye is exclusively fixed in one direction, that the danger of loss or the prospect of advantage in another quarter has been overlooked; and although the abounding resources of the country have maintained the exports at a high figure, this flattering result has been due more to the super-abundant bounty of Nature than to the demand of other nations for our protected manufactures.

For nearly the lifetime of a generation, therefore, American industries have been thus protected, until the practice has assumed the force of a tradition, and is clothed in the mail of conservatism. In their mutual relations, these industries resemble the activities of a modern ironclad that has heavy armor, but an inferior engine and no guns;

From Alfred T. Mahan, "The United States Looking Outward," *Atlantic Monthly*, LXVI (December 1890), pp. 816–24.

mighty for defense, weak for offense. Within, the home market is secured; but outside, beyond the broad seas, there are the markets of the world, that can be entered and controlled only by a vigorous contest, to which the habit of trusting to protection by statute does not conduce.

At bottom, however, the temperament of the American people is essentially alien to such a sluggish attitude. Independently of all bias for or against protection, it is safe to predict that, when the opportunities for gain abroad are understood, the course of American enterprise will cleave a channel by which to reach them. Viewed broadly, it is a most welcome as well as significant fact that a prominent and influential advocate of protection, a leader of the party committed to its support, a keen reader of the signs of the times and of the drift of opinion, has identified himself with a line of policy which looks to nothing less than such modifications of the tariff as may expand the commerce of the United States to all quarters of the globe. Men of all parties can unite on the words of Mr. Blaine, as reported in a recent speech: "It is not an ambitious destiny for so great a country as ours to manufacture only what we can consume, or produce only what we can eat." In face of this utterance of so shrewd and able a public man, even the extreme character of the recent tariff legislation seems but a sign of the coming change, and brings to mind that famous Continental System, of which our own is the analogue, to support which Napoleon added legion to legion and enterprise to enterprise, till the fabric of the Empire itself crashed beneath the weight.

The interesting and significant feature of this changing attitude is the turning of the eyes outward, instead of inward only, to seek the welfare of the country. To affirm the importance of distant markets, and the relation to them of our own immense powers of production, implies logically the recognition of the link that joins the products and the markets,—that is, the carrying trade; the three together constituting that chain of maritime power to which Great Britain owes her wealth and greatness. Further, it is too much to say that, as two of these links, the shipping and the markets, are exterior to our own borders, the acknowledgement of them carries with it a view of the relations of the United States to the world radically distinct from the simple idea of self-sufficingness? We shall not follow far this line of thought before there will dawn the realization of America's unique position, facing the older worlds of the East and West, her shores lapped by the oceans which touch the one or the other, but which are common to her alone.

Coincident with these signs of change in our own policy there is a restlessness in the world at large which is deeply significant, if not ominous. It is beside our purpose to dwell upon the internal state of Europe, whence, if disturbances arise, the effect upon us may be but partial and indirect. But the great seaboard powers there do not only stand on guard against their continental rivals; they cherish also aspirations for commercial extension, for colonies, and for influence in distant regions, which may bring, and even under our present contracted policy, have already brought them into collision with ourselves. The affair of the Samoa Islands, trivial apparently, was nevertheless eminently suggestive of European ambitions. America then roused from sleep as to interests closely concerning her future. At this moment internal troubles are imminent in the Sandwich Islands, where it should be our fixed determination to allow no foreign influence to equal our own. All over the world German commercial and colonial push is coming into collision with other nations: witness the affair of the Caroline Islands with Spain; the partition of New Guinea with England; the yet more recent negotiation between these two powers concerning their share in Africa, viewed with deep distrust and jealousy by France; the Samoa affair; the conflict between German control and American interests in the islands of the western Pacific; and the alleged progress of German influence in Central and South America. It is noteworthy that, while these various contentions are sustained with the aggressive military spirit characteristic of the German Empire, they are credibly said to arise from the national temper more than from the deliberate policy of the government, which in this matter does not lead, but follows, the feeling of the people, a condition much more formidable.

There is no sound reason for believing that the world has passed into a period of assured peace outside the limits of Europe. Unsettled political conditions, such as exist in Hayti, Central America, and many of the Pacific islands, especially the Hawaiian group, when combined with great military or commercial importance, as is the case with most of these positions, involve, now as always, dangerous germs of quarrel, against which it is at least prudent to be prepared. Undoubtedly, the general temper of nations is more averse from war than it was of old. If no less selfish and grasping than our predecessors, we feel more dislike to the discomforts and sufferings attendant upon a breach of peace; but to retain that highly valued repose and the undisturbed enjoyment of the returns of commerce, it is necessary to argue upon somewhat equal terms of strength with an adversary. It is the preparedness of the enemy, and not acquiescence in the existing state of things, that now holds back the armies of Europe.

On the other hand, neither the sanctions of international law nor the justice of a cause can be depended upon for a fair settlement of differences, when they come into conflict with a strong political necessity on the one side opposed to comparative weakness on the other. In our still-pending dispute over the seal-fishing of Bering Sea, whatever may be thought of the strength of our argument, in view of generally admitted principles of international law, it is beyond doubt that our contention is reasonable, just, and in the interest of the world generally. But in the attempt to enforce it we have come into collision not only with national susceptibilities as to the honor of the flag, which we ourselves very strongly share, but also with a state governed by a powerful necessity, and exceedingly strong where we are particularly weak and exposed. Not only has Great Britain a mighty navy and we a long, defenseless seacoast, but it is a great commercial and political advantage to her that her larger colonies, and above all Canada, should feel that the power of the mother country is something which they need, and upon which they can count. The dispute is between the United States and Canada, not the United States and England; but it has been ably used by the latter to promote the solidarity of sympathy between herself and her colony. With the mother country alone an equitable arrangement, conducive to well-understood mutual interests, could readily be reached; but the purely local and peculiarly selfish wishes of Canadian fishermen dictate the policy of Great Britain, because Canada is the most important link uniting her to her colonies and maritime interests in the Pacific. In case of a European war, it is probable that the British navy will not be able to hold open the route through the Mediterranean to the East; but having a strong naval station at Halifax, and another at Esquimalt, on the Pacific, the two connected by the Canadian Pacific Railroad, England possesses an alternate line of communication far less exposed to maritime aggression than the former, or than the third route by the Cape of Good Hope, as well as two bases essential to the service of her commerce, or other naval operations, in the North Atlantic and the Pacific. Whatever arrangement of this question is finally reached, the fruit of Lord Salisbury's attitude can hardly fail to be a strengthening of the sentiments of attachment to, and reliance upon, the mother country, not only in Canada, but in the other great colonies. Such feelings of attachment and mutual dependence supply the living spirit, without which the nascent schemes for Imperial Federation are but dead mechanical contrivances; nor are they without influence upon such generally unsentimental considerations as those of buying and selling, and the course of trade.

This dispute, seemingly paltry, yet really serious, sudden in its appearance, and dependent for its issue upon other considerations than its own merits, may serve to convince us of many latent and yet unforseen dangers to the peace of the western hemisphere, attendant upon the opening of a canal through the Central American Isthmus. In a general way, it is evident enough that this canal, by modifying the direction of trade routes, will induce a great increase of commercial activity and carrying trade throughout the Caribbean Sea; and that this now comparatively deserted nook of the ocean will, like the Red Sea, become a great thoroughfare of shipping, and attract, as never before in our day, the interest and ambition of maritime nations. Every position in that sea will have enhanced commercial and military value, and the canal itself will become a strategic centre of the most vital importance. Like the Canadian Pacific Railroad, it will be a link between the two oceans; but, unlike it, the use, unless most carefully guarded by treaties, will belong wholly to the belligerent which controls the sea by its naval power. In case of war, the United States will unquestionably command the Canadian Railroad, despite the deterrent force of operations by the hostile navy upon our seaboard; but no less unquestionably will she be impotent, as against any of the great maritime powers, to control the Central American canal. Militarily speaking, the piercing of the Isthmus is nothing but a disaster to the United States, in the present state of her military and naval preparation. It is especially dangerous to the Pacific coast; but the increased exposure of one part of our seaboard reacts unfavorably upon the whole military situation. Despite a certain great original superiority conferred by our geographical nearness and immense resources,—due, in other words, to our natural advantages, and not to our intelligent preparations,— the United States is woefully unready, not only in fact, but in purpose, to assert in the Caribbean and Central America a weight of influence proportioned to the extent of her interests. We have not the navy, and, what is worse, we are not willing to have the navy, that will weigh seriously in any disputes with those nations whose interests will there conflict with our own. We have not, and we are not anxious to provide, the defense of the seaboard which will leave the navy free for its work at sea. We have not, but many other powers have, positions, either within or on the borders of the Caribbean, which not only possess great natural advantages for the control of that sea, but have received and are receiving that artificial strength of fortification and armament which will make them practically inexpugnable. On the contrary, we have not on the Gulf of Mexico even the beginning of a navy yard which could serve as the base of our operations. Let me not be misunderstood. I am not regretting that we have not the means to meet on terms of equality the great navies of the Old World. I recognize, what few at least say, that, despite its great surplus revenue, this country is poor in proportion to its length of seaboard and its exposed points. That which I deplore, and which is a sober, just, and reasonable cause of deep national concern, is that the nation neither has nor cares to have its sea frontier so defended, and its navy of such power, as shall suffice, with the advantage of our position, to weigh seriously when inevitable discussions arise,—such as we have recently had about Samoa and Bering Sea, and which may at any moment come up about the Caribbean Sea or the canal. Is the United States, for instance, prepared to allow Germany to acquire the Dutch stronghold of Curaçao, fronting the Atlantic outlet of both the proposed canals of Panama and Nicaragua? Is she prepared to acquiesce in any foreign power purchasing from Hayti a naval station on the Windward Passage, through which pass our steamer routes to the Isthmus? Would she acquiesce in a foreign protectorate over the Sandwich Islands, that great central station of the Pacific, equidistant from San Francisco, Samoa, and the Marquesas, and an important post on our lines of communication with both Australia and China? Or will it be maintained that any one of these questions, supposing it to arise, is so exclusively one-sided, the arguments of policy and right so exclusively with us, that the other party will at once yield his eager wish, and gracefully withdraw? Was it so at Samoa? Is it so as regards Bering Sea? The motto seen on so many ancient cannon, Ultima ratio regum, is not without its message to republics.

It is perfectly reasonable and legitimate, in estimating our needs of military preparation, to take into account the remoteness of the chief naval and military nations from our shores, and the consequent difficulty of maintaining operations at such a distance. It is equally proper, in framing our policy, to consider the jealousies of the European family of states, and their consequent unwillingness to incur the enmity of a people so strong as ourselves; their dread of our revenge in the future, as well as their inability to detach more than a certain part of their forces to our shores without losing much of their own weight in the councils of Europe. In truth, a careful determination of the force that Great Britain or France could probably spare for operations against our coasts, if the latter were suitably defended, without weakening their European position or unduly exposing their colonies and commerce, is the starting-point from which to calculate the strength of our own navy. If the latter be superior to the force that can thus be sent against it, and the coast be so defended as to leave the navy free to strike where it will, we can maintain our rights; not merely the rights which international law concedes, and which the moral sense of nations now supports, but also those equally real rights which, though not conferred by law, depend upon a clear preponderance of interest, upon obviously necessary policy, upon self-preservation, either total or partial. Were we now so situated in respect of military strength, we could secure our perfectly just claim as to the seal fisheries; not by seizing foreign ships on the open sea, but by the evident fact that, our cities being protected from maritime attack, our position and superior population lay open the Canadian Pacific, as well as the frontier of the Dominion, to do with as we please. Diplomats do not flourish such disagreeable truths in each other's faces; they look for a *modus vivendi*, and find it.

While, therefore, the advantages of our own position in the western hemisphere, and the disadvantages under which the operations of a European state would labor, are undeniable and just elements in the calculations of the statesman, it is folly to look upon them as sufficient for our security. Much more needs to be cast into the scale that it may incline in favor of our strength. They are mere defensive factors, and partial at that. Though distant, our shores can be reached; being defenseless, they can detain but a short time a force sent against them. With a probability of three months' peace in Europe, no maritime power would now fear to support its demands by a number of ships with which it would be loath indeed to part for a year.

Yet, were our sea frontier as strong as it now is weak, passive self-defense, whether in trade or war, would be but a poor policy, so long as this world continues to be one of struggle and vicissitude. All around us now is strife; "the struggle of life," "the race of life," are phrases so familiar that we do not feel their significance till we stop to think about them. Everywhere nation is arrayed against nation; our own no less than others. What is our protective system but an organized warfare? In carrying it on, it is true, we have only to use certain procedures which all states now concede to be a legal exercise of the national power, even though injurious to themselves. It is lawful, they say, to do what we will with our own. Are our people, however, so unaggressive that they are likely not to want their own way in matters where their interests turn on points of disputed right, or so little sensitive as to submit quietly to encroachment by others, in quarters where they have long considered their own influence should prevail?

Our self-imposed isolation in the matter of markets, and the decline of our shipping interest in the last thirty years, have coincided singularly with an actual remoteness of this continent from the life of the rest of the world. The writer has before him a map of the North and South Atlantic oceans, showing the direction of the principal trade routes and the proportion of tonnage passing over each; and it is curious to note what deserted regions, comparatively, are the Gulf of Mexico, the Caribbean Sea, and the adjoining countries and islands. A broad band stretches from our northern Atlantic coast to the English Channel; another as broad from the British Islands to the East, through the Mediterranean and Red Sea, overflowing the borders of the latter in order to express the volume of trade. Around either cape —Good Hope and Horn—pass strips of about one fourth this width, joining near the equator, midway between Africa and South America. From the West Indies issues a thread indicating the present commerce of Great Britain with a region which once, in the Napoleonic wars, embraced one fourth of the whole trade of the Empire. The significance is unmistakable: Europe has now little interest in the Caribbean Sea.

When the Isthmus is pierced this isolation will pass away, and with it the indifference of foreign nations. From wheresoever they come and whithersoever they afterward go, all ships that use the canal will pass through the Caribbean. Whatever the effect produced upon the prosperity of the adjacent continent and islands by the thousand wants attendant upon maritime activity, around such a focus of trade will centre large commercial and political interests. To protect and develop its own, each nation will seek points of support and means of influence in a quarter where the United States has always been jealously sensitive to the intrusion of European powers. The precise value of the Monroe doctrine is very loosely understood by most Americans, but the effect of the familiar phrase has been to develop a national sensitiveness, which is a more frequent cause of war than material interests; and over disputes caused by such felings there will preside none of the calming influence due to the moral authority of international law, with its recognized principles, for the points in dispute will be of policy, of interest, not of conceded right. Already France and England are giving to ports held by them a degree of artificial strength uncalled for by their present importance. They look to the near future. Among the islands and on the mainland there are many positions of great importance, held now by weak or unstable states. Is the United States willing to see them sold to a powerful rival? But what right will she invoke against the transfer? She can allege but one,—that of her reasonable policy supported by her might.

Whether they will or no, Americans must now begin to look outward. The growing production of the country demands it. An increasing volume of public sentiment demands it. The position of the United States, between the two Old Worlds and the two great oceans, makes the same claim, which will soon be strengthened by the creation of the new link joining the Atlantic and Pacific. The tendency will be maintained and increased by the growth of the European colonies in the Pacific, by the advancing civilization of Japan, and by the rapid peopling of our Pacific States with men who have all the aggressive spirit of the advanced line of national progress. Nowhere does a vigorous foreign policy find more favor than among the people west of the Rocky Mountains.

It has been said that, in our present state of unpreparedness, a trans-isthmian canal will be a military disaster to the United States, and especially to the Pacific coast. When the canal is finished the Atlantic seaboard will be neither more nor less exposed than it now is; it will merely share with the country at large the increased danger of foreign complications with inadequate means to meet them. The danger of the Pacific coast will be greater by so much as the way between it and Europe is shortened through a passage which the stronger maritime power can control. The danger lies not merely in the greater facility for dispatching a hostile squadron from Europe, but also in the fact that a more powerful fleet than formerly can be maintained on that coast by a European power, because it can be so much more promptly called home in case of need. The greatest weakness of the Pacific ports, however, if wisely met by our government, will go far to insure our naval superiority there. The two chief centres, San Francisco and Puget Sound, owing to the width and the great depth of the entrances, cannot be effectively protected by torpedoes; and consequently, as fleets can always pass batteries through an unobstructed channel, they cannot obtain perfect security by means of fortifications only. Valuable as such works will be to them, they must be further garrisoned by coast-defense ships, whose part in repelling an enemy will be coördinated with that of the batteries. The sphere of action of such ships should not be permitted to extend far beyond the port to which they are allotted, and of whose defense they form an essential part; but within that sweep they will always be a powerful reinforcement to the sea-going navy, when the strategic conditions of a war cause hostilities to centre around their port. By sacrificing power to go long distances, the coast-defense ships gains proportionate weight of armor and guns; that is, of defensive and offensive strength. It therefore adds an element of unique value to the fleet with which it for a time acts. No foreign states, except Great Britain, have ports so near our Pacific coast as to bring it within the radius of action of their coast-defense ships; and it is very doubtful whether even Great Britain will put such ships at Vancouver Island, the chief value of which will be lost to her when the Canadian Pacific is severed,—a blow always in the power of this country. It is upon our Atlantic seaboard that the mistress of Halifax, of Bermuda, and of Jamaica will now defend Vancouver and the Canadian Pacific. In the present state of our seaboard defense she can do so absolutely. What is all Canada compared with our exposed great cities? Even were the coast fortified, she could still do so, if our navy be no stronger than is as yet designed. What harm can we do Canada proportionate to the injury we should suffer by the interruption of our coasting trade, and by a blockade of Boston, New York, the Delaware, and the Chesapeake? Such a blockade Great Britain certainly could make technically efficient, under the somewhat loose definitions of internatioanl law. Neutrals would accept it as such.

The military needs of the Pacific States, as well as their supreme importance to the whole country, are yet a matter of the future, but of a future so near that provision should immediately begin. To weigh their importance, consider what influence in the Pacific would be attributed to a nation comprising only the States of Washington, Oregon, and California, when filled with such men as now people them and are still pouring in, and controlling such maritime centres as San Francisco, Puget Sound, and the Columbia River. Can it be counted less because they are bound by the ties of blood and close political union to the great communities of the East? But such influence, to work without jar and friction, requires underlying military readiness, like the proverbial iron hand under the velvet glove. To provide this, three things are needful: First, protection of the chief harbors by fortifications and coast-defense ships, which gives defensive strength, provides security to the community within, and supplies the bases necessary to all military operations. Secondly, naval force, the arm of offensive power, which alone enables a country to extend its influence outward. Thirdly, it should be an inviolable resolution of our national policy that no European state should henceforth acquire a coaling position within three thousand miles of San Francisco,—a distance which includes the Sandwich and Galapagos islands and the coast of Central America. For fuel is the life of modern naval war; it is the food of the ship; without it the modern monsters of the deep die of inanition. Around it, therefore, cluster some of the most important considerations of naval strategy. In the Caribbean and the Atlantic we are confronted with many a foreign coal depot, and perhaps it is not an unmitigated misfortune that we, like Rome, find Carthage at our gates bidding us stand to our arms; but let us not acquiesce in an addition to our dangers, a further diversion of our strength, by being forestalled in the North Pacific.

In conclusion, while Great Britain is undoubtedly the most formidable of our possible enemies, both by her great navy and the strong positions she holds near our coasts, it must be added that a cordial understanding with that country is one of the first of our external interests. Both nations, doubtless, and properly, seek their own advantage; but both, also, are controlled by a sense of law and justice drawn from the same sources, and deep-rooted in their instincts. Whatever temporary abberation may occur, a return to mutual standards of right will certainly follow. Formal alliance between the two is out of the question, but a cordial recognition of the similarity of character and ideas will give birth to sympathy, which in turn will facilitate a coöperation beneficial to both; for, if sentimentality is weak, sentiment is strong.

3

HYSTERIA

ERNEST R. MAY

Early in 1897, when Spain's first reforms began taking effect in Cuba, public indignation in the United States seemed to cool. Democrats in Congress, it is true, continued to talk about Cuba even after McKinley succeeded in appeasing Republican jingoes. When Morgan demanded a vote on a joint resolution acknowledging Cuban belligerency, insisting that "the mind of the people of the United States is agitated and all their hearts are full of this subject," only nineteen senators held out for rereferral to committee, even though passage was plainly not desired by the administration, and only fourteen refused to approve the resolution itself. The forty-five senators who voted "aye" foresaw that Speaker Reed would prevent action by the House; still they testified by their votes that they believed the public eager for some kind of action.

Rank and file politicians certainly took this view. The National Association of Democratic Clubs, meeting in Washington in July, 1897, resolved: "The day should be hastened by all proper means which shall see the lone star of Cuba fixed forever in the constellation of American States, and we demand the immediate recognition of the belligerent rights of the Cuban people." The National League of Republican Clubs merely replied that the President could "be relied upon to interpose his good offices to end . . . [the] struggle with the greatest promptitude consistent with wise administration." Kentucky Republicans wrote a demand for intervention into their platform. Iowa Re-

---

From *Imperial Democracy* by Ernest R. May, pp. 133–147. Copyright 1961 by Ernest R. May. Reprinted by permission of Harcourt Brace Jovanovich, Inc.

publicans almost did so. When Congress came into session in December, Democrats were reported as planning to press the Cuban issue. Many in the President's own party refused to say whether or not they would vote for a recognition resolution against opposition from the White House.

On the whole, however, these senators and representatives seemed to be still under the influence of the Maceo incident and the excitement of the preceding winter. Though circulation-hungry New York dailies played up lurid events and other papers copied their stories, there had been only one eruption of public feeling on the Cuban issue since the inauguration of McKinley. The case of Evangelina Cisneros, a Cuban girl allegedly jailed for defending her honor against a Spanish officer, produced a petition signed by over a million women. But this petition had been circulated by and in Hearst newspapers, and the agitation died down as soon as a Hearst reporter aided the girl to escape.

When the session of 1897–1898 opened and McKinley asked the Congress to give him more time, his strong but vague message promised action if Cuba were not pacified in the near future. Administration spokesmen claimed that Spain's autonomy decree and the removal of Weyler were fruits of McKinley's diplomacy. A poll by the New York *Herald* showed majorities in both the Senate and the House privately opposed to any Congressional action, though Senator John H. Mitchell of Oregon, like other administration supporters, predicted that a recognition resolution would be forced through both Houses. Nothing of the sort happened.

Congressmen found to their astonishment that they were not pressed as they had been in the previous session. Only a few memorials and petitions came in. Morgan told a Junta representative that he and Lodge thought it desirable to fight for Hawaiian annexation before renewing a campaign for intervention in Cuba. Others tried to reassure the Junta that McKinley meant to do something more in the near future. This procrastination may have been in some cases reaction to a suit filed in Illinois by a printer who claimed that the Junta had never paid him $3,500 due for manufacturing bonds. At least two senators, Mason of Illinois and Hernando DeSoto Money of Mississippi, had been given some of these bonds. But this would only explain why they failed to raise the issue on their own initiative. The more important fact was that the public did not appear to be clamoring for action as it had a year earlier.

Congress's inaction did not cause McKinley to become unwary. From time to time the White House issued announcements calculated to keep jingoes at bay. At the opening of the session, for example, it was made known that the North Atlantic squadron, the main force of the navy, would winter off Key West, as near as possible to Cuba. Both the Spanish government and American conservatives were told that the move was merely routine preparation for spring maneuvers. Jingo newspapers, however, interpreted it as preparation for the "further and other action" of which McKinley had spoken in his annual message.

The President took precautions lest congressmen return from the Christmas recess fired up to gratify bellicose constituents. The New York *Herald* reported the White House increasingly concerned about suffering among Cubans in reconcentration camps. If deaths from sickness and starvation did not lessen, said the *Herald*, the President might well feel that conditions had reached the breaking point he had forecast. On Christmas Eve the State Department issued an appeal in the name of the President for private contributions to help relieve the suffering, and it was noised about that the President himself contributed the first five thousand dollars. Moreover, by arrangements pressed on the Spanish legation, the money, food, and medicine were to be sent in naval vessels. The announcement of this departure from precedent, more than the relief appeal itself, was sure to warm and quieten the jingoes.

Almost immediately, events required the President to do more. On January 12, 1898, riots broke out in Havana. Led by soldiers still loyal to Weyler, the demonstrations were really directed against three newspapers that had criticized the departed general, and violence subsided as soon as their presses had been smashed. To Consul General Lee and American reporters, however, the commotion had seemed at first the beginning of anarchy in the city. The President evidently paled at a nightmare vision of Americans being shot, hanged, and butchered while Congress was in session, for the State Department signaled Lee that if communications were interrupted the fleet would move. Subsequent dispatches showed the riots to be over and Americans in no danger, but the Spanish minister was informed that a fresh outbreak might oblige the President not only to send ships but also to land troops.

The riots, brief and harmless though they had been, revived the danger of Congress's taking up the Cuban issue. As it happened, diplomatic and consular appropriations were being considered by the House at the time. Not even the best efforts of Speaker Reed prevented Democrats from dragging Cuba into the debate. At least one Republican, William Alden Smith of Michigan, went to the Speaker and eventually to the White House to say that he could not afford to remain silent much longer; the pressure from his constituents was too great. Despite the relative quiet in the Senate, conservative leaders confessed that they were only half-sure of their ability to keep the Senate in line behind the President.

Chairman Hitt of the House Foreign Affairs Committee, who was widely regarded as an administration spokesman, finally rose in the House to declare that since the Democrats insisted on talking about Cuba, it was well that the subject be discussed openly and candidly. He went on,

> We have seen in the time that the President has been in charge what he has tried to do and how much he has accomplished. Can we not trust him? We know that spirit that animates the captain of the ship. Events that have recently transpired at Havana and are impending warn us how grave is his responsibility . . . and . . . indicate how near we may be to a critical hour. What will be done? The President, while he does not favor the recognition of belligerency as a specific cure or as advisable, has intimated where the line of duty will take him, acting not by halves, but facing the whole question.

He quoted McKinley's comments on possible armed intervention, and concluded, "We should all of us be ready to do our duty like patriotic Americans, standing firmly behind the President when he takes a step necessary for the vindication of the honor and protection of the interests of our country."

An unnamed high official denied that Hitt had spoken for the President, and even such a practiced observer as the American correspondent of the London *Times* remained unsure whether the speech had been inspired. But the possibility that Hitt's words were McKinley's was enough to force the Democrats temporarily to lay aside the Cuban issue.

Before they could rally, the President had taken the further step of posting the *Maine* to Havana. The question of stationing a warship there had been discussed ever since the outbreak of the rebellion.

Cleveland and his Secretary of the Navy had refused appeals from Lee on the ground that there was too much risk of an inflammatory incident. The McKinley administration, bent on keeping Congress cool, could not be so indifferent to Lee's warnings of possible danger to American residents.

Lee was advised in June, 1897, that a naval vessel would be sent if he ever thought its presence imperative. As soon as he began telling of possible Weyler-ite uprisings, the Department of State arranged with the navy for the *Maine* to go to Key West. Following the Havana riots the State Department directed Lee to send out some message every day. If a day passed without one, the *Maine* was to sail.

This arrangement had obvious disadvantages, since Spaniards were apt to feel affronted if the ship suddenly turned up after a new riot. Even the cautious, pacific Secretary of the Navy concluded that it would be safer on all counts simply to station the ship at Havana, and on January 24 Day asked the Spanish minister blandly if, in view of the improvement in Spanish-American relations, the *Maine* could not pay a courtesy call at Havana. The President knew that dispatch of the ship would arouse little criticism, for even the New York *Evening Post* and the New York *Staatszeitung* had said editorially that the Havana riots might signal the failure of autonomy and hence make necessary some new gestures by the administration. He could take comfort principally from the fact that the *Maine's* dispatch would help to calm the zealots.

Hardly had the ship reached Havana, however, before a sensational news story broke at home. A New York newspaper published a private letter written by the Spanish minister, Dupuy de Lôme. In it the minister described the President, according to the official translation, as "weak and a bidder for the admiration of the crowd, besides being a would-be politician (*politicastro*) who tries to leave a door open behind himself while keeping on good terms with the jingoes of his party." The minister admitted to the letter, and the administration had no choice but to demand his recall. The Spanish government meanwhile hurriedly accepted de Lôme's resignation and the State Department was left to plead with Madrid for some apology that it could exhibit to Congress and the press. A few grudging words of regret sufficed, and the administration declared the episode closed.

The de Lôme incident marked the point at which time began to run out. In the week following publication of the letter there was every indication that Congress and the country verged on new demonstrations like those that had followed Maceo's death. Three recognition resolutions appeared in the Senate. One came from Allen, a Kansas Populist, one from Frank J. Cannon, a Utah Silver Republican, the third from Mason of Illinois, who, as an orthodox Republican, had usually been found on the administration's side. In support of his resolution, Mason made as fiery a speech as any other, damning unpatriotic Wall Street speculators who would not let the nation do its duty to humanity.

In Mason's home state. Governor John R. Tanner issued an official proclamation, asking contributions for Cuban relief but declaring that the real remedy was not charity but recognition. The New York state assembly passed a recognition resolution despite opposition from all Republican leaders in the body. Lodge wrote Henry White even before the de Lôme letter, "feeling in this country is steadily rising in favor of active intervention." Three days after de Lôme's letter had been published, a worried Bostonian wrote the Secretary of the Navy: "The jingo members of Congress and vile unscrupulous, jingo, yellow journals have so wrought up and stirred popular feeling that we seem to be slanting on the verge of a war with Spain with all its terrible consequences." One newspaper with supposed inside sources of information reported on February 13 that a delegation of Republican congressmen had visited McKinley to demand that he force a crisis with Spain.

Nowhere was there clearer evidence of the threatened public outbreak than in McKinley's own state of Ohio. During December and early January, the President had fought to have the state legislature elect Hanna to a full six-year term as senator. Though Day, other Ohioans in Washington, and even outsiders like Theodore Roosevelt had been pressed into service, Hanna triumphed by only one vote. In mid-February the state Republican League met. Representatives of Senator Foraker's faction were prepared to do battle with the followers of McKinley and Hanna. The issue they chose was a proposed resolution for recognition of Cuba. Though the President's friends fought it stubbornly, contending that it was insulting to the administration, their fight was useless and the resolution passed 437–283. Coupled with indications from other states, this vote showed beyond any doubt that Republican jingoes would not long remain patient.

On February 14, notice to this effect was formally served. The Foreign Relations and Foreign Affairs Committees introduced almost identical resolutions which the two Houses passed without delay. They called upon the administration to publish the reports of American consuls in Cuba. Some members of the two committees presumably knew that these reports drew an unrelieved picture of Spanish military failure and of suffering among the Cuban civil population. It had already been noised in the press that all the consular corps regarded autonomy as a failure. McKinley did not have to deliver the correspondence at once, but he knew that the moment when he did would be the moment when Congress began to discuss a declaration of war.

Then, early on the morning of February 16, the President was awakened to receive a telegram from Lee. Dated 12:30 A.M., it read: "*Maine* blown up and destroyed to-night at 9:40 P.M." Subsequent telegrams reported the dead at about 260, the cause of the explosion unknown.

The initial reaction seemed, it is true, to be merely dismay. Hearst and a few other publishers denounced Spain and called for war. In search of support, their reporters interviewed hundreds of erstwhile jingoes. They found many who would say that war would be inevitable if Spain had deliberately blown up the *Maine*, but suprisingly few who held Spain to blame or advocated immediate war. Ordinarily bellicose journals such as the St. Louis *Republic* and the New York *Press* said the *Maine's* explosion was a misfortune that need not effect Spanish-American relations. Publisher Whitelaw Reid of the New York *Tribune* wrote optimistically to his Washington correspondent, "In one way the horrible disaster . . . may prove a sort of blessing in disguise. It really looks as if it might sober our . . . jingoes a little."

Momentarily, indeed, these seemed a reaction much like that which had followed Cleveland's Venezuela message. Many businessmen had already come out against intervention in Cuba, and business journals promptly called for patience and self-restraint in the *Maine* case. In New York "all the reputable community" was reported against war and incensed at yellow journals that called for it. In Chicago financiers were said to be resolutely in favor of continued peace. One Chicago broker criticized the Cubans as "nothing but mongrels, not fit for self-government." Two eminent business figures, Cleveland industrialist Myron T. Herrick and Omaha railroad lawyer Charles F. Manderson, wrote the President assuring him that no one they knew was even excited about the *Maine*.

Many of the clergy suddenly joined businessmen in calling for peace. On the first Sunday after the explosion, three Methodist ministers in Brooklyn gave pacific sermons. So did a leading Methodist in Cleveland. A week later an Episcopalian in Washington denounced "wild clamors for blood, blood, blood." In Chicago a Baptist, a Methodist, and a Universalist all called for peace. Boston Congregationalist and Unitarian groups issued similar appeals; so did religious newspapers, including some that had long been bemoaning Cuba's condition. The Baptist Chicago *Standard* declared. "The religious weeklies . . . have been almost without exception opposed to war. . . . A great conservative force thus exerted has done much to guide public opinion in safe channels." The French ambassador reported to his government, "In nearly all the churches pastors have given pacific sermons; this is especially noteworthy because there is in the passions aroused against Spain something of old Huguenot and Puritan hatreds."

Jewish spokesmen took the same side. In Chicago, Reform leader Emil Hirsch pleaded for cautious diplomacy, and orthodox Rabbi Joseph Stolz denounced "savages" who cried for war. Though the Roman Catholic clergy feared the charge of sympathizing with Spain, Irish and Italian clerics both deplored the possibility of violence. Some went so far as to say that it would be sinful for American Catholics to fight Spanish Catholics.

Joined with businessmen and clergymen were German-American leaders. A *Literary Digest* survey of the German language press found only one sheet, Hearst's New York *Morgen Journal*, that was not firmly for peaceful arrangements with Spain.

There was some reason for believing in the spring of 1898 that a movement for peace, even more powerful than the one of 1895–1896, was getting under way. There was even some evidence of backtracking on the part of important jingo groups. On March 2 representatives of the national G.A.R. met jointly in Atlanta, Georgia, with representatives of the United Confederate Veterans. Though the Commander-in-Chief of the G.A.R., General John P. S. Govin, had been active in the Cuban agitation in Pennsylvania, he now made a speech calling for cool heads and support of the President, whatever direction he took. The Chicago Union League Club, where the Committee of One Hundred had had its start, listened to advocates of peace, gave them standing ovations, and booed members who sought to speak for war. The Union League Club of San Francisco passed a resolution condemning war agitation and backing the President. Many of these sermons, editorials, and resolutions were ambiguous; nevertheless they served to create an appearance of stiffening opposition to jingoism.

The passing days brought little evidence, however, that utterances by peaceful-minded clergymen and businessmen were having any effect on the general public. A minority of Protestant ministers joined the public clamor. In Chicago Baptist Poindexter S. Henson blamed the *Maine* sinking on "the procrastinating policy of those at the head of our nation, who have failed to deal honestly and courageously in behalf of an oppressed people." Newspapers reported sermons for intervention by a number of Baptists, Methodists, and Presbyterians. In Boston, where peace sentiment was supposed to be strongest, a Congregationalist equated "jingoism" with "strong and pure patriotism." In Chicago a leading Campbellite minister pleaded for war, and in San Francisco a Unitarian declared that it would be a service to Spain as well as to Cuba. In Terre Haute, Indiana, an Episcopal clergyman promised to do all in his power "to make Spanish the prevailing language of hell." In an address before a ministerial association in St. Louis, Methodist Bishop Charles C. McCabe declared, "There are many things worse than war. It may be that the United States is to become the Knight Errant of the world. War with Spain may put her in a position to demand civil and religious liberty for the oppressed of every nation and of every clime." Another Methodist bishop, John F. Hurst of Washington, D.C., wrote the President, exhorting him to free Cuba, adding, "Who knoweth whether thou art not come to the Kingdom for such a time as this?" Since, as in 1896, manifestations of public feeling preceded utterances by clergymen, this bellicose minority of preachers did not supply the only leadership, though their dissent may have fortified in favor of war laymen who would otherwise have had sober second thoughts. The public movement, however, was independent of them or any well-defined leadership group.

Across the country, thousands gave themselves up to emotional excesses like those of tent-meeting revivals. Theater audiences cheered, stamped, and wept at the playing of the Star-Spangled Banner. The antiwar New York *Herald* reported "war fever" in Jersey City and Hoboken. The conservative Portland, Oregon, *Morning Tribune* admitted that enthusiastic war talk could be heard on every street corner. Similar reports came from smaller towns. There were mob scenes in which effigies of Spanish statesmen were burned in Troy, New York,

Metropolis, Illinois, Pittsburg, Kansas, and Somerset, Kentucky. The St. Louis *Republic* reported fervor for Cuban independence and war with Spain in suburban communities like Kirkwood, Webster Groves, and Ferguson, Missouri, and in Clay City and Mount Vernon, Illinois. Colonel Henry A. Newman, coming in from Randolph County in central Missouri, said he himself opposed war, but "everything is war talk up in our part of the country, and patriotism is oozing out of every boy who is old enough to pack feed to the pigs." The editor of the Carson City *Appeal* declared that in Nevada, "the clamor for war is heard everywhere. Many people . . . are for war . . . on general principles, without a well-defined idea of the why or wherefor." A New York Democratic leader, just returned from a southern tour, reported resentment against Spain to be intense throughout the South.

Some of the fervor was anti-Catholic. In St. Louis the utterances of those few Catholic priests who spoke up for Spain were reproduced on "Cuba Libre" handouts. In Boston the Reverend Justin D. Fulton, Baptist author of such tracts as "Washington in the Lap of Rome," charged the administration with failing to act through fear of seven hundred thousand armed Catholics. In New York the editor of *The Converted Catholic* accused all Catholics of treasonable sympathy for Spain.

A number of Catholics retaliated by testifying their enthusiastic willingness to fight. An Indiana unit of the Catholic Knights of America offered to volunteer. A priest in Los Angeles declared, "The butcheries in Cuba must cease at any cost," and another in New York told his congregation, "We must show our true spirit as American citizens." Irish Catholic groups in Boston, New York, Chicago, Denver, and San Francisco proclaimed their enthusiasm for the Cuban cause and willingness to fight. Italians in Missouri and Alabama offered to raise companies for war. One said, "every Italian who has made America his home is only waiting a call to arms in order to prove his loyalty to this country."

Congressmen and cabinet officers received increasingly offensive letters, many scrawled in pencil on crude paper. Two typical examples came to Navy Secretary John D. Long (from Haverhill, Massachusetts): "If we wer in Spaines place and they in ours they would wipe us of the map as regards the Maine it was a planed plot and De Lome is at the bottom of it . . . the people are indignent wake up the president people in general will not stand it much Longer"; (from Chicago):

"Who else is to blame but you McKinley & Hanna & Reed. Who are working for the interest of the monied people of the U.S. between the actions of you three demagoges you have caused the Glorious Maine to be blown up . . . Why on earth don't you resign you *old fosil.*"

By the seventh week after the *Maine* disaster, these passions were beginning to take the form of anger against the President. In a Colorado community McKinley was hanged in effigy. In New York theaters, as the Hearst papers gleefully reported, the President's picture was sometimes hissed. A Massachusetts man wrote to Senator Chandler, "There is a growing discontent every where in the East in the dilley dally of the Administration on the Cuban question." The French ambassador, writing to Paris of spreading anti-McKinley feeling, observed, "A sort of bellicose fury has seized the American nation."

In the face of this undiminished mass passion, some pacific business and church leaders showed signs of weakening. The ordinarily staid New York *Journal of Commerce* published an almost hysterical editorial: "if popular passion is permitted to force the Administration into war, what is the conclusion suggested to our own masses? Simply that they may have whatever mad follies they hanker after, provided they raise their clamor to the requisite pitch." Wall Street was reported increasingly gloomy and convinced of the inevitability of war. Business journals swung toward the position that war might be necessary, and the same shift occurred among religious weeklies like the *Christian Index,* which warned, "the president will have to act, or an outraged nation will, through its congress, act for themselves."

Though the President's own views and acts were closely guarded secrets, businessmen, lawyers, and clergymen could see with increasing clarity the danger that McKinley might change front and make himself leader of the war forces. The further peril, if business and religious leaders appeared isolated and antipatriotic, was all too obvious. By conscious or unconscious processes of rationalization, ci-devant leadership groups eased from resolute pacifism toward a more ambivalent position. Whitelaw Reid wrote to McKinley: "The impression I got on crossing the continent was that the more intelligent classes are not greatly affected by the sensational press; but . . . I have never seen a more profound or touching readiness to trust the President, and await his word."

Many in "the more intelligent classes" needed no more than an excuse to abandon their obviously unpopular pacifism and, like other minority groups, to affirm their patriotism. In the middle of March Senator Redfield Proctor of Vermont returned from a brief trip to Cuba and delivered a speech in the Senate. He described the suffering that he had seen, and declared that Spain would never give up and the rebels would never give in; the only solution was American intervention. A relatively undistinguished Vermont politician, once Secretary of War under Harrison, Proctor said little that was new. His conversion to interventionism would not have caused great remark nor would his speech have been published across the nation had it not been for the widespread rumors that he had gone to Cuba as McKinley's observer and that his speech had been cleared with the President.

Businessmen, clergymen, and previously conservative newspaper editors seized upon this straw in the wind. The *Wall Street Journal* reported that Proctor's speech "converted a great many people in Wall Street who have heretofore taken the ground that the United States had no business to interfere in a revolution on Spanish soil." Clergymen and religious newspapers began dissociating themselves from businessmen. A San Francisco Congregationalist preached, "If there is to be a war with Spain it will be on the ground that humanity is our republic, our country the world. The passion for business is the least Christian." A Congregationalist in St. Louis declared his mind changed by Proctor's speech: "It were better far to paralyze the business of Wall Street than paralyze our national life." Consciously or unconsciously, many public leaders decided that it was no longer safe to resist the passion for war.

Politicians had naturally been even more alive to these currents in public emotion. Some Populists and agrarian Democrats had begun calling for war as soon as the *Maine* sank, among them Senator Marion Butler of South Carolina, the Populist Governor of Kansas, and William J. Stone, a Bryan Democrat from Missouri. So had local Populist and Democratic groups in Indiana, Illinois, Colorado, and California. Later, some historians were to suppose that the clamor for war originated among southern and western farmers. On the evidence, however, they were no more in a frenzy than northern and eastern urbanites. Their political leaders had simply broken already with most conservative community leaders on account of the free silver issue and thus had nothing to lose by speaking out.

Before long, Democrats who were not silverites showed willingness to gamble that war fever could not be cured. Hannis Taylor, who had been Cleveland's minister to Spain, called for immediate intervention, not on account of the *Maine* but simply to free Cuba. Olney said, in a rare public appearance: "No foreign question arises nowadays, but as soon as it is hinted that the United States should interfere and play its part in a manly fashion, the cry of 'jingo' goes up." Bryan, as the national party leader, was careful not to commit himself too soon. At first he refused comment other than to say that in a crisis the country would be united. At the end of March he called in newspaper reporters and announced, "the time for intervention has arrived. Humanity demands that we shall act. Cuba lies almost within sight of our shores, and the sufferings of her people cannot be ignored unless we, as a nation, have become so engrossed in money-making as to be indifferent to distress." If the administration failed to act, it was evident that Democrats would exploit the Cuban issue to the full.

Many Republicans made it clear that they could not support the administration if it resisted the public demand. Republican governors in Illinois, Indiana, and Vermont joined the war movement. Speaking to the State Board of Agriculture, Vermont's governor said: "The spirit of Bunker Hill still lives, and 'Uncle Sam' will soon stretch out his long, bony hands and give those who are seeking freedom their liberty." Republican senators and representatives in Congress began hinting broadly that if the President failed to move, Congress would do so.

Administration supporters began to tremble. The conservative Chicago *Times-Herald*, published by H. H. Kohlsaat, suddenly abandoned its pacific stand, declaring: "Intervention in Cuba . . . is immediately inevitable. Our own internal political conditions will not permit its postponement. Who that has marked the signs of the times does not see that 'war for Cuban liberty' looms before us as the only rallying standard of the legions of our national discontent." Senator Lodge, who, though a jingo, was also a firm supporter of the administration, wrote an earnest letter to the President, reporting virtual unanimity among the voters in Massachusetts. He cited a staunch Republican, the chairman of the Board of Selectmen in Nahant, who said that if the Cuban question were not settled at once, "it will become very hard to vote for the Republican party." Lodge went on to report:

I put the same questions over and over again & always got answers like these & was told that "Everybody felt that way." . . . [I]f the war in Cuba drags on through the summer with nothing done we shall go down in the greatest defeat ever known. . . . I know that it is easily & properly said that to bring on or even to threaten war for political reasons is a crime & I quite agree. But to sacrifice a great party & bring free silver upon the country for a wrong policy is hardly less odious. On a great, broad question like this, when right & wrong are involved I believe profoundly in the popular instinct & what that instinct is no one who goes out among the people . . . can doubt for one moment.

Some conservative Republicans and Democrats continued to believe that public feeling would come under control if the administration only waited the clamor out. The majority in Congress evidently did not agree. Senator Spooner wrote gloomily at the beginning of April: "Apparently Congress cannot keep its head. It looks . . . as if a majority had their watches out, waiting for the arrival of a particular hour . . . to force the hand of the President, and let loose the dogs of war."

At the outset of the Cuban rebellion, few in the United States except a handful of Cuban-Americans had been intensely interested. Now, three years later, neighborhoods, suburbs, small towns, and rural counties simply caught fire. No section, no type of community, no occupational group was immune. Vocal opposition by much of the Protestant clergy and the religious press, silence on the part of the G.A.R. and other organization leaders, and resolute disapproval from the most successful businessmen—many of whom had sympathized with the rebels from the beginning, but who now dreaded an open conflict—barely checked the fever for war. In numberless and nameless leaders and followers, emotion had become unshakable conviction. A frightened elite retreated from resistance to acquiescence. Politicians in one party, the Democratic, prepared to make capital of the issue, while those in the other, the Republican, more terrified of the opposition than of Spain, begged the administration to capitulate and make war for the sake of party survival and domestic peace.

4

INSULAR IMPERIALISM AND
THE OPEN DOOR:
THE CHINA MARKET AND THE
SPANISH-AMERICAN WAR
THOMAS McCORMICK

The territorial expansion of the United States, as the chief of the State Department's Bureau of Foreign Commerce asserted in 1900, came as "an incident of the commercial expansion." "The recent acquisitions," he continued, "are but outposts of our future trade, and their chief importance consists not in their own resources and capabilities, but in their unquestionable value as gateways for the development of commercial intercourse with . . . the Far East."

America's insular acquisitions of 1898 were not primarily products of "large policy" imperialism. Hawaii, Wake, Guam, and the Philippines were not taken principally for their own economic worth, or for their fulfillment of the Manifest Destiny credo, or for their venting of the "psychic crisis." They were obtained, instead, largely in an eclectic effort to construct a system of coaling, cable, and naval stations into an integrated trade route which could facilitate realization of America's one overriding ambition in the Pacific—the penetration and, ultimately, the domination of the fabled China market.

These developments emerged from the cauldron of economic catastrophe. The "long depression" of the 1870's and 1880's, capped by the terrible panic of 1893, had led America's political and business leaders to embrace the heretical analysis that industrial overproduction lay at the heart of the nation's economic ills. Spurred by conse-

Thomas McCormick, "Insular Imperialism and the Open Door," © 1963 by the Pacific Coast Branch, American Historical Association. Reprinted from *Pacific Historical Review*, Volume 32, Number 2, pp. 155–169, by permission of the Branch.

quent fears of economic stagnation and social upheaval, they increasingly turned their gazes oceanward in search of outlets for their industrial glut. In essence, they sought America's new frontier in the markets of the world.

Eschewing formal imperialism, the nation's leaders chose, as the major *modus operandi* of economic expansion, the Open Door, the policy, as defined and adopted in 1895, of "keeping foreign markets open" and securing "equal and liberal trading advantages." The choice, in part, reflected an aversion to the material and spiritual burdens of extensive colonialism. It also indicated, however, a buoyant assurance that American economic supremacy, given such equal commercial access, would win a sizeable share of world markets. Never rigid, the Open Door policy was to be supplemented by a limited dose of "insular imperialism" in the vast Pacific, where the technology of the day demanded island stepping-stones to the major market areas. The modification took no exception to the prevailing opinion that colonialism in large, densely-populated areas, such as China, was undesirable and unnecessary.

Many reasons propelled this economic expansion toward China. Memories of the clipper ship heyday of merchant capitalism, the influence of European writers, the blandishments of American missionaries: all played a part. Uppermost, however, was China's ignominious defeat at the hands of Japan in 1894–1895, which many American businessmen and diplomats believed would teach China "the folly of [its] exclusive and conservative policy." Thus, to many influential Americans, the Sino-Japanese War heralded the long-awaited awakening of the Chinese colossus, a development which would "probably have the effect of opening vast markets to us."

Subsequent developments in China belied such optimism. In 1895 and 1896, the international rivalry over Chinese indemnity loans and the completion of the Li-Lobanov pact marked an ever-quickening drive for exclusive economic privileges by the great powers. The process did not bode well for America's own inflated business hopes. So alarmed with the Cleveland administration that it abruptly forsook its laissez faire attitude toward American corporate interests in China and ordered its minister in Peking to use all his "personal and official influence" to win equality of economic opportunity for American "commercial enterprise." This inadequate response, however, could not stem the tide, and the encroachments upon Chinese integrity

reached flood-water proportions during the early McKinley administration with the famous "sphere of influence" partitioning. The "Sick
Man of Asia" seemed on his deathbed, and his threatened demise
promised a similar fate for the American hope of an Open Door frontier in the Celestial empire.

The growing crisis in China evoked great alarm in American business and government circles. Prompting most of the immediate apprehension were the Russian and German encroachments in Manchuria
and Shantung, areas which absorbed nearly two-thirds of America's
exports to China. Cognizant of this, the American minister in China,
Charles Denby, cried loudly to the "Home Office" that "partition
would . . . destroy our markets." He urged "an energetic protest . . .
against the dismemberment of China." The newly-formed Committee
on American Interests in China, numerous chambers of commerce,
several commercial papers, and other business groups added their
fervent assent.

Thus prodded, the State Department inquired pointedly of Germany
and Russia as to "what would be the effect on foreign trade" of their
new leases. The German response concurred in the American policy of
"holding China open to foreign commerce," while the Russian reply
was similarly reassuring. But the latter, especially, did not jibe with
admonitions from the business and diplomatic communities that Russia secretly planned "the absorption of Manchuria in her Customs
area." So pervasive and persuasive were these suspicions that many
previous promoters of Russo-American cooperation, such as Theodore
Roosevelt, reversed fields and cast their lot with the administration's
Anglophile elements in defining Russia as America's chief adversary
in the Orient.

Unassuaged then by the diplomatic responses, the McKinley administration found itself, by the spring of 1898, viewing the China
problem with a critical attention second only to that of the Cuban
issue. Yet the concern educed only watchful waiting (albeit, very
watchful). Even the dramatic British proposal for joint support of the
Open Door in China could not jar American policy off its quiescent
center. Already preoccupied with Cuba, the United States lacked the
commercial-military bases in the Pacific necessary, in the Mahanite
thinking of the day, to implement a more affirmative economic and
diplomatic policy. Within the year, the war with Spain was to eliminate these obstacles and pave the way for America's own Open Door

policy, the policy (so Minister Denby affirmed in early 1898) of preserving equal commercial "access" and "the autonomy of China" in the hope of "an immense development of trade."

From the very beginning of the Spanish-American War, the McKinley administration intended to retain a foothood in the Philippines as an "American Hong Kong," a commercial *entrepôt* to the China market and a center of American military power. Formulation of this policy commitment began seven months before hostilities with Spain; it began with Presidential examination of a Navy Department memorandum authored by Assistant Secretary Theodore Roosevelt. This multipurpose paper made one especially bold suggestion: in event of war with Spain, the Asiatic squadron "should blockade, and if possible take Manila." Temporarily put in abeyance by a short-lived *detente* with Spain in late 1897, the suggestion was revived and made the basis of Roosevelt's famous February 25 orders instructing Commodore George Dewey to "start offensive operations in the Philippines" after eliminating the Spanish fleet. Often viewed simply as a conspiratorial effort by "large policy" extremists, this interpretation misses two more significant facts: first, that Roosevelt's superiors accepted his orders concerning Philippine operations even though they unceremoniously countermanded fully two-thirds of the other miscellaneous orders issued concurrently by the Assistant Secretary; second, that the administration thereafter permitted the Naval War Board to incorporate the February 25 orders into its overall strategy plans for the Pacific. Clearly, while Roosevelt's actions may have been precipitate, they fell within the main lines of the "larger policies" of the administration. Of these, Roosevelt, as he privately admitted, was largely "ignorant."

With the outbreak of war, the McKinley administration rushed to implement its designs upon the likeliest *entrepôt*, Manila, by determining to send an army of occupation to the Philippine capital. It made this decision on May 2 before full-blown rumors of Dewey's victory at Manila Bay reached Washington, and formally issued the call for Philippine volunteers on May 4, three days before an anxious Navy Department received authoritative word that the Asiatic squadron was safe. The determined size of the army force was to be "not less than twenty thousand men"—four times the number recommended by Dewey "to retain [Manila] and thus control the Philippine Islands."

On May 11, McKinley and his cabinet gave definite form to American aims by approving a State Department memorandum calling for

Spanish cession of a suitable "coaling station," presumably Manila. The islands as a whole were to remain with Spain. Shortly thereafter, on June 3, when it had become apparent that the great distance between Manila and Honolulu demanded an intermediate coaling and cable station, the President broadened the American position to include an island in the Marianas. The choice made was Guam, and the United States Navy promptly seized it.

As of early June, then, administration intent envisioned only postwar control of Manila and Guam as way stations to the Orient. But dramatic events swiftly undercut this limited resolve and, for a critical fortnight, set American policy aimlessly adrift upon uncertain seas. First of all, the emergence of the Philippine insurgents as "an important factor" crystallized administration belief (as one American diplomat later noted) that "Spain cannot control; if we evacuate, anarchy rules." What then; bestow the largess of Philippine independence? The mere posing of the alternative raised an even more threatening specter of European intervention against a weak, fledgling republic, an intervention warned against by American diplomats in Berlin and Paris and lent specific credibility by German actions and attitudes. Either possibility—nationalistic revolution or rival intervention— might well render the isolated American position in Manila less than useful.

Between the horns of this cruel dilemma American policy lay immobilized—immobilized at a time when the growing crisis in China least afforded the luxury of prolonged indecision. On the one hand, intensified rumors that Russia regarded her South Manchurian leases as "integral portions of Russian territory" weakened the already shaky underpinnings of the Open Door in that key commercial area. At the same time, England's extension of the Hong Kong settlement and her monopolistic approach to Yangtze Valley developments indicated that nation's growing estrangement from her traditional Open Door approach, and threatened to leave American policy in China diplomatically isolated. In this deteriorating framework, any sustained impasse over Philippine policy incurred the obvious risk of letting America's grandiose hopes in China go by default. Against the formidable hosts of Philippine insurgency, German antagonism, and crisis in China, the American policy commitment of June 3 seemed an ineffectual one indeed. Cognizant of this, the McKinley administration, in mid-June, made a determined effort to break the bind by initiating three dramatic and interrelated moves in Hawaii, China, and the Philippines designed to increase American influence in the Western Pacific.

On June 11, the administration reactivated the sagging debate on Hawaiian annexation in the hope of strengthening America's hand in the Pacific basin. In the ensuing congressional debate, administration spokesmen hammered one theme with greater constancy than others: "we must have Hawaii to help us get our share of China." America, so the argument went, needed Hawaii not only for its own economic or cultural worth, but also for its commercial and military value as a stepping-stone to the China market. The influential Iowa congressman, William P. Hepburn, captured the theme best when he declared: "I can distinguish between the policy that would scatter all over the islands of the sea and the lands of the earth and that policy which would secure to us simply those facilities of commerce that the new commercial methods make absolutely essential."

Other annexationists offered their own variations. Hawaii, they declared, would give the United States "strategic control of the North Pacific," "a permanent share in the mighty commerce which beats its wings in the waves of the broad Pacific," "this half-way house to the great markets of the East," "a harbor which will enable us to protect with our fleet our commerce in the Far East," a necessary "crossroads" for "our rapidly increasing commerce with the mighty hordes with whom we shall trade . . . across the Pacific," "our essential stepping-stone and base." The theme was mainly a Republican one, but a few Democrats and one Populist bolted party lines to swell the chorus.

Significantly, anti-annexationists did not dispute the desirability of commercial expansion into Asia. Some even admitted the necessity of commercial-military bases as accoutrements to this expansion, but argued that the Pearl Harbor lease of 1886 or the Kiska holding in the Aleutians already met such needs. Most, however, stressed the laissez faire, free trade approach that "commercial expansion" could best be realized "by competition of quality and price," not by "annexation of territory." The point did not carry. On June 15, the House passed the annexation resolution by an overwhelming vote, 209 to 91. Three weeks later, after redundant and desultory discussion, the Senate affirmed the measure by a similar ratio. Thus, on July 8, with McKinley's signature, America acquired her halfway house to the Orient. The acquisition followed by four days the occupation of Wake

Island, a move intended to meet the technological necessities of an additional cable point between Hawaii and Guam.

Synchronous with the push on Hawaiian annexation, the administration initiated the first step in an American economic offensive in China itself by proposing a government commercial commission to China to recommend measures for trade expansion. Secretary of State William R. Day's supporting letter to Congress made it pointedly clear that the internal economic situation necessitated a vigorous commercial expansion in China. Declaring that an industrial production "of large excess above the demands of home consumption" demanded "an enlargement of foreign markets," the Secretary concluded that "nowhere is this consideration of more interest than in its relation to the Chinese Empire." Aware that "the partition of commercial facilities" in China threatened America's "important interests," he still contended that "the United States . . . is in a position to invite the most favorable concessions to its industries and trade . . . provided the conditions are thoroughly understood and proper advantage is taken of the present situation." Congress, to be sure, failed to appropriate the necessary monies. The reason, significantly, was because it considered such one-shot missions an inadequate substitute for a thoroughgoing reform of our consular representation in China. Nevertheless, the administration proposal, coupled with intensified consular activities later in the summer, served clear notice of American intent to take "proper advantage . . . of the present situation" in order to play a more active role in China.

Simultaneously, on June 14, the administration capped its trio of dramatic moves by shelving the earlier decision to return the Philippines to Spain, thus opening the disposition of the islands to further examination. With this open-ended shift, there began a progressive but reluctant redefinition of the desired area of American sovereignty: from Manila, to Luzon, and finally to the entire group. For two months after the June 14 move, American policy remained seemingly ambivalent on the question of extent. Even the Armistice agreement of August appeared to avoid confrontation of the issue by reserving the question of "control, disposition, and government" for final peace negotiations. The ambiguity was more apparent than real, for McKinley had already crushed an internal move headed by his own secretary of state to limit American commitment to Manila. In sealing this extremity, he left open only the question of how far to journey toward

the other—Luzon or the entire group? The beginning of the final negotiations in early October found this problem still unresolved. While the
American peace commissioners were instructed to work only for retention of Luzon, they were also to "accumulate all possible information"
on the possible necessity of controlling the whole archipelago. Less
than one month later, on October 25 McKinley himself finally cut the
knot by broadening his instructions to include all the Philippines.

In this evolution of Philippine policy, America's commercial stake
in China was of considerable importance. Indeed, it played the primary
role in the thinking of the business and government elite that chiefly
shaped McKinley's decisions. It also played a significant, though not
paramount, part in the outlook of the military advisers who exercised
a more limited but still crucial influence upon the President's policies.

Between June and October, business and government circles united
vigorously around a policy of retaining all or part of the Philippines.
Significantly, their rationale stressed the intrinsic economic worth of
the islands far less than their strategic relationship to China—both as
a commercial *entrepôt* and a political-military lever. Moreover, it emphasized that Manila alone would not suffice for these purposes; that
the United States would have to take Luzon and perhaps the whole
group. In part this support for enlarged control reflected the pervading
fear that native revolution or European penetration might undermine
the viability of American power in Manila. It also indicated a growing
belief, born of newly accumulated information, that the economic in-
terdependence of the archipelago made efficient division most difficult.
Charles H. Cramp, America's leading shipbuilder, aptly illustrated the
impact of both factors upon influential Americans when he declared:
"[Manila] is the emporium and the capital of the Philippines . . . and it
exists because of that fact. . . . Can anyone suppose that with Manila in
our hands and the rest of the Philippine territory under any other
Government, that city would be of any value?"

Numerous business associations, as well as prominent individual
businessmen, pushed the viewpoint that trade interests in China demanded American control in the Philippines. Led by the National Association of Manufacturers and the American Asiatic Association,
many special business organizations urged retention of the Philippines "for the protection and furtherance of the commercial interests
of our citizens in the Far East." At the same time, save for a few
prominent dissenters, McKinley's many personal friends in the cor-

porate world gave similar counsel. Typical was the advice of Irving M. Scott, manager of the Union Iron Works, that America needed the Philippines as "a point of observation at or near the centre of activity." Predicting that "the world is ours commercially" if we preserved peace and the Open Door, Scott urged that "the implements must be on hand, the position must be secured, and a vigilant watch kept on every encroachment." Noting that "the first move has been made in China," he concluded that "nothing has so effectually stopped it as the occupation of Manila."

Most of McKinley's close associates in the government (many of whom were themselves products of the business community) pressed similar views upon their chief. The redoubtable Mark Hanna, State Department economic expert Frederic Emory, the American Minister to China Charles Denby, his successor Edwin H. Conger, Comptroller of the Currency Charles G. Dawes, Assistant Secretary of the Treasury Frank A. Vanderlip, to name a few, all shared in general the conviction (as Vanderlip stated) that an American-controlled Philippines would be "pickets of the Pacific, standing guard at the entrances to trade with the millions of China and Korea, French Indo-China, the Malay Peninsula, and the islands of Indonesia."

Exerting a more narrow influence upon McKinley's Philippine policy was a third group, the military. In general, the President's military advisers shared the widespread concern over the strategic relationship of the archipelago to the Asian mainland. Yet, attracted by the siren's call of *imperium* (in which they would play a prominent role), many military spokesmen also promoted retention of the Philippines as the first step toward an expansive territorial imperialism. In the main, their hopes were dashed as McKinley refused to heed their advice for a general American expansion into Micronesia and the islands of the South China Sea. Military advice, however, could claim one significant result: it resolved the President's ambivalence (shared by the business and government elite) between taking Luzon or the entire group by convincing him that the islands were an indivisible entity: that strategically and economically they were highly interdependent. Especially persuasive were the lengthy and articulate reports of Commander R. B. Bradford and General Francis V. Greene. Coming in late September and early October, they proved to be the decisive factors in broadening the President's instructions to their ultimate dimensions.

The great repute of these business and government groups, coupled with their ready access to the Chief Executive, gave much weight to their contention (shared, in part, by the military) that American interests in China necessitated retention of the Philippines. But this view also gained a powerful though unwanted ally in the twin crisis in China itself during the fall of 1898. One side of the crisis was the intensified partitioning of railroad concessions by the European powers. Begun in the aftermath of the Sino-Japanese War, the division of concession spheres had advanced greatly by late summer of 1898. Russia and Germany had established *de facto* monopolization of Manchurian and Shantung railroads, respectively, while England bent her own efforts to strengthening her hold in the Yangtze Valley. British acceptance of the modified Open Door policy and the ratification of the Anglo-German railroad accord of September showed unmistakably that the Open Door had no current relevance to the world of railroad investments. From the American point of view, the development augured ill for its own economic interests. To be sure, it did not greatly injure American investors. At this stage there was still little American financial interest in Chinese investments; and what little existed was assured profitable employment by the British in the Yangtze Valley. The solidification of railroad spheres, however, did threaten the important American export trade of Manchuria and North China by requiring American goods to travel from treaty port to market over Russian and German railroads. The prospect was not inviting, for these products might well meet railroad rate discrimination which, in raising transportation costs, would render American articles less competitive.

Meanwhile, America's economic dreams faced another menace from a different quarter in China. In September of 1898, a successful coup d'etat by conservative, anti-foreign elements managed to crush the pro-western, reform party surrounding the young Chinese Emperor. The new government immediately initiated administrative measures viewed by the United States as inimical to "commercial development" and the "pendulum of progress." More seriously, the conservative forces failed to control anti-foreign uprisings inspired by their own *putsch*. Centered along projected Manchurian railroads, the violent and unstabilizing demonstrations offered both the excuse and the opportunity for potential Russian intervention to save her great railroad interests. The mere suggestion of such a development was sufficient to conjure up visions of a further fragmented China and a vitiated Open Door.

These developments in China spawned first alarm, then action in the McKinley administration. The first move came in September with official renewal of inquiries to Russia and Germany concerning trade policies in their respective spheres. While the German response seems satisfactory, the evasive Russian declaration that her "administrative regulations" on foreign trade were still undetermined appear to be a foreboding retreat from earlier positions. Thus accentuated, State Department concern germinated a second move in October with favorable action upon a textile industry petition concerning the Russian threat in China. Noting that one-half of America's cotton textile exports to China went to Russian-dominated areas, the petitioners demanded a "vigorous policy" to prevent "these markets" from being "eventually closed to our trade." Immediately, the Department responded by instructing its embassy in St. Petersburg to "use every opportunity to act energetically" against Russian adoption of discriminatory trade policies in Manchuria. Quite obviously, the American government regarded the crises in China as dangerous enough to warrant substantial American reaction. Presumably, the situation was sufficiently threatening to impart added urgency and impact to the already influential opinion that America's commercial aspirations in China necessitated retention of the Philippines.

There can be no doubt that the Chinese question, illuminated by the opinion of business, government, and the military and by the growing crises in China, had progressive impact upon the shaping of America's Philippine policy. Nowhere is that fact made more significantly and dramatically apparent than in the private, candid, and lengthy exchange of opinions between McKinley and his peace commissioners at a White House meeting on September 16. The President, speaking somberly and with none of his frequent evasiveness, explained his reasons for retaining all or part of the archipelago. Almost all of them were negative, embraced with obvious reluctance. The only positive and assertive determinant was his conviction that "our tenure in the Philippines" offered the "commercial opportunity" of maintaining the Open Door, a policy which McKinley defined as "no advantages in the Orient which are not common to all." "Asking only the open door for ourselves," he told his commissioners, "we are ready to accord the open door to others." Explaining further, he made it clear that retention was no first step in an orgy of imperialism and jingoism, but simply a limited though important accoutrement to commercial expansion. "The commercial opportunity . . . associated with this opening," he declared, "depends less on large territorial possessions than upon an adequate commercial basis and upon broad and equal privileges." The statement was more than rhetoric. Before the conclusion of peace, McKinley was to turn his back on jingoistic pressure to acquire all the Carolines and the Marianas from Spain, thus further illustrating that commercial needs, not Manifest Destiny, guided American decision-making in the Pacific basin; that the Open Door, not colonialism on a vast scale, was to remain the vehicle of American expansion.

McKinley's linking of the Philippines question with the Open Door in China found ready favor with the majority of his peace commissioners. Indeed, the dominant triumvirate of Cushman K. Davis, William P. Frey, and Whitelaw Reid favored retention of the Philippines largely out of consideration for the future of American economic expansion in China. Reid's response to McKinley's remarks of September 16 was not atypical, when he "spoke of the great importance of the Philippines with reference to trade in China." Noting the previous acquisition of Hawaii, he concluded that "if to this we now added the Philippines, it would be possible for American energy to . . . ultimately convert the Pacific Ocean into an American Lake."

Initiated then, in September, within the conscious framework of the Chinese question, the peace negotiations with Spain concluded three months later on an identical note. Article IV of the treaty made clear the intimacy that bound Philippine and China policy by keeping McKinley's earlier promise that we would accord the Open Door in the Philippines, provided we received reciprocal treatment elsewhere in the Orient. In actuality, this American Open Door was limited both in time and scope; however, administration spokesmen regarded the proviso as the key to future American policy in the Far East. Alvey A. Adee, long-time power inside the State Department, stated quite unequivocally that "the open door paragraph is the most important"; and Whitelaw Reid, dominant figure in the peace commission, insisted that the impartial "revenue tariff" for the Philippines "enables Great Britain and the United States to preserve a common interest and present a common front in the enormous development in the East that must attend the awakening of the Chinese Colossus."

The final treaty arrangement on the Philippines was the outgrowth of an evolving set of circumstances dating back to 1895, when the combined impact of American depression and the Sino-Japanese War offered both the need and the hope that China might become the great absorber of America's industrial surplus. Subsequent developments, culminating in the partitioning of late 1897 and early 1898, critically threatened the hope, but in no way dissipated the need. They did, however, dictate the desirability of finding some vigorous means of safeguarding America's present and future commercial stake in the Chinese Empire. Fortuitously, perhaps, the Spanish-American War provided just such an opportunity, and the McKinley administration was quick to exploit it. The result was the effective thrust of American influence into the far Pacific. From Honolulu, through Wake and Guam, to Manila stretched a chain of potential coaling, cable, and naval stations to serve as a commercial and military avenue to the Orient. Only the construction of an isthmian canal remained to complete the system.

The grand scheme was not, in the narrow sense, imperial. The insular possessions in the Pacific were not pieces of empire, per se, but stepping-stones and levers to be utilized upon a larger and more important stage—China. Paradoxically, American expansion was designed, in part, to serve an anti-imperial purpose of preventing the colonization of China and thus preserving her for Open Door market penetration: *imperium in anti-imperio*. All this McKinley captured in his presidential message of December 5, 1898, when he declared that our "vast commerce . . . and the necessity of our staple production for Chinese uses" had made the United States a not "indifferent spectator of the extraordinary" partioning in China's maritime provinces. Nevertheless, he continued, so long as "no discriminatory treatment of American . . . trade be found to exist . . . the need for our country becoming an actor in the scene" would be "obviated." But, he concluded, the fate of the Open Door would not be left to chance; it would be, he stated, "my aim to subserve our large interests in that quarter by all means appropriate to the constant policy of our government." Quite obviously, the fruits of the Spanish-American War had enormously multiplied the "appropriate . . . means" available to American policy-makers, and had set the stage for the illusory search of America for that holy commercial grail—the China market.